LANGUAGE
AND COGNITION

LANGUAGE
AND COGNITION

ALEXANDER R. LURIA
PROFESSOR OF PSYCHOLOGY
MOSCOW UNIVERSITY

Edited by
JAMES V. WERTSCH

V.H. WINSTON & SONS
1981 Washington, D.C.

1807 1982

A Wiley-Interscience Publication
JOHN WILEY & SONS
New York   Chichester   Brisbane   Toronto   Singapore

Translation of this study was supported through the Special Foreign
Currency Program of the National Library of Medicine, National
Institutes of Health, Public Health Service, U.S. Department of Health
and Human Services, Bethesda, MD.

Library of Congress Catalogue Card Number: 81-70188
ISBN 0-471-09302-5

Composition by Marie A. Maddalena, Scripta Technica, Inc.
Printed in the United States of America
10 9 8 7 6 5 4

Contents

Editor's Introduction

As is so often the case with innovators in science, Alexander Romanovich Luria developed a theoretical approach that does not fit neatly into a single tradition, or even into a single discipline. His scientific concerns were extremely wide ranging by today's standards. Thus, Western readers often were led to conclude that he lacked an integrative theoretical focus and that the different problems he investigated simply reflected different interests during various periods in his long intellectual career. Luria's recent autobiography (1979) has done much to dispel this notion. In it, we see that although there is little doubt Luria modified and expanded his ideas from the time of his early research in the 1920s to his final work before his death, certain general themes guided his thinking. Once these themes had become integrated into his scientific approach, they continued to guide it in subsequent years or decades.

The present book touches on virtually all aspects of Luria's thinking about psychology and language. It covers such a broad range of issues since it derives from lectures that Luria developed in order to introduce university students to some of the general concerns of contemporary Soviet psychology. While individual topics in his approach have been examined in his other writings (sometimes in greater detail than here), this volume represents one of the few opportunities

1

Luria had to outline the overall picture that directed the course of his thinking. Since Luria's autobiography identifies many of the forces that went into his intellectual and personal development, we will not review them here. Rather, we will identify a few of the major themes that guided his research approach near the end of his life. In some cases, these themes are specifically mentioned and discussed in this volume. In other cases, they are not explicitly discussed but are no less powerful in their influence on the way Luria approached a research or clinical problem.

It is reasonable to identify three major influences that guided Luria's thinking during the latter part of his career. First, we see the influence of Vygotsky (1896–1934). Even in those writings where Luria says little or nothing about him, Vygotsky's impact on Luria's approach to a problem was so profound that one is likely to misconstrue the general direction of his argument if one fails to take this into consideration. The second influence on Luria's approach came from linguistics and semiotics. In this connection, we will see that the ideas of Jakobson and other linguists had an important influence on the way Luria posed research questions about language development and aphasiology. The third major influence was the account of the physiological foundations of human psychological activity developed in Russian and Soviet research. This volume is replete with references to figures such as Pavlov and Bernshtein. Their development of the theory of "higher nervous activity," a theory which is *not* simply a form of behaviorism, provided the origins for Luria's account of cortical functioning and its relationship with human psychological activity.

Although all three of these factors influenced Luria's anlaysis of language and cognition, it is possible to rank them, to some degree, in terms of how fundamental they were to his approach. This ranking is a reflection of Luria's intellectual biography in the sense that his early collaboration with Vygotsky had a profound impact on all subsequent developments in his thinking. Thus it is clear that Vygotsky's influence created the basic framework *within* which linguistic and neurophysiological ideas were interpreted. Vygotsky himself was concerned with how linguistic and neurophysiological phenomena fit into an account of human cognition. In fact, one can identify the origins of almost every aspect of Luria's approach in Vygotsky's writings from the 1920s and 1930s. However, this does not mean that Luria simply added in a few minor details to a complete theoretical framework. His development of Vygotsky's approach in light of modern linguistic and neurophysiological research constitutes a major accomplishment.

One does not have to search far to find Luria's ackonwledgment of Vygotsky. For instance, he once wrote:

> Vygotsky was a genius. After more than half a century in science I am unable to name another person who even approaches his incredible analytic ability and foresight. All of my work has been no more than a working out of the psychological theory which he constructed. (1978)

In order to identify some of the specific ways that Vygotsky influenced Luria's ideas, we will outline three major themes that characterize the research of both men: (1) the use of genetic (or developmental) explanation, (2) the search for the social origins of human psychological functioning, and (3) an emphasis on the role of sign systems in mediating social and individual processes. These three themes provided the cornerstones of Vygotsky's attempt to reformulate psychology on Marxist foundations. They have guided the research of Luria as well as the research of Vygotsky's other followers (e.g., D. B. El'konin, P. Ya. Gal'perin, A. N. Leon'tev, and A. V. Zaporozhets).

The method of genetic explanation (what Luria terms the "comparative evolutionary method" in Chapter 15) provides the epistemological foundations for Vygotsky's and Luria's approach to the study of mind. Simply stated, genetic explanation is the notion that in order to understand human social and psychological processes, one must trace them back to their origins. Like Vygotsky, Luria applied this method in a variety of "genetic arenas." Naturally, historical change was very important in the development of a Marxist psychology. Historical analysis played such an important role in Vygotsky's writings that Soviet scholars (e.g., Smirnov, 1975) refer to his approach as the "cultural-historical" theory of mind. The importance of this genetic arena for Luria can be noted in this volume in its numerous references to historical differences in languages, cultures, and modes of thinking. Chapter 14 is concerned solely with these issues. In that chapter, the reader will find an overview of Luria's early research in central Asia. Western psychologists would categorize this research as cross-cultural. The reader will detect that a more appropriate term from Luria's perspective might be "cross historical." This is because Luria's primary concern was with how cultural instutution that appear at different points in socioeconomic history influence human reasoning processes.

However, Vygotsky's and Luria's use of genetic explanation was by no means limited to the sociohistorical arena. They also examined phylogenetic, ontogenetic, and microgenetic change. Ontogenetic and microgenetic comparisons play a particularly important role in this volume. Luria examines the ontogenesis of word meaning in Chapter 3 and the ontogenesis of the directive function of speech in Chapter 6. Although he does not use the term "microgenesis" in this volume, this genetic arena occupied an important position in his reasoning. We use the term "microgenesis" to refer to the unfolding of a single psychological act, usually over the course of seconds or milliseconds.

For Luria, the microgenetic arena was especially important in the analysis of speech production and comprehension. His account of these processes is based on a series of successive stages in the production or comprehension of single utterances. Thus, he approached speech production as a process whereby a speaker moves through a sequence of steps beginning with a motive and ending with an expanded speech utterance. In addition to using this microgenetic framework in his analysis of speech production (Chapter 10) and speech comprehension (Chapter 12), Luria relied on it in formulating his typology of disturbances in speech processing which result from focal brain lesions (Chapters 15 and 16). In general, each of his categories of speech disturbance corresponds with a stage in the microgenesis of speech production or comprehension.

Luria's microgenetic analysis of speech processes have specific precursors in the writings of Vygotsky (1934/1962). Vygotsky's account of speech production involved notions such as motive and inner speech which are now a part of Luria's analysis. However, Luria (1947, 1975) and his colleagues (e.g., Akhutina, 1975, 1978) have developed these notions much further on the basis of their research in aphasiology.

One of the most important results of Luria's use of the microgenetic method is that he was led to develop a more complete account of speech production and comprehension processes than typically appears in psycholinguistics. This, in turn, led him to consider a variety of syndromes not usually included in the study of speech disturbances. For example, his examination of the effects of frontal lobe lesions on speech production is something that is seldom included in accounts of speech disorders. Although he clearly distinguished between such frontal lobe syndromes and disturbances which affect the language code itself, his method led him to argue that an account of speech processes that does not take into account all aspects of this functional system is incomplete in an essential way.

Occasionally, Luria contrasted the method of genetic explanation with a research approach concerned with the psychological consequences of focal brain lesions. We would argue that while this second approach involves additional assumptions and methods, it still is based on genetic explanation. This is so for at least two reasons. First, as already noted, Luria conceived of disturbances in psychological processes in terms of disruptions in a sequence of stages in microgenesis. Thus, his classification and interpretation of speech disorders rests on assumptions inherent in the microgenetic method. Second, when dealing with the breakdown and subsequent remediation of speech processes that are affected by focal brain lesions, Luria often based his analyses and predictions on the order in which various types of abilities appear in the history of society and in ontogenesis. To some degree, he conceived deterioration as following the reverse order of ontogenesis and rehabilitation as following the same order. For example, in his discussion of speech production disorders in Chapter 15, he writes of the "process of remediation or reverse development of the defect."

Hence, one major theme in Vygotsky's writings that influenced Luria's ideas is that psychological phenomena must be analyzed on the basis of how they develop. Although the notion of genetic explanation is not explicitly discussed in detail in this volume, it is inherent in virtually every aspect of Luria's argument.

The second Vygotskian theme that influenced Luria is the notion that higher psychological processes have their origin in social interaction. Obviously, this second theme is not completely independent of the first. One can see how the method of genetic explanation is already "built into" it. Luria explicitly deals with this theme in Chapter 1, where he argues that in order to overcome the "crisis in psychology," we must understand the relationship between human consciousness and material activity. He states this Vygotskian position by arguing:

> One must seek the origins of conscious activity and "categorical" behavior not in the recesses of the human brain nor the depths of the spirit, but in the external conditions of life. Above all, this means that one must seek these origins in the external processes of social life, in the social and historical forms of human existence.

Unlike writers such as Janet (1936) and Vygotsky (1934/1962, 1978, in press (a), in press (b)), this was not something that Luria focused on a great deal in his writings. However, as in the case of genetic explanation, it occupied a major place in the set of assumptions that guided his theoretical and empirical research. Inherent in many aspects of his approach is the notion that human cognition is a product of the cultural-historical milieu in which it evolves and can be examined in terms of the internalization of social interaction. These assumptions form the basis of his critique of figures such as Piaget and Chomsky who argue for a quite different account of the origins of cognition and language.

This second Vygotskian theme is reflected in many of the arguments Luria develops in this volume. For example, his argument about the role of speech in the regulation of thinking is based on the claim that this regulation first appears on the social plane, especially in interaction between a child and his/her mother. In his account of the ontogenesis of voluntary acts (in Chapter 6), he makes this point by arguing:

> ... the ontogenesis of voluntary action begins with the practical act that the child performs in response to the command of the adult. Clearly, this hypothesis is basic to modern scientific psychology. It views complex ontogenetic processes not as resulting from biological development, but from social forms of human activity.

These statements are then followed by a review of Soviet research on adults' speech to children and the argument that self-regulative cognitive activity arises through the internalization of social interaction.

The importance of social interaction in Luria's approach to psychological phenomena is evident in other aspects of his argument as well. For example, in his examination of speech production and comprehension, he often reminds us of the importance of the fact that these processes emerged in the process of carrying out social interaction. In this connection, he writes (in Chapter 10):

> There are two crucial factors involved in analyzing an expanded speech utterance. First, the utterance is part of ongoing social interaction which involves the communication of information from one person to another.

To the outside observer, it would appear that this statement would have to play a crucial role in any account of psycholinguistic and neurolinguistic processes. However, the Chomskian emphasis on examining what language *is* before examining *how it is used* has led many Western investigators away from emphasizing social interactional phenomena. As a result, Luria includes several questions and phenomena in his analyses of speech production and comprehension that are typically not covered in Western approaches. For instance, he considers the differences among oral dialogic, oral monologic, and written speech to be very important. This issue arises, for Luria, because of his concern with the social functions and origins of language activities. His statement in Chapter 11 is evidence of that:

> There is yet another basic difference in the psychological structure of written and oral speech. This difference is due to the fact that these two types of speech have different origins. Oral speech evolves naturally in the process of social interaction between children and adults. This speech is sympractical in its earliest stages and later becomes a special independent form of oral speech communication.... Written speech emerges as the result of special learning.

From quotes such as these, one can begin to appreciate the important role that social interaction played in Luria's account of individual psychological processes. In addition to giving rise to the issues we have identified, this theme stands behind many other ideas which are part of his approach. For example, in order to understand his treatment of the distinction between sense and meaning (especially in connection with Stanislavskii's ideas), one must appreciate Luria's concern with the Vygotskian theme that human psychological processes originate in social interaction.

The third Vygotskian theme reflected in Luria's thinking is that social and psychological processes are mediated by sign systems. While neither Vygotsky nor Luria limited the notion of a sign system to language, they both argued that language played a preeminent role in mediation. Furthermore, they argued that semiotic functions, such as the generalizing or abstracting function, would be difficult, if not impossible, to carry out in the absence of language.

Just as the second theme is closely tied to the first, this third, "semiotic" theme is closely tied to the second. In fact, it is what makes the second theme viable. This follows from Vygotsky's and Luria's argument that social (or "interpsychological") and individual (or "intrapsychological") functioning are linked by the fact that the same mediational means are used in both. That is, they not only argued that social interaction gives rise to psychological processes, they also specified the means—speech—that mediated both and therefore linked them.

This line of reasoning is what led to Vygotsky's ideas about the role of egocentric and inner speech in the emergence of human cognition. An important aspect of his argument was that the primary concern was speech ("rech' ") or speaking activity ("rechevaya deyatel'nost'") rather than language ("yazyk"). While language (i.e., the linguistic system) serves as the tool or mediational means, the emphasis in psychological analysis was on the transition from social *practice* or *activity* to psychological *activity*. The distinction between language and speech becomes even more important when one considers that Vygotsky and Luria used the term "rech'" (speech) in Russian to refer to a broader class of phenomena than is not usually assumed when the word "speech" is used in English. Their notion of speech is certainly not limited to the neurophysiological processes involved in phonation. Furthermore, it is not limited to the transfer of information.

This broad interpretation of the notion of speech led Vygotsky and Luria to include phenomena such as the motive in their analyses. Thus, Vygotsky argued that:

> To understand another's speech, it is not sufficient to understand his words—we must understand his thought. But even that is not enough—we must also know its motivation. No psychological analysis of an utterance is complete until that plane is reached. (1934/1962, p. 151)

This understanding of the factors involved in speech is reflected (in this volume) in Luria's insistence that the motive be included in an account of speech processes. For example, it appears in his analysis of speech production and speech production disturbances associated with lesions to the prefrontal zone of the cerebral cortex. Luria also investigated the role of the motive in speech by analyzing Stanislavskii's methods for training actors (cf. Chapter 13).

Luria's discussion, in Chapter 3, of the distinction between sense ("smysl") and meaning ("znachenie") is another manifestation of this separation of speech and language in the Vygotskian approach. Again, while not overlooking the important role that the language system (and its associated *meaning*) plays in mediating human cognition, Luria ultimately was interested in the use of language in particular settings. That is, he was ultimately interested in the activity of speech (and its associated *sense*).

Perhaps the best example of how these three Vygotkian themes influenced Luria is his account of the regulative function of speech. In order to account for the most advanced form of regulative speech—inner speech—he used genetic explanation to trace it from its earlier social interactional origins (Chapter 6). It is interesting to note that where Luria used the notion of inner speech in analyzing self-regulation and speech production, many other investigators would be tempted to use models of representational and information processing mechanisms that do not mention speech. They might ask why the notion of speech needs to be involved at all. As Vygotsky (1934/1962) said, "Silent 'pronouncing' of words is not equivalent to the total process of inner speech." The answer is not that Luria believed that subvocal speech production activity is necessarily involved.

Rather, "inner *speech*" is the term used by Luria to refer to internal psychological processes because these processes are viewed as deriving from and reflecting the structural properties of social speech. That is, the use of this term results from the method of genetic explanation and the claim that mediated psychological functioning arises out of mediated social interaction.

The ideas and accomplishments of all of the figures in the Vygotskian school of Soviet psychology cannot be examined in this Introduction. However, we must mention at least one member of this school who was an equal partner with Luria in developing Vygotsky's ideas, namely, A. N. Leont'ev. In the 1920s, when Vygotsky came to Moscow, Luria and Leont'ev joined him to form what is known as the "troika." Whereas Luria developed Vygotsky's ideas in the areas of neurophysiology, neuropsychology, developmental psychology, neurolinguistics, and cross-cultural studies, Leont'ev (1959, 1978, in press) developed the philosophical foundations of a general Marxist psychology. His approach was based on the Marxist category of activity ("deyatel'nost' "). Together with Luria, Leont'ev played an extremely important role in developing contemporary Soviet psychology. Any attempt to identify all of the ways that Leont'ev's theory of activity influenced Luria would require a treatment beyond the scope of this Introduction. However, it is worth noting that terms from Leont'ev's theory of activity, such as "activity," "action," "operation," "goal," and "motive," appear in many places in this volume (especially in Chapter 10 and 12). These are clearly drawn from his development of Vygotsky's original theoretical framework.

Before leaving the issue of how Vygotsky's ideas influenced Luria, an additional observation about a terminological issue is in order. This observation has to do with the term *consciousness* ("soznanie"). As is always the case when translating writings from one scientific tradition for readers from another, certain terms have no acceptable equivalents. Although the English term *consciousness* is widely used, the term is not used in Western cognitive and developmental psychology and in aphasiology as it is used by Soviet scholars in these disciplines. The major reason for this problem with "paradigm specific" terms is that, unlike their Western colleagues, Vygotsky and others constructed Soivet psychology on the basis of ideas proposed in Marxist philosophy.

Any attempt to provide a complete explanation of how Western and Soviet scholars differ in their interpretation of the notion of consciousness would take us far beyond the problems we can address in this Introduction. Therefore, we will simply make a few comments. First, we should note that the Vygotskian concept of consciousness is concerned with how the individual reflects the sociocultural environment in which he/she functions. This, of course, derives from Marx and has already been mentioned in connection with the second theme that characterized Vygotsky's and Luria's thinking. Without exploring all of the implications of such an assumption, we should note that it argues against claims about universal characteristics of consciousness. Rather, it has led investigators like

Luria to examine the psychological consequences of different socioeconomic and cultural environments.

Secondly, Vygotsky's and Luria's understanding of consciousness is that it includes affective as well as cognitive phenomena. Actually, both writers eschewed the very distinction between affect and cognition in theory. However, it is important to realize that they both focused primarily on cognitive phenomena in practice. Thus, in the present volume, Luria broaches the topic of affect when dealing with volition, sense, and motive, but his primary concern is with what would be termed cognitive phenomena in Western psychology.

Given these facts, it might seem that the best solution to the problem of translating the term *"soznanie"* (consciousness) would be to invent a new term. However, in an attempt to avoid additional barbarisms and to be consistent with existing practices in translation, we have decided to retain the term *consciousness* throughout the text. It is our opinion that by encountering this term in all of its various contexts in this volume the reader will come to understand what Luria had in mind when he used it. However, we have not followed this practice (and used the term *cognition* instead) in the title of the volume, where the term by necessity appears in a relatively decontextualized setting. Of course, similar questions arise in the case of other terms as well. In particular, words such as *activity* ("deyatel'-nost' "), *action* ("deistvie"), *operation* ("operatsiya"), and *sense* ("smysl") must be recognized as being paradigm specific.

If Vygotsky provided the broad theoretical framework for Luria's work, Luria himself did a great deal to develop it. This is obvious if we consider the second major influence on Luria's work—research in linguistics and semiotics. Given Vygotsky's great interest in these fields, it is clear that this was a natural direction for Luria to expand the framework.

There are many linguists whose ideas influenced Luria in one way or another. They range from such early figures as Svedelius (1897) and Trubetskoi (1939) to such contemporary investigators as Apresyan (1974), Bierwisch (1972), Chomsky (1957, 1965), Mel'chuk (1974), and Zholkovskii (1964). The linguist who had the greatest influence on Luria's thinking during the past few decades, however, was Roman Jakobson (1942, 1971a, 1971b, 1971c, 1971d; Jakobson, Fant, and Halle, 1952; Jakobson and Halle, 1956).

It should not be assumed that the relationship between Luria and Jakobson consisted solely of Jakobson's influence on Luria. Rather, it would be more appropriate to emphasize the mutual influence involved. Thus, in writing some of his early papers on aphasia, Jakobson referred to Luria as one of the "outstanding experts [who] assign high importance to linguistic problems involved in the study of aphasia . . . . " (1971a, p. 231).

Through his writings and personal contact, Jakobson influenced Luria's ideas in many ways, but the most obvious impact was in connection with Luria's classification of aphasias. There is still a great deal of debate among aphasiologists about the merits of this classification scheme, but not many would question that it provides one of the few existing comprehensive frameworks for categorizing speech disorders. The important point about this scheme, for our present purposes, is that it is based on linguistic principles that were a part of Jakobson's proposal for aphasiology. His influence can be seen in the set of dichotomies that Luria has used to distinguish aphasia types.

The first dichotomy used to classify aphasia syndromes contrasts encoding with decoding, or speech comprehension processes with speech production processes. Luria used this distinction when organizing the two chapters in this volume which are devoted to the analysis of disturbances in the psychological processing of language (Chapters 15 and 16). In his recent writings, Luria (1975) has attributed this distinction to Vygotsky's (1934/1962) concern with the processes whereby a motive and a thought are converted into speech and vice versa. However, it is interesting to note that Jakobson (1971a) proposed that the first question to ask when categorizing aphasia syndromes is whether encoding or decoding is primarily affected.

In the case of the second major distinction in Luria's system of classifying aphasia syndromes, Jakobson clearly played the role of innovator. This is the distinction between what Luria terms "syntagmatic" and "paradigmatic" levels of organization and disruption in speech processes. These terms were originally proposed by de Saussure (1922), but it was Jakobson's (1971b) analysis of them and his related notions of the two modes of arrangement in speech—combination and selection—that provided the primary source of Luria's ideas on this topic. In one of his papers on aphasia, Jakobson wrote:

> Two different factors, selection and combination, play an essential role in any speech event. If, for instance, I intend to tell something about my father, I have to make a conscious or subconscious choice of one of the possible terms—father, parent, papa, dad, daddy; then, if I want to say that he is in bad shape, again I select one of the suitable words: ill, sick, indisposed, not healthy, ailing. Selections are one aspect of the twofold event, and the combination of the two selected entities, "Father is sick" is its other aspect. The entities among which we make our selection are mutually connected by various forms and degrees of similarity in all its varieties: likeness, similitude, equivalence, resemblance, analogy, diverse grades of specification, contrast. Contrary to selection, which is based on an internal relation, combination involves the external relation to contiguity in its various forms and degrees: neighborhood, proximity, and remoteness, subordination and coordination. (1971b, pp. 308–309)

Jakobson (1971b) argued that the distinction between selection and combination was very closely related to what Luria (1962/1966) had termed "sensory" and "efferent" aphasia. However, he proposed that the inclusion of linguistic principles in categorization schemes could provide precision and insights that would be unavailable in an account based solely on neuropsychological principles.

While the most obvious evidence of Jakobson's influence on Luria can be seen in the latter's distinction between syntagmatic and paradigmatic speech disorders, one can find other points of influence as well. For example, Luria's notion of the "codes" involved in the structure of language and his understanding of the phoneme owe a great deal to Jakobson.

The third major factor that influenced Luria's research was the Russian and Soviet tradition of research on the physiological and neurophysiological foundations of psychology. As was the case with linguistic research, Luria's genius at integrating contemporary research into a Vygotskian framework is apparent here.

This source of input to Luria's ideas has often been misinterpreted in the West. The biggest problem in this regard has arisen because of a tendency to equate Pavlovianism with behaviorism. As authors like Mecacci (1979) have pointed out, this has led to a great deal of confusion about the nature of Soviet psychology. The crucial issue here is that Luria was interested in Pavlov (1960) and others (e.g., Bernshtein, 1967) because of their analysis of the neurophysiological mechanisms involved in psychological processes. This is obviously not the same as being interested in behaviorism.

While Luria did not use the term "higher nervous activity" ("vysshyaya nervnaya deyatel'nost' ") extensively in his own writings, this is the Soviet field of research that guided his thinking on neurophysiological phenomena. As Mecacci (1979) points out, some of the precursors of the Soviet theory of higher vervous activity can be found in the writings of Sechenov (1961) and Bekhterev (1973). However, it was Pavlov's research that provided the real foundations for this line of inquiry. His approach constituted a break with earlier Russian physiology and with Western physiology and physiological psychology because of his interest in the neurodynamic processes that account for behavior. His analysis of the processes of inhibition and excitation plays a central role in Luria's account of the relationship between cortical functioning and psychological processes.

After Pavlov's death in 1936, other Soviet investigators made further advances in neurophysiology that allowed Luria to develop his ideas even further. For example, Bernshtein (1967) developed a sophisticated account of the physiology of movement. His approach was based on principles that subsequently were proposed in cybernetic analyses in the West. Along with other scholars, such as Anokhin (1949, 1969), Bernshtein developed an approach that allowed Luria to propose more sophisticated neurophysiological foundations for a Vygotskian framework than had previously been available.

In this volume, Luria's application of neurophysiological constructs within his Vygotskian theoretical framework is perhaps best illustrated in Chapter 6. There he discusses the development of the regulative function of speech. On the one hand, we see him dealing with the issue of how a child develops self-regulative abilities by transferring sociohistorically evolved mediational means (especially speech) from the interpsychological plane to the intrapsychological plane of functioning. Thus we see that he posed the problem in terms of the Vygotskian concerns with genetic explanation, the social origins of psychological processes, and semiotic mediation. On the other hand, Luria specified how this ontogenetic process depends on certain neurophysiological conditions. This aspect of his approach gives rise to his statements about the development of selective excitation and inhibition in the cortex. It is only by considering both the Vygotskian foundations and the neurophysiological mechanisms that one can understand Luria's overall approach.

The specific explanatory mechanism that Luria used to incorporate neurophysiological phenomena into a Vygotkian theoretical framework was the notion of "functional system." In the case of self-regulative speech, he points out in Chapter 6 that:

> ... we attempted to join both links (speech and motor) of the child's response into one "functional system." In this functional system the verbal response played a regulative role, reinforcing the adult's verbal command.

As in so many other areas of Luria's work, the foundations for the notion of the functional system can be found in Vygotsky's writings. However, here again we see that Luria made some important contributions of his own. In particular, he utilized the physiological models provided by Anokhin (1949, 1969) and Bernshtein (1967) to develop the notion of functional system in several respects.

The important point here is that by drawing from a variety of disciplines, Luria's integrative genius led to an approach to the study of language and cognition that is perhaps unparalleled in the breadth of phenomena it describes. One is hard pressed to identify another modern author who has devised an account of human consciousness that extends from linguistic and aesthetic phenomena on the one hand to neurophysiological phenomena on the other.

Our account of the factors that influenced Luria's understanding of language and cognition is far from complete. While there is little doubt his approach evolved as a result of integrating ideas from linguistics and neurophysiology into a Vygotskian theoretical framework, the reader of this volume will note that many other factors were involved as well. For example, in outlining our three themes, we have not dealt with the influence of other major figures in aphasiology, such as Goldstein (1948), Head (1926), Jackson (1932), and Pick (1913), and we have only touched on the importance of other students of Vygotsky, such as A. N. Leont'ev (1959).

In his epilogue to Luria's autobiography, Michael Cole (1979) pointed out that the trait that perhaps characterized Alexander Romanovich above all else was his boundless energy and enthusiasm, a trait which he retained to the very end of his life. Luria was constantly searching for new perspectives and empirical findings that could help him in his quest to understand the relationship between cortical processes and human psychological functioning. As a result, the reader will find numerous references to Soviet and Western works written shortly before death. For example, beginning in early 1976, he began to read the works of Norwegian social psychologist Rommetveit (1968, 1974) and decided he needed to return to the writings of Wittgenstein (1972) in order to develop further insights into the functions of language. In some cases, one can argue that he was too quick to assimilate ideas and that they sometimes added very little to his approach or even detracted from it. For example, it is my opinion that some of his attempts to utilize ideas from transformational generative grammar in his psychological accounts of language processing were inappropriate. However, there are few scholars in the world today who can say that they have crossed so many disciplinary boundaries while making such important and original contributions to our understanding of thought and language.

As Macdonald Critchley observed in his foreword to the English translation of Luria's *Traumatic Aphasia*, we cannot predict the fate of Luria's approach. If Alexander Romanovich were alive today, he undoubtedly would continue to be the first to criticize his own ideas and to call for further revision. From the present perspective, however, one must agree with Critchley that an appropriate summary of the Western investigator's impression of Luria's work can be found in Sydney Smith's statement that ". . . the further he went West the more convinced he felt that wise men came from the East . . . "

James V. Wertsch
Northwestern University

REFERENCES

Akhutina, T. V. *Neirolingvisticheskii analiz dinamicheskoi afazii.* [A neurolinguistic analysis of dynamic aphasia]. Moscow: Izdatel'stvo Moskovskogo Universiteta, 1975.

Akhutina, T. V. The role of inner speech in the construction of an utterance. *Soviet psychology*, Spring, 1978, XVI (3), 3–30.

Anokhin, P. K. (Ed.), *Problemy vysshei nervnoi devatel'nosti.* [Problems of higher nervous activity]. Moscow: Academy of Medical Sciences, SSSR, 1949.

Anokhin, P. K. Electroencephalographic analysis of the conditioned reflex. In K. H. Pribram (Ed.), *Brain and Behavior. 3. Memory mechanisms.* Harmondsworth, England: Penguin, 1969.

Apresyan, Yu. D. *Leksicheskaya semantika.* [Lexical semantics]. Moscow: Nauka, 1974.

Bekhterev, V. M. *General principles of human reflecology: The objective study of personality.* New York: Arno Press, 1973.

Bernshtein, N. A. *The coordination and regulation of movements.* Oxford: Pergamon, 1967.

Bierwisch, M. Ueber einige semantischer Darstellung. In F. Kiefer (Ed.), *Semantik und generative grammatik.* Frankfurt: Athenäum, 1972.

Chomsky, N. *Syntactic structures.* The Hague: Mounton, 1957.

Chomsky, N. *Aspects of the theory of syntax.* Cambridge, Mass.: MIT Press, 1965.

Cole, M. Epilogue: A portrait of Luria. In A. R. Luria. *The making of mind: A personal account of Soviet psychology.* Edited by M. Cole and S. Cole. Cambridge, Mass.: Harvard University Press, 1979.

Goldstein, K. *Language and language disorders.* New York: Grune and Stratton, 1948.

Head, H. *Aphasia and kindred disorders of speech.* London: Cambridge University Press, 1926.

Jackson, J. H. Notes on the physiology and pathology of language. In *Selected writings of John Hughlings Jackson.* London: Hodder and Stouton, 1932.

Jakobson, R. O. *Kindersprache, Aphasie und allgemeine Lautgesetze.* Uppsala: Almquist and Wiksell, 1942.

Jakobson, R. O. Aphasia as a linguistic topic. In *Selected writings.* Vol. II. The Hague: Mouton, 1971a.

Jakobson, R. O. Linguistic types of aphasia. In *Selected writings.* Vol. II. The Hague: Mouton, 1971b.

Jakobson, R. O. Toward a linguistic classification of aphasic impairments. In *Selected writings.* Vol. II. The Hague: Mouton, 1971c.

Jakobson, R. O. Two aspects of language and two types of aphasic disturbances. In *Selected writings.* Vol. II. The Hague: Mouton, 1971d.

Jakobson, R. O., Fant, C. G. M. and Halle, M. *Preliminaries to speech analysis.* Cambridge, Mass.: MIT Press, 1952.

Jakobson, R. O. and Halle, M. *Fundamentals of language.* The Hague: Mouton, 1956.

Janet, P. *L'intelligence avant le langage.* Paris: Ernest Flammarion, 1936.

Leont'ev, A. N. *Problemy razvitiya psikhiki.* [Problems in the development of mind]. Moscow: Izdatel'stvo Moskovskogo Universiteta, 1959.

Leont'ev, A. N. *Activity, consciousness, and personality.* Englewood Cliffs, N.J.: Prentice-Hall, 1978.

Leont'ev, A. N. The problem of activity in psychology. In J. V. Wertsch (Ed.), *The concept of activity in Soviet psychology.* White Plains, N.Y.: Sharpe, in press.

Luria, A. R. *Travmaticheskaya afaziya.* Moscow: Izdatel'stvo Akademii Meditsinskikh Nauk SSSR, 1947. (English translation: *Traumatic Aphasia.* The Hague: Mouton, 1970.)

Luria, A. R. *Vysshie korkovye funktsii cheloveka i ikh narushenie pri lokal'nykh porazheniyakh mozga.* Moscow: Izdatel'stvo Moskovskogo Universiteta, 1962. (English translation: *Higher cortical functions in man.* New York: Basic Books, 1966.)

Luria, A. R. *Osnovnye problemy neirolingvistiki*. Moscow: Izdatel'stvo Moskov-skogo Universiteta, 1975. (English translation: *Basic problems of neurolinguistics*. The Hague: Mouton, 1976.)

Luria, A. R. Introductory comment on dust jacket. In L. S. Vygotsky. *Mind in society: The development of higher psychological processes*. Edited by M. Cole, V. John-Steiner, S. Scribner and E. Souberman. Cambridge, Mass.: Harvard University Press, 1978.

Luria, A. R. *The making of mind: A personal account of Soviet psychology*. Edited by M. Cole and S. Cole. Cambridge, Mass.: Harvard University Press, 1979.

Mecacci, L. *Brain and history: The relationship between neurophysiology and psychology in Soviet research*. New York: Brunner/Mazel, 1979.

Mel'chuk, I. A. *Ocherk teorii yazokovikh modelei "Smysl-Tekst"*. [Outline of the theory of "Sense-Text" linguistic models]. Moscow: Nauka, 1974.

Pavlov, I. P. *Conditioned reflexes: An investigation of the physiological activity of the cerebral cortex*. New York: Dover, 1960.

Pick, A. *Die agrammatischen Sprachstorungen*. Berlin: Springer, 1913.

Rommetveit, R. *Words, meanings and messages*. New York: Academic Press, 1968.

Rommetveit, R. *On message structure: A framework for the study of language and communication*. London: Wiley, 1974.

Saussure, F. de. *Cours de linguistique generale*. Paris: Payot, 1922.

Sechenov, I. M. *Selected physiological and psychological works*. Moscow: Foreign Languages Press, 1961.

Smirnov, A. A. *Razvitie i sovremennoe sostoyanie psikhologicheskoi nauki v SSSR*. [The development and current state of psychology in the USSR]. Moscow: Pedagogika, 1975.

Svedelius, C. *L'analyse du langage*. Uppsala, 1897.

Trubetskoi, N. S. *Grundzuge de Phonologie*. Prague: Cercle Linguistique de Prague, 1939.

Vygotsky, L. S. *Myshlenie i rech'*. [Thinking and speech]. Moscow: Sotsekriz, 1934. (English translation: *Thought and Language*. Cambridge, Mass.: MIT Press, 1962.)

Vygotsky, L. S. *Mind in society: The development of higher psychological processes*. Edited by M. Cole, V. John-Steiner, S. Scribner and E. Souberman. Cambridge, Mass.: Harvard University Press, 1978.

Vygotsky, L. S. The genesis of higher mental functions. In J. V. Wertsch (Ed.), *The concept of activity in Soviet psychology*. White Plains, N.Y.: Sharpe, in press. (a)

Vygotsky, L. S. The development of higher forms of attention in childhood. In J. V. Wertsch (Ed.), *The concept of activity in Soviet psychology*. White Plains, N.Y.: Sharpe, in press. (b)

Wittgenstein, L. *Philosophical investigations*. Oxford: Blackwell, 1972.

Zholkovskii, A. K. On the rules of semantic analysis. In *Mashinnyi perevod i prikladnaya lingvistika*. [Machine translation and applied linguistics, No. 8]. Moscow, 1964.

Chapter 1

The Problem of Language and Consciousness

The psychological structure of language, its role in communication and in the formation of consciousness, is perhaps the most important branch of psychology.

The crucial problem of consciousness concerns how humans reflect the real world in which they live (i.e., how they form a subjective image of the objective world). Most importantly, humans are not limited to the direct impressions of their surroundings; they are able to transcend the bounds of sensory experience and penetrate further into the essence of things than is possible by direct perception. Humans are able to abstract individual characteristics of things, to perceive the relationships into which things enter.

Lenin pointed out repeatedly that the study of cognition, and hence of science, is not so much a study of things in and of themselves, as the interrelationship among them. A glass tumbler may be a subject of study in physics if we are interested in its material makeup, in economics if we approach it from the perspective of value, or in aesthetics if we are primarily interested in its aesthetic value. We perceive things not only visually, but also by virtue of their connections and

17

associations. Thus, we go beyond the bounds of sensory experience and form abstract concepts which enable us to penetrate more deeply into the essence of things.

Humans not only perceive things; they also reason about them or draw conclusions from their direct observations. They are sometimes able to draw conclusions even if they have no direct personal experience. If a person is given two premises of a syllogism, such as: (1) in all regional centers there are post offices and (2) X is a regional center, he/she can easily derive at the conclusion that in the place called X there is a post office, although he/she may never have been in this regional center or even heard of it. Humans, therefore, not only can go beyond immediate perception, they also are able to draw conclusions on the basis of reason without direct concrete experience. This suggests that humans possess far more complex means of receiving and processing information than immediate perception.

What we have said so far may be formulated in another way. Humans are characterized not only by sensory, but also by *rational*, cognition. Humans have the ability to penetrate more deeply into the essence of things than is possible through immediate perception by sensory organs. In other words, with the transition from the animal world to human history, a great advance from sensory to rational perception takes place. That is why the classics of Marxism have quite rightly pointed out that the transition from sensory to the rational experience is no less important than the transition from inorganic to living matter.

This may be illustrated by a single example taken from facts obtained from evolutionary psychology. I have in mind the Buitendiyk's Experiment, which illustrates better than any other the differences between human and animal thinking. Buitendiyk's observations were carried out on a number of animals belonging to different species, such as birds, dogs, and monkeys. Several small jars were arranged in front of the animal. A piece of bait was placed in a jar while the animal was watching, and the jar was covered. Naturally, the animal ran to the jar, turned it over, and obtained the bait. Next, the bait was placed under a second jar. If the animal did not see the bait under this new jar, it would run to the first jar. Only when it did not find the bait there would it run to the second, where it was obtained. This procedure was repeated several times, the bait being placed each time under the next jar in a series. The experiment showed that in animal behavior traces of the previous visual experience dominates, and the abstract principle "next" if not formed.

In contrast, even a child of 3½ or 4 years of age easily grasps the principle "next," and after a few trials stretches his/her hand toward the jar that had never hidden bait but occupied the "next" position.

What we have said so far supports the notion that, unlike animals, humans possess new forms of reflecting reality—forms which are not visual and concrete but are abstracted through experience, forms which are not sensory but are rational. The ability to transcend the bounds of immediate concrete[1] experience is a fundamental feature of human consciousness.

How can we explain the transition in humans from concrete experience to abstract experience, from the sensory to the rational? This fundamental problem has been asked repeatedly in psychology for over a century. Psychologists can be divided into two camps on the basis of how they approached this problem. Psychologists who belonged to the idealist camp acknowledged the fundamental fact of the transition from sensory to rational experience, the fact that in contrast to animals humans possess qualitatively new forms of cognitive activity. However, they could find no explanation for this transition. Although they described the fact, they refused to *explain* it. A second group of psychologists—the mechanists—tried to approach psychological phenomena in a deterministic way, but they limited themselves to explaining only the elementary psychological processes and preferred to remain silent on the question of consciousness. They ignored the issue of the transition from sensory to rational experience by limiting themselves to the study of elementary behavioral phenomena, such as instincts and habits. The American behaviorists were in this camp.

Let us consider in a greater detail the positions of these two camps of psychologists. The idealist psychologists (e.g., Dilthey, 1901; Spanger, 1926, 1929) argued that the highest level of abstract behavior, behavior determined by abstract categories, characterizes humans. However, from this they immediately concluded that such level of abstract consciousness is the expression of peculiar spiritual powers inherent in the human mind. They argued that the ability to transcend the bounds of sensory experience and operate on the basis of abstract categories is a property of the spiritual world that is manifested in humans but missing in animals. This was the basic position of many dualist accounts, the most striking example of which was Descartes'.

Descartes' basic postulate was that animals act according to mechanistic laws and their behavior can be explained in a strictly deterministic way. He argued, however, that such a deterministic explanation of behavior is not valid for humans. In contrast to animals, humans operate on the basis of a spiritual principle, making abstract thinking and conscious behavior possible. This principle cannot be deduced from material phenomena. Its roots go back into the properties of the spirit. These ideas provide the foundation for Descartes' dualistic conception. Kant's views were close to those of Descartes. For Kant, all conscious activity could be divided into two kinds: the a posteriori, i.e., categories which can be deduced from

---

[1]The word "concrete" is the translation of a word ("neglyadnyi") Luria uses quite frequently in the early sections of this volume. In other contexts, it is often translated as "visual." For Luria, something is concrete to the extent that it is processed with a minumum of cognitive effort. In particular, he used this term when treating the issue of how humans can deal with their environment without invoking the abstract categories and reasoning processes that characterize consciousness.—*J. V. Wertsch*

the subject's experience, and the a priori, i.e., those categories which are embedded in the depths of the human spirit. The essence of human consciousness, according to Kant, is precisely that it can go beyond the bounds of concrete experience. Consciousness is a transcendental process, a process of passing beyond sensory experience to inner essences and categories. The mechanisms of this process lead to a transition from sensory experience to generalized rational processes which are embedded in the human spirit.

Kantian ideas have influenced idealistic thinking in the 20th century. One of the most important neo-Kantians was German philosopher Cassirer, whose work *The Philosophy of Symbolic Forms* (1953) is of fundamental importance. According to Cassirer, certain symbolic forms are characteristic of the human spirit. These are expressed in signs, in the language of abstract concepts. It is precisely the ability to think and to organize their behavior within the framework of "symbolic forms" (i.e., not only within the limits of sensory experience) that distinguishes humans from animals. This ability to think and act in symbolic forms derives from the fact that humans possess spiritual properties which animals lack.

Philosophers of the idealistic camp argue that these principles can be described but cannot be explained. It is on this basis that the whole of contemporary phenomenology, the doctrine regarding the essential forms of the spiritual world, is founded. The ultimate form of this doctrine is reached in the works of German philosopher Husserl. Phenomenology proceeds from the following simple proposition: No one has any doubt that the sum of the angles of a triangle is equal to two right angles. This can be studied and described, but it would be foolish to ask, "Why is it that the sum of the angles of a triangle equals two right angles?" This fact is given as a known basic a priori phenomenological characteristic of geometry. Geometry is constructed in accordance with the strictest laws and can be studied and described, but it does not require explanations such as those found in physics and chemistry. Precisely in the same manner as we describe geometry, we can also describe the phenomenology of spiritual life, i.e., those laws that characterize complex forms of abstract thinking and categorical behavior. All these laws can be described, but they cannot be explained. By virtue of such assertions, idealistic philosophy as well as idealistic psychology are cut off both from the natural sciences and from any kind of scientific psychology.

So far, we have been talking about the philosophical foundations of dualism. Now we turn to problems of psychology. For the most important psychologist of the 19th century, Wilhelm Wundt, there existed, first of all, elementary processes—feelings, sensations, perceptions, attention, and memory. These processes follow elementary natural laws and are accessible to scientific (and sometimes physiological) explanations. However, he argued that in human mental processes there are also phenomena which go beyond the limits of direct sensation, perception, and memory. These processes are especially evident in which Wundt called "apperception," i.e., active human perception, perception arising out of the active orientation of humans' will or volition. According to Wundt, these processes of active, abstract perception go beyond the limits of sensory experience. They relate to higher spiritual phenomena. They can be described, but it is not possible to explain them because basic a priori categories of the human spirit are inherent in them. Wundt's theory of apperception was further elaborated in the beginning of the 20th century. In its wider formulations, it became the basis of a particular trend in psychology that came to be known as the Würzburg School.

Psychologists who belonged to the Würzburg School, such as Kulpe, Ach, Messer, and Bühler, began analyzing the laws which govern the most complex forms of consciousness. They concluded that consciousness and thinking cannot be considered as forms of sensory experience. Thinking occurs without the participation of visual images or words; it is a special category of mental processes at the basis of which lie precisely the spiritual properties mentioned above. According to the Würzburg School, thinking comes from "direction" or "intention" derived from the human spirit. It is formless and nonsensory, follows its own laws, and cannot be reduced to elementary physiological laws.

The experiments that provided the basis for these conclusions are well known. They were carried out on highly qualified subjects—professors and senior lecturers who were able to observe their inner world and to describe the processes that they had observed. The tasks used were quite complex. For instance, subjects were asked to comprehend the sense of the sentence, "Thinking is so unusually difficult that many prefer simply to draw conclusions." Then they were asked to say whether it was correct or not. They would think, repeat the sentence to themselves and say, "Aha, of course, it is correct. Thinking is really so difficult that it is simpler to avoid the labor involved in thinking. It is better to come straight to a conclusion." In another case, the following sentence was presented: "The laurels of pure will are dry leaves which will never turn green." It is not difficult to see that each part of this sentence is something concrete—"laurels," "dry leaves," "will turn not green." However, the essence of this sentence does not lie either in "dry leaves" or in "greenness"; its essence lies in the fact that "pure will" is such an abstract concept that it is never expressed in sensory experience and cannot be reduced to sensory experience. When the subjects were asked what exactly they experienced as they were forming their conclusions, it turned out that they could say nothing. The process of abstract thinking was so far removed from reality that it had no sensory basis; it did not evoke any images or words. In fact, it was necessary to get away from images in order to penetrate into the meaning of the second sentence. As a rule, subjects arrived at the conclusion "intuitively," on the basis of some "logical process" which a person goes through when perceiving such a sentence. On this basis, the Würzburg psychologists argued that humans possess some kind of "logical feeling" or experience of the correctness or incorrectness of an idea, a feeling similar to that we experience when we are given a syllogism and arrive immediately at a logical conclusion. This conclusion is not made on the basis of a single personal experience, but on the basis of a "logical process"; and this "logical process," according to the Würzburg School, is precisely that primary property of the spiritual world which distinguishes humans from animals and distinguishes the rational from the sensory.

Members of the Würzburg School obtained similar results when they conducted simpler experiments. For example, subjects were asked to find the genus of a species ("chair—furniture"), or the species of a genus ("furniture—chair"), or a part of a whole, or the whole of a part. In these cases, too, the process of rational conclusion flowed automatically. According to these psychologists, it was based neither on sensory experience nor on verbal reasoning. The phenomena studied were quite different from those examined in the psychology or psychophysiology of sensation and perception.

It is interesting to note that the dualism which marked the work of these psychologists and which distinguished sharply between elementary "sensory experience" and "nonsensual, categorical" consciousness or thinking emerged very strikingly, even among physiologists. To illustrate this, we name only two among the important foreign physiologists—Charles Sherrington, one of the founders of the reflex theory, and John Eccles, a noted physiologist and the founder of the current theory of the synaptic functioning of the neuron. Both scientists are very distinguished in their own field, but both turn to idealism as soon as they approach the question of explaining the higher psychological processes of consciousness and thinking.

Sherrington published two books toward the end of his life—*The Brain and Its Mechanisms* (1934) and *Man on His Nature* (1942)—in which he advanced the thesis that a physiologist is unable to explain the spiritual world and that the human spirit, the world of voluntary acts, is a reflection of the spiritual world. The brain is viewed simply as a conduit of this spiritual world.

John Eccles, who published a number of works, the last of which is *Facing Reality* (1970), arrived at a very similar conclusion. He proceeded from the premise that reality is not the reality we perceive through our senses. It is not the external world in which humans live. The basic reality for Eccles was the reality of the inner world; it was what humans live through themselves and what remains inaccessible to others. The position of Ernst Mach, already known to us, lies at the basis of Eccles' subjective idealism.

What is the explanation of the fact that humans can perceive themselves, evaluate themselves, and be aware of their states? Eccles said that this is not to be explained by examining material processes, as the materialists hold, but in special neural devices, which serve as "detectors" of the spiritual world beyond. Eccles even tried to calculate the size of these detectors.

It is not difficult to comprehend the dead ends reached by a dualism which starts by contrasting sensory experience with rational experience and then refuses to provide a scientific explanation of the latter. All of these positions adopted by philosophers and psychologists serve the valuable role of drawing our attention to an important sphere, i.e., the sphere of rational, categorical experience. However, their negative aspect lies in the fact that, having drawn attention to this abstract, categorical thinking and to the pure voluntary act, these scholars refused to arrive at a scientific explanation of that type of reality. They did not try to approach these phenomena as a product of the complex development of humans and human society. Rather, they assumed that this kind of reality arises out of a special "spiritual experience" which has no material roots and belongs to an absolutely different sphere of being. That view precludes a scientific treatment of the most important side of human mental life.

It is therefore understandable that psychologists who were not satisfied with these idealist views should seek new avenues to open the way to a causal scientific explanation of these very complex mental phenomena. The views of the idealist psychologists, which we have discussed very briefly, could not, of course, satisfy those psychologists who consider it their main task to find a scientific, deterministic explanation of the phenomena involved. Thus, in an effort to refute them, an opposing view was developed in psychology. Psychologists of this opposing school took their cue from the basic proposition of empiricist philosophers who asserted that "anything which exists in thought must exist earlier in sensory experience" ("Nihil est in intellectu, quod non fuerit primo in sensu"). Their goal was to approach the phenomena of thinking through the same methods which can be used to approach the elementary phenomena of sensory experience.

Although the basic proposition of empiricist philosophy is undoubtedly sound, attempts to operationalize this proposition in "empirical" or classical experimental psychology immediately gave rise to other, equally insurmountable difficulties. While trying to explain highly complex forms of thinking, researchers of this school of thought proceeded, in practice, from an opposite *mechanistic* standpoint. In its earliest stages, these positions arose in the assertion that the human mind is a *tabula rasa* on which experience inscribes its letters. While correctly pointing out that without experience nothing can happen, researchers of this school approached the study of highly complex, abstract or "categorical" thinking from a perspective based on reductionism. They argued that in order to understand the laws of thinking, it is sufficient to postulate two elementary processes—a representational or sensory image on the one hand, and the association or connection of these sensory experiences on the other. According to them, thinking is nothing but the association of sensory representations.

The views of these associationist psychologists, who occupied center stage in 19th century psychology and who accepted the ideas of the analytical natural science of that time, were completely counter to the notion that complex forms of abstract thinking are unique or independent. All of these psychologists proceeded from the hypothesis that even the most complex forms of thinking can be understood as a series of visual representations, and that the assumption of "a priori categories" (in particular the positions of the Würzburg School) does not reflect any reality and is therefore unacceptable in principle. These views gave rise to a number of schools of associationist psychologists of the 19th century, among whom one can name Herbert in Germany, Beck in England, and Taine in France. That is why in the works of those psychologists who dealt with sensations, representations, and associations one will find neither a chapter on thinking nor a description of what distinguishes animal behavior from human conscious activity.

The most extreme form of this approach can perhaps be found in the writings of members of the "objective" science of behavior—the American behaviorists. From the very start, the behaviorists refused to study abstract thinking. For them, the subject of psychology was behavior, and behavior itself was understood to consist of responses to stimuli. The bonds between stimuli and responses were formed through repetition. In other words, it was a process formed in accordance with Pavlov's account of a conditioned reflex. The behaviorists never undertook the analysis of the physiological mechanisms of behavior and it was this that basically set their views apart from the doctrine of higher nervous activity. They limited themselves to analyzing the external phenomenology of behavior, which they explained in an oversimplified manner. They tried to approach all human behavior in the same way as they approached animal behavior. This was possible because of their view that behavior consists solely of the simple formation of habits. Therefore, if we examine psychology textbooks written by behaviorists (including those written until very recently), we find chapters on instincts and habits, but not a single chapter on topics such as volition, thinking, or consciousness. For the authors of these textbooks, abstract ("categorical") behavior does not exist and cannot, therefore, be the topic of scientific analysis.

Now let us turn to an appraisal of the viewpoint of this group of psychologists. A positive characteristic of their work was that they tried not only to describe, but also to explain, psychological phenomena. The weakness of their approach lay in their reductionism, i.e., attempting to reduce the highest forms of psychological processes (with all their complex nature) to elementary operations. They refused to recognize the specific nature of the highly complex type of conscious categorical behavior. It is difficult to give a better definition of behavioristic reductionism than the one given by one of their own writers, T. Taylor. In the foreword to his textbook of psychology which came out in 1974, he writes:

> ... it is known that the subject matter of psychology is behavior, which can be traced from the amoeba to the human being. The attentive reader will easily see that the basic standpoint of this book is the standpoint of reductionism. The reductionist tries to explain phenomena by reducing them to the parts which constitute the whole. The biological bases of behavior can be reduced to movements of muscles and contractions of glands, which in their turn are the result of chemical processes. These chemical processes can be understood from the changes that take place in molecular structures,

which in their turn lead to changes in the correlations of atoms on the submolecular level and are expressed in mathematical indices. A logical extension of reductionism will enable us to express man's behavior also in mathematical concepts. (Retranslated from Russian.—*J. V. W.*)

Naturally, an approach based on such a proposition precludes the possibility of dealing with the complex forms of conscious activity that characterize humans and are the product of complex social evolution.

A crisis in psychology arose as a result of the clash between these two approaches. This crisis, which had taken final shape by the first quarter of the 20th century, was expressed in the fact that psychology was practically split into two, quite independent, disciplines. One of them, "descriptive psychology" or "the psychology of spiritual life" ("Geisteswissenschaftliche Psychologie") acknowledged the existence of the higher, complex forms of psychological life, but denied the possibility of explaining them. Thus, it was limited to a phenomenology or description. The other approach, "explanatory" or scientific psychology ("Erklarende Psychologie"), understood its task as one of building a scientifically-based psychology. However, it limited itself to an explanation of the elementary psychological processes and refused to provide any explanation of the more complex forms of psychological life.

There was one way to resolve this crisis. The study of human psychology must examine the more complex forms of conscious activity, but, at the same time, it must not be aimed at *describing* these forms as a manifestation of spiritual life. Rather, it must *explain* the origin of these forms of conscious activity on the basis of processes which are amenable to analysis. In other words, the problem was to retain a study of the more complex forms of consciousness as the first, basic aim of psychology, while ensuring a materialistic and a deterministic approach to their causal explanation.

What could be done to resolve the crisis? An answer was provided by L. S. Vygotsky, one of the founders of Soviet psychology. In many respects he determined the course of the development of Soviet psychology in the following decades. What was Vygotsky's proposal? His basic position sounds paradoxical. It is as follows: *In order to explain the highly complex forms of human consciousness one must go beyond the human organism. One must seek the origins of conscious activity and "categorical" behavior not in the recesses of the human brain or in the depths of the spirit, but in the external conditions of life. Above all, this means that one must seek these origins in the external processes of social life, in the social and historical forms of human existence.*

Let us examine this statement in greater detail. We proceeded from the position that the subject matter of psychology is not only the inner life of humans, but *the reflection in this inner life of the external world* (i.e., the active inter-action between humans and external reality). The human organism, with its needs and unique, historically evolved forms of activity, reflects the conditions in the external world and processes the information which reaches it. In biology, this is known as the process of metabolism, the assimilation by the organism of sub-stances needed by the organism and secretion of products resulting from its me-tabolism. In the more complex physiological processes, the basis of life is the reflected image of the internal and external influences. The organism receives information and subjects it to refraction through the prism of its needs or pur-poses, processes it, creates a model of its own behavior, and builds a certain scheme of expected results with the help of advance stimulation. If its behavior coincides with these schemes, it ceases. If, however, its behavior does not coincide with these schemes, the stimulation again circulates along the same path, and an active search for the solution continues (Bernshtein, 1967; Miller, Galanter, and Pribram, 1960).

Exactly the same thing applies to the highly complex forms of conscious life. However, in this case it is not a question of assimilation of material stimuli. Rather it is a question of processing the highly complex information which reaches humans. They process this information through sense activity and with the help of language.

As we have already stated, humans differ from other animals because, with the transition to *sociohistorical existence, to labor*, and to the forms of social life associated with it, all basic categories of man's behavior undergo a radical change. Human activity is founded on social labor and the division of social labor. These aspects of human life give rise to new forms of behavior that are indepen-dent of biological motives. Direct, instinctive behavior yields to complex, indirect behavior. Thus, from the point of view of biology, it would be meaningless to scatter seeds on the ground instead of eating them, drive away wild animals and birds instead of catching them, or grind and polish stones without considering their future use. Social labor and the division of labor result in indirect behavior, which is subject to social, as well as biological, stimuli. It is precisely these factors that give rise to new, nonbiological human needs. Thus are formed those specific-ally human forms of mental activity. This activity can give rise to initiating stimuli and goals which, in turn, lead to specific *acts*. These acts are carried out by the appropriate set of operations. The structure of the complex forms of human activity has been worked out in detail in Soviet psychology by A. N. Leont'ev (1959, 1975). We will not, therefore, dwell on this question in greater detail here.

The second decisive factor determining the transition from animal behavior to human conscious activity is the appearance of *language*. As Engels correctly pointed out, it was in the process of social labor that the need arose for people to say something to each other, to specify the situation in which they are partici-pating, and to convey the information which emerges as a result of the division of labor. During the initial stages, this language was closely ties to gestures, and an inarticulate sound could mean either "Be careful!" or "Pull harder!" The exact meaning of such a sound depended on factors such as the situation in which it was used, the action needed, the gesture accompanying it, and the tone in which it was uttered. The birth of language led to the gradual appearance of a whole system of codes signifying objects and actions. This system of codes later began to differentiate signs, acts and relationships, and finally led to the formation of complex codes of sentences that could be used to form complex utterances.

That system of codes came to assume a decisive importance for the further development of human conscious activity. Language, at first, was very closely connected with practical activity, i.e., it had a "sympractical character." Gradually, it began to become separated from practice and constitute a system of codes adequate for expressing any information. However, as we shall see, there was a long period of time during which this system of codes retained a close connection with concrete human activity.

Language, in the course of social history, became the decisive instrument which helped humans transcend the boundaries of sensory experience, to assign symbols, and to formulate certain generalizations or categories. Thus, if humans had not possessed the capacity for labor and had not had language, they would not have developed abstract, "categorical" thinking. That is why we should not seek the origins of abstract thinking and categorical behavior, which mark a sharp change from the sensory to the rational, within human consciousness or within the human brain. Rather, we should seek these origins in the social forms of human historical existence. Only in this way (which differs radically from all the teachings of traditional psychology) can we explain the appearance of complex forms of conscious behavior that are uniquely human.

This constitutes the basic position of a Marxist psychology. The fundamental significance of these principles should not be underestimated. In order to determine what distinguishes humans from animals, or in order to understand the transition from sensory to rational experience, from the concrete to the abstract, one must not remain within the circle of subjective experiences or consider only the internal processes of the brain. Instead, one must turn to an analysis of the objective forms of human historical existence, of social practice, which make use of instruments and language. One must examine conscious processes as the product of these forms of social life. Only thus can we find an explanation of the forms of "categorical" behavior characteristic of humans.

It is not difficult to see that by adopting such an approach, conscious activity will be the basic subject of psychology. However, we shall at the same time make the complex forms of human conscious activity the object of a deterministic analysis. We shall not refuse to *explain* the highly complex phenomena involved. The basic difference between our approach and that of traditional psychology will be that we are not seeking the origins of human consciousness in the depths of the "soul" or in the independently acting mechanisms of the brain (where we shall find nothing). Rather, we are operating in an entirely different sphere—in humans' actual relationship with reality, in their social history, which is closely tied to labor and language.

We shall, therefore, approach the problems of consciousness and abstract thinking by linking them with the problem of language. Thus, we shall seek the roots of these complex processes in the social forms of human existence, in the actual use of that language which enables us to abstract, codify, and generalize signs and objects. This is the essence of language. As we have already said, language was initially tied inextricably to practice and then gradually began to take shape as a system sufficient in itself for the expression of any abstract relationship or thought.

Before proceeding any further, we must consider yet another fundamental question: Is language, and the forms of conscious activity connected with it, unique to humans? Is it not true that animals also possess language? If so, how does this language differ from truly human language?

The idea that language also exists in the animal world is often encountered in literature. For example, writers frequently point out that when the leader of a flight of cranes begins to trumpet, the whole flock of birds rises in alarm; or when the leader of a herd of deer lets out a cry, the entire herd follows that deer because they understand the danger signal. Finally, and most interestingly, it is often said that bees have their own social "language," expressed in the so-called "bee dance." It is said that a bee that has returned from gathering honey informs others where it has come from, whether the source of honey is far away, and in which direction they should fly to get it. This information is conveyed by the bee through "dances," through figures that it describes in the air. These dances indicate both the direction and the distance of the source. All of these facts seem to suggest that animals have language. Thus, if animals do have language and can convey information just like humans can, then the entire argument that we have proposed above falls to the grounds (Frisch, 1923, 1967).

In this connection, questions arise as to whether any kind of language really exists among animals, and if it does, whether it really is a language or is only something similar to language, a "language" in a relative sense of the word. During the past few decades, the issue of animal "language" has attracted a great deal of attention. This interest began with the studies of Frisch on the "language" of bees (1923) and was followed by a considerable number of studies devoted to sound communication among birds. Finally, there have been several research studies into what may be called nonverbal communication among apes. A number of American psychologists have published their findings in this area during the last 10 years (e.g., Gardner and Gardner, 1969, 1971; Premack, 1971a, 1971b). Their studies have been devoted to analyzing whether an ape can be taught to speak. For this purpose, apes were taught to use visual, rather than vocal, signs.

For instance, an oval meant "pear," a square—"nut," a line—"to give," a dot—"I don't want," etc. It was claimed that the data showed that apes could use this "vocabulary" after prolonged training. Consequently, there was lively discussion as to whether language exists even among animals as an innate form of behavior.

As far as we are concerned, the question poses no theoretical difficulty. One must understand only that by language we have in mind a complex system of codes, signifying objects, attributes, actions, and relationships. On the basis of these entities, it is possible to carry on the complex functions of coding and transferring of information and the mediation of highly complex systems. A "language" lacking these characteristics is a quasi-language. All these attributes are, in fact, characteristic of human language. If a human being says "briefcase," he/she not only indicates a certain object in the speech situation, but, as we shall see later, analyzes it and introduces it into a certain system of associations and relationships. If a person says "brown," he/she abstracts something about this briefcase, indicating only its color. If he/she says "lies," he/she abstracts from the object its position, showing that it is lying and not moving. If he/she says, "This briefcase is lying on the table" or "This briefcase is standing near the table," he/she abstracts a relationship or conveys a whole message. A developed language, therefore, represents a system of codes adequate for conveying or denoting any information, even information that is not tied to practical activity.

Can we apply this definition to the language of animals? The answer is no. Human language designates things or actions, properties and relations, and hence conveys and processes objective information. The natural "language" of animals, however, does not designate a stable object, attribute, property, or relationship. Rather, it only expresses *a condition* or *what the animal is going through*. Thus, instead of conveying objective information, it only infects others with the same feelings the animal producing the sign experience (as in the case of the leader of the flock of cranes or of the herd of deer) and evokes a certain conditioned response movement. The crane experiences alarm, the alarm is expressed by its cry, and the cry infects the other members of the flock with the same feeling. A deer who reacts to danger by raising its ears, turning its head, straining the muscles of its body and running, and sometimes by emitting a cry, expresses its condition. Consequently, the signal emitted by an animal is an expression of its affective condition, and the reception of this signal indicates the infection of others by the same condition—nothing more.

The same argument can also be applied to the "language" of bees. A bee is guided back to its hive by a number of indicators still not well known to us (probably the angle of the sun or perhaps the magnetic field). This bee experiences a degree of exhaustion. When it goes through its dance upon arriving back at the hive, it expresses its condition (which is determined objectively by a number of factors, still not adequately understood). The bees that perceive this dance and infected by these conditions, are drawn into them, and in this way receive the information. But this information does not designate an object, action, or relationship. It reflects the particular condition of the bee that has returned from a long flight.

Recent studies which involve teaching an artificial "language" to apes call for another interpretation. We would argue that here we have a case of complex forms of the artificial development of conditioned responses which resemble human language in its external characteristics. However, this development does not constitute any special form of activity that arises among these apes naturally. This problem is the subject of lively debate at the present time and we shall not deal with it in detail here.

All of this leads to the conclusion that there is a fundamental difference between human language (as a system of objective codes, evolved in the process of social history and designating objects, actions, properties, and relationships) and animal "language" (which is nothing but external signals expressing affective states). In the latter case, the "decoding" of the signs is not the decoding of an objective code, but the involvement of other animals in similar common experience. Consequently, the "language" of animals is neither a means of designating objects nor a means for abstracting properties, and cannot be considered a means of generating abstract thinking. Hence, any reference to language among animals does not in any way refute what we have said before.

Humans differ from animals because of the existence of human langauge—a system of codes that designates external objects and their relationships, and helps to arrange these objects into certain sytems of categories. This system of codes leads to the formation of abstract thinking, to the formation of "categorical" consciousness. We shall, therefore, consider the problem of consciousness and of abstract thinking in terms of its close relationship with the problem of language.

Chapter 2
The Word and Its Semantic Structure

As we have already stated, our central concern is with the role of language in the formation of human consciousness. This leads us to pose several important questions. What, in the structure of language, enables us to abstract and generalize the properties of the external world, in other words, to form concepts? What are the characteristics of language that constitute the psychological basis for discursive thinking? What are the characteristics of language that make it possible to transmit the cumulative experience of generations?

The basic element of language is the *word*. A word can be used to refer to objects and to identify properties, actions, and relationships. Words organize things into systems. That is to say, words *codify our experience*. In what follows, we shall deal with such issues as how words come into being, how the semantic structure of a word is constructed, and how the structure of a word enables us to refer to objects and assign attributes and relations.

ORIGINS OF THE WORD:
FROM SYMPRACTICAL TO SYNSEMANTIC WORD STRUCTURE

One can only speculate about the origins of the word in protolanguage and protohistory. Although many theories attempt to explain the origin of words, we still know very little about it. What is clear is that words did not originate as a means for expressing affective conditions or states. If they had, the so-called languages of animals would in no way differ from those of humans.

We have every reason to believe that the word arose as a result of labor, which is a form of material action. As Engels repeatedly pointed out, the roots of the first word should be sought in the history of labor and social interaction. There is good reason to believe that during the first stages of history, words were *intertwined with practice*; they did not yet have an independent existence—i.e., during the early stages of language development, words had a *sympractical character*. They acquired their meaning only from concrete practical situations and activities. According to this line of reasoning, when humans interacted with one another in order to perform elementary acts of labor, the word was intertwined with these acts. If, for instance, a group had to lift a heavy object, such as a tree trunk, the word "ah" could mean either "Careful!" or "Come on, lift the log!" or "Exert yourself!" or "Be careful with that thing!" However, it was impossible to decipher the meaning of this word outside the context of the labor situation. It was impossible to do so because the meaning of the word changed depending on the situation. It became comprehensible only from gestures (in particular, pointing gestures), from the intonation of the speaker, and from the whole situation. Thus, the primitive word had an unstable diffuse meaning, which acquired concreteness from the sympractical context.

Apparently, the entire history of human language is the history of the emancipation of the word from practical life and the evolution of speech as an independent activity. This activity makes use of language and its elements (i.e., words) in an independent system of codes. The process of emancipating the word from its sympractical context involves the transition of language to a *synsemantic system*. As we shall see later, the most developed form of this independent synsemantic code is seen in *written language*.

While we know very little about the protohistory of language, we do know something about the origin of the word in ontogenesis (i.e., the development of a child). In contrast to what was believed at one time, ontogenesis never parallels phylogenesis (i.e., the development of species). The sociohistorical development of language, like that of all mental processes, originates in the social process of labor. However, the development of language in ontogenesis does not occur in the process of labor. It occurs during the acquisition of human experience and communication with adults.

It may appear that the language of a small child begins with babbling during infancy and that the development of language simply involves the extension of these initial sounds. Many generations of psycholinguists believed that. However, this is not the case. In effect, babbling is the expression of a state and not the designation of objects. Many sounds found in babbling are not later repeated in the child's speech. The first words uttered by a child are often either less distinct or quite different in their phonological structure[2] from the babbling of an infant. We would argue that in order to learn the sounds in a linguistic system, the child must inhibit the sounds in babbling. This argument applies to many aspects of the ontogenesis of children's voluntary movements. For example, it was formerly assumed that the grasping reflex emerges from innate reflexes. Only a few days after birth, a child can have such a strong grasping reflex that it is possible for an adult to lift the child by offering him/her two fingers. However, it has been demonstrated that nothing emerges out of this grasping reflex. It cannot in any way be taken as the prototype of future voluntary movements. Just the reverse is true. It is necessary to inhibit the grasping reflex before voluntary movement appears. The grasping reflex is a subcortical act, whereas voluntary movement is a cortical act. The latter has a quite different origin and occurs only when the grasping reflex is inhibited.

The same developmental sequence occurs in the case of speech. The first words arise not from the child's babbling sounds, but from the linguistic sounds the child learns by perceiving the speech of older people. Children's language is always initially connected with their *action* and with their interaction with adults. In contrast to babbling, children's first words do not express a state, but are directed toward and designate an object. However, initially these words are sympractical; they are closely tied to action. If the child is playing horses and utters "tpru!,"[3] this utterance may mean "horse," "sledge," "Sit!," "Let's go!," and/or "Stop!," depending on the situation and on the accompanying gestures and intonation. Therefore, a child's first words are directed toward an object but remain inseparable from action. It is only in later stages that the word begins to be separated from action and to acquire an independent character. While we can only speculate on how this process occurred in social history, we can follow it very closely in ontogenesis.

Shortly after the appearance of such rudimentary, sympractical words (approximately at the age of 18 to 20 months), the child begins to acquire the morphology of the word. Then, instead of "tpru!" he/she begins to utter "tprun'ka!" thus adding the suffix -n'ka to the diffuse word "tpru!". The meaning of the word "tprun'ka" is less diffuse than its precursor. Instead of all the meanings associated with the uses of "tpru," the meaning of "tprun'ka" is restricted to "horse," "sledge," or "cart." With the addition of this suffix, it acquires the

---

[2]We are using the term "phonological" structure as it is used in linguistics (e.g., Trubetskoi, 1939; Jakobson, 1971). It refers to the way sounds are organized in a language with certain signs that possess a significance which makes a difference in meaning. The phonological system differs from the phonetic structure of language in that the latter is concerned with the physical characteristics of speech sounds irrespective of their phonological significance.

[3]The Russian interjection, usually used for horses. It is somewhat similar to the English "Whoa!"—*J. V. Wertsch*

character of a noun and begins to have a clear objective meaning. It becomes independent of its sympractical context. Typically, it is at this time (i.e., when words begin to acquire differentiated morphological forms) that we notice an enormous increase in the child's vocabulary. Formerly, there had been amorphous words which could designate practically anything. As a result, the child was able to manage with a small number of words which took on different meanings, depending on the situation, gesture, and intonation. If the meaning of each word is then restricted (e.g., the word "tprun'ka" can designate only an object), the child is forced to extend his/her vocabulary. Whereas the child's vocabulary had consisted of 12 to 15 words, its range now jumps to 60, 80, 150, or 200 words. This leap in size of the child's vocabulary has been studied by many investigators (e.g., Stern and Stern, 1928; McCarthy, 1954; Brown, 1973).

Thus, ontogenetic observations support the notion that words initially appear in a sympractical context and only gradually become separated from action to become independent signs which designate objects, actions, and properties (and later, also relationships). In our opinion, this shift from sympractical to synsemantic speech represents the real birth of the differentiated word, i.e., the word as an element of the complex system of codes and language. Since we have elsewhere (Luria and Yudovich, 1956) dealt with this process, whereby the word is liberated from its sympractical context and becomes an element of an independent code, we shall not go into detail here.

THE SEMANTIC STRUCTURE AND FUNCTION OF THE WORD

Let us now turn to the central issue of the psychological structure of the word. We have already said that every word designates a thing, an attribute, an action, or a relationship. Does this mean, therefore, that the analysis of a word involves nothing more than its capacity to be used to refer to an object? Does the semantic structure of a word involve nothing more than the representation of an object?

Let us consider these two questions. The basic function of a word is its "referential" function. In psychology, this claim reflects an acceptance of the position introduced into Soviet psychological literature by Vygotsky (1934, 1956, 1960). According to him, any word possesses an *object reference*. It can function as a substitute for an object. A word is always directed toward an object. It may designate an object ("briefcase" or "dog"), an act ("lie" or "run"), a property ("leather briefcase" or "bad-tempered dog"), or a relationship ("the briefcase is lying on the table" or "the dog is running out of the forest"). That a word can designate different objects is reflected in the fact that it can assume the form of a noun (when designating an object), a verb (when designating an action), an adjective (when designating a property), or a copula, preposition, or conjunction (when designating a relationship).

What advantage accrues to humans by having at their disposal words which have an object reference? The enormous advantage is that their world doubles. In the absence of words, humans would have to deal only with those things which they could perceive and manipulate directly. With the help of language, they can deal with things which they have not perceived even indirectly and with things which were part of the experience of earlier generations. Thus, the word adds another dimension to the world of humans. It enables them to deal with things without having to have those things present. Animals have one world, the world of objects and situations which can be perceived by the senses. Humans have a double world.

Furthermore, humans can elicit these images at will even in the absence of the objects. As a result, humans not only can regulate their perception, they can also regulate their memory by using images. They can control their actions. That is to say, words give rise not only to a duplicate world, but also to a form of *voluntary action* which could not exist without language.

In addition, humans can act internally; this means that they can carry out trial and error thinking and other cognitive actions in the absence of real objects. Thus, they can compare the weights of two objects without having to have the objects in front of them. This is possible because humans can mobilize all the features involved in their linguistic representational system.

The final advantage of this second world that we shall mention here is that humans can transmit information and knowledge from one individual to another, thus making it possible for us to acquire the experience of previous generations.

As we said earlier, an animal has only two ways of organizing its behavior. This organization can be based on the "inherited experience" embedded in its instincts, or by acquiring new forms of behavior through its own object experience. Humans, on the other hand, are not forced to depend solely on their personal experience. They can obtain experience from others because speech can serve as a source of information. The greater part of humans' experience (both in everyday life and in formal educational settings) is derived in this uniquely human way. This aspect of human mental development has been studied in detail by A. N. Leont'ev (1959, 1975).

THE WORD AND ITS SEMANTIC FIELD

It would be wrong to consider a word only as a label used to designate an individual object, action, or property. The semantic structure or a word is far more complex, as has been repeatedly observed in linguistics. It is well known that many words possess not one, but several meanings. For instance, the Russian word "kosa" may mean either "a girl's long braid," "a scythe for cutting grass," or "a narrow sandy shoal jutting out into the sea." The Russian word "klyuch" may designate either a key to open a door or a spring (i.e., a source of water). The

Russian word "podnyat'" (to raise), which at first may appear to designate a single definite action, is also in reality polysemantic. It may mean "to lean down and pick up something from the floor" (e.g., to pick up a handkerchief), "to raise something upward" (e.g., raise one's hand), "to ask a question" (e.g., raise the question), or in general "to start any action which changes a former state" (e.g., to raise a din, to raise a point in conversation). Such words are well known in Russian as well as in other languages, and they are usually called "homonyms." Cases in which we see multiple meanings for a single, seemingly simple and unambiguous word are not something rare. Rather, "polysemy" is the rule rather than the exception (Vinogradov, 1953; Shcherba, 1957). Therefore, we see that identifying the object reference of a word is really a matter of selecting the meaning required from several possible candidates.

The specification of a word's meaning can be accomplished by means of "semantic markers" or "semantic features." These features specify the meaning of the word and separate this meaning from other possible meanings. Very often a word's meaning is determined by the situation or *context* in which it is used, and sometimes by the *tone* with which it is pronounced (e.g., "On kupil sebe shlyapu." vs. "On—shlyapa!").[4]

Many investigators argued that a word almost never has a single, fixed object reference and it would be more correct to say a word almost always has many meanings, that it is polysemantic. That is precisely why many writers argue that in order to establish the correct object references of a word, the science of linguistics alone (or lexicography—one of its branches) is insufficient and that the choice of the object reference is determined by many factors, both linguistic and psychological. Among these factors are the specific context in which the word is used and its inclusion in a concrete situation (cf. Rommetveit, 1968, 1974).

The multiplicity of word meanings is not, however, exhausted by the phenomenon of "polysemy," which we have just mentioned. Perhaps the most important fact here is that in addition to the "referential" or "denotative" meaning of a word, there is a wide range of what has come to be known as "associative" meanings. As noted by several authors (e.g., Deese, 1962; Noble, 1952), a word not only indicates an object; it also elicits several additional associations. Among these associations are elements of words similar in meaning on the basis of the concrete situation in which the word appears, on the basis of previous experience, etc. Thus, the word "garden" may involuntarily call to mind such words as "tree," "flowers," "bench," "rendezvous," etc., and the word "kitchen-garden" may lead to words such as "bed" (i.e., where plants are grown—*J.V.W.*), "potatoes," "onions," "spade," etc. In this way, a word becomes the central point for an entire chain

---

[4] Literally, "He bought himself a hat" ("shlyapu") and "He is a shlyapa" (i.e., a helpless/unpractical person), the implication being that there is nothing under the hat.—*J. V. Wertsch*

of images generated by it and for words connotatively connected with it. The speaker or listener selectively inhibits some of these images and connotatively connected words so as to choose, in the given situation, the "closest" meaning or the "denotative" meaning that is needed.

These complexes of associative meanings, which involuntarily emerge when a certain word is perceived, have been studied in great detail by investigators such as Kent and Rosanoff (1910), Deese (1962), and Luria (1930). On the basis of this research, a new concept was introduced into science, the concept of the "semantic field" which surrounds every word (e.g., Trier, 1934; Porzig, 1934). The problems of the "connotative" meanings of words had been studied in detail in Soviet linguistics by Klimenko (1970). We shall deal below with the methods of objective analysis of "semantic fields" carried out by Riess (1940) and Razran (1949) abroad and by Shvarts (1948, 1954), Vinogradova (1956), Vinogradova and Eisler (1959), Luria and Vinogradova (1959, 1971) in our country.

All of this research indicates that from a psychological point of view the analysis of a word is far from being limited to an invariable and monosemantic object reference. It supports the notion that a semantic field exists for every word and, as a consequence, that both the process of naming and the process of perceiving a word really ought to be considered a complex process of selecting the closest meaning from the word's entire semantic field.

The existence of such a semantic field is vividly illustrated in the literature on the difficulties in word recall. This is the "tip of the tongue" situation where the real word is replaced by another, more widely known word taken from the common semantic field. This phenomenon has been described by Brown and McNeill (1966). We will see later how important this is and how it should be taken into account when considering changes in the processes of naming or understanding a word in patients with brain damage.

THE CATEGORICAL MEANING OF A WORD

Up to this point, we have been concerned with how a word functions to designate an object, action, or property. However, this does not exhaust the roles that a word plays in reflecting reality and in processing information. Another important aspect of the word, which Vygotsky called its *meaning*, concerns "categorical" or "conceptual" meaning.

By the "meaning" of a word, we understand the capacity of a word not only to substitute or represent objects, not only to elicit associations, but also to *analyze objects*, to isolate and generalize their properties. A word not only substitutes for a thing, but also analyzes it by *introducing it into a system of complex associations and relations*. It is this abstracting and generalizing function that is known as its meaning.

Let us turn to a more detailed analysis of this second characteristic of the word. We have already said that every word not only designates an object but also *singles out its essential property*. This is very easy to see when we analyze the root of a word. For example, the Russian word "stol" (table) has the root STL, and this root is connected with the words "stlat'" (to lay out), "postilat'" (to spread), and "nastil" (flooring). When we utter the word "*stol*," we single out the property of the word. We see that this word involves something that can be laid or spread out, something upon which one can write, dine, or work. This analytical or abstracting function of a word can easily be seen in complex words of recent origin. Thus the word "samovar" (sam ovar) designated an object which boils by itself ("sam"—self, "varit'"—to boil). This function of isolating or abstracting a property is an extremely important function of the word.

In addition to referring to an object and abstracting its properties, the word also *generalizes objects* by relating them to other objects in a category. The word "stol" designates any table. For example, it may designate a writing table, a dining table, a card table, a square or round table, a table with four legs or three legs, a leaf table, or a simple table. This generalizing function of the word is very important. Thus, when we use a word to refer to some object, we automatically include it in a specific category. This means that a word is a *unit of thought*. It is a unit of thought because the powers of abstraction and generalization are the most important functions of thinking.

We should also note that a word is not only an instrument for thinking, but also a means for *communication*. Every instance of communication requires that a word not only denote a specific object, but also introduce a generalized concept. If a speaker has a particular table in mind, but the listener does not grasp the generalized sense of the word, the speaker would never be able to convey his/her thought. However, the word "table" does have a generalized meaning. As a result, the hearer can understand the speaker; as a result, when a speaker mentions a generalized thing, he/she is able to convey the meaning of this thing. Thus, by abstracting and generalizing the property of an object, a word becomes an *instrument of thought and a means of communication*. All of this shows that a word not only duplicates the world, it also serves as a powerful *instrument for analyzing this world*. The word takes one beyond the world of sensory experience and leads to rational experience.

However, this does not exhaust our analysis of word meaning. There is one more component, which we have not analyzed so far. In many developed languages (e.g., Russian, German, and in Turkic languages), the word involves another meaning component—inflections. Inflections change with the various uses of the word. For example, if we analyse the word "chernil'nitsa" (ink stand), we see that its case status is indicated by inflections.[5] By changing a word's inflections, we do

---

[5]In other languages which do not make use of inflections (e.g., English and French), the role of inflections is taken over by auxiliary words such as prepositions and conjunctions.

not change its meaning. In this case, the word is concerned with an object related to dyes ("chern"), to instrumentality ("-il"), to receptacles ("-nits-"), etc. However, the functional role of the object may change. In the nominative case or the so-called "citation" form, "chernil'nitsa" simply indicates the existence of the object. In the accusative case ("chernil'nitsu"), it indicates that the thing is the object of some action (e.g., "Ya vizhu chernil'nitsu."–I see the inkpot.). In the genitive case, it is used to indicate a part of an object ("krai chernil'nitsi"–the edge of the inkpot), or to indicate the absence of the object ("U menya net chernil'nitsi."–I do not have an inkpot.). With the help of the instrumental inflection ("chernil'nitsei"), we indicate that the object is used for some instrumental purpose. In other words, inflections give rise to *new psychological possibilities for a functional designation of an object*. They enable us not only to correlate the object to a certain category, but also to indicate the form of the action which the object performs in a given context.

This is precisely what enables us to say that language is a *system of codes adequate for independently analyzing an object and expressing any of its features, properties, and relationships*. The word is the foundation of the system of codes which ensures the transition from the sensory to the rational world.

LEXICAL FUNCTIONS AND THE VALENCY OF WORDS

Let us now focus on some additional issues which will become important when we take up the analysis of sentence structure. Several investigators have noted that some of the words which are part of a given semantic group are characterized by greater "availability" than others. A word's availability determines the difficulty with which it can be chosen from among many items. It is explained partly by the context, partly by its habit strength and frequency of occurrence (Miller, 1967; Morton, 1971; Katz, 1966, 1972), and partly by speaker's attitudes and direct experience (Rommetveit, 1968, 1974). However, very often a word's availability depends on its *lexical connections*.

It is not difficult to understand that the word "doctor" elicits the word "to treat," that "broom" reminds us of "to sweep," that "axe" calls forth the word "to chop," and that the word "needle" makes us think of the word "to sew." This is even more clearly the case for words denoting actions (i.e., verbs) and properties (i.e., adjectives).

It has been customary to distinguish between intransitive verbs, which do not require an object ("sleep," "starve," "live") and transitive verbs, which require a word to complement them. To this latter class belong such verbs as "drink" (something), "desire" (something), "give" (something), "buy" (something), "borrow" (something, from someone), etc. (cf. Fillmore, 1972; Fodor, Bever, Garrett, 1968a; Zholkovskii, 1964, 1967). The same can be said of adjectives. They usually require the presence of a noun. The choice of a noun is determined both by proximity in meaning and by the frequency of occurrence of the combinations (e.g., "red"–flag, "Soviet"–Union, "ripe"–apple, "sharp"–knife).

These facts about how certain words, when isolated, leave us with a feeling of incompleteness are concerned with the word's valence. Valence is a factor that determines the readiness with which certain words are evoked when presented with others. That is why it is an important factor in the process of word selection.

We still have not addressed the issue of the lexical functions of words. These functions tie a word into the system of other words, and are of great significance in sentence production. The problem of word valence has been studied in Soviet linguistics. Those who have dealt with this problem have identified a few basic categories of lexical functions. For example, such investigators as Mel'chuk (1970, 1974), Zholkovskii and Mel'chuk (1969), and Apresyan (1974) have identified the following connections: "incip-" or "to start" (e.g., "it has started raining," "the verse comes to mind"); "fin-" or "to finish" (e.g., "the quarrel has ended," "autumn is over"); "func-" or "to function" (e.g., "a cook has the function of preparing food," "a clock has the function of telling time"); and "caus-"–"to cause" (e.g., "an engine causes motion," "a push causes movement"). Semantic groups like these give rise to the connections among words and determine one word's probability of occurrence after another. It is not difficult to see that this goes beyond the simple assertion that a word refers to a thing and that it identifies and generalizes a property of an object.

That words differ in their tendency to elicit other words (i.e., in their valencies) is of great importance (cf. Fodor et al., 1968a; Fillmore, 1972; Kiefer, 1972). Thus, the words "love" and "hate" have one valency (love–whom, hate–whom); the words "chop" and "dig" have two valencies (chop–what, and with what; dig–what, and with what); the words "buy" and "sell" have three valencies (buy–what, from whom, and for how much; sell–what, to whom, and for how much). The Russian word "odolzhit'" (lend, borrow) has four valencies (lend-borrow–what, to whom, from whom, and for how long).

Recent linguistic reserach has demonstrated that in Russian there are words which have no more than three or four (or a maximum of five) valencies. Consequently, every word has a limited number of lexical connections. As we shall see, this idea will become important when we deal with sentence production.

SUMMARY

We can summarize our argument in a few propositions. A word as an element of language refers to an object, property, or relation. Language consists of complex codes which introduce the object thus denoted into a system of links and associations. The word is a product of social evolution. In the process of this evolution, it separated from the sympractical context and becomes an independent system.

The development of language is the process of the word's emancipation from its sympractical character and its synsemantic growth. The basic structure of a word is very complex. A word involves *object reference* and *meaning*. It enables humans to go beyond the limits of their direct perception, thus achieving that *leap from the sensory to the rational world*, which is essential for human consciousness. Finally, a word has certain "lexical functions" which lead to the formulation of certain classes of sense relations; it also has the means at its disposal for connecting some words with others, thus ensuring the transition from individual words to their synsemantic bonds. All this constitutes a highly important mechanism that enables the word to become the main instrument of human conscious activity.

Chapter 3
The Development of Word Meaning in Ontogenesis

We have examined the word as the basic unit of language and have shown that its signification involves two main aspects: (1) *object reference*—its function of referring to an object, property, action, or relation and (2) *meaning*—its function of isolating and generalizing various features of an object, thereby relating the object to a system of categories. Those aspects of signification make it possible for the word to fulfill the enormous potential it has accrued over the course of social history. Therefore, one can consider the word as a *basis for generalization* (and therefore an instrument of thinking) as well as a *means of social interaction*.

One of the most important discoveries of Soviet psychology, made over 40 years ago by Vygotsky, is that these aspects of a word's signification change during a child's development. Vygotsky (1934) formulated it in the proposition that the *meaning of the word develops* both in its structure and in the psychological processes which underlie it. His basic proposition involved the *systematic development of word meaning*.

Vygotsky's basic claim was that during ontogenesis there are important changes in the operations of referring to an object, abstracting features from the object, coding these features, and placing the object into a system of categories. He claimed that different psychological processes characterize word meaning at different stages in ontogenesis.

Vygotsky related this notion about the growth of word meaning to the development of *consciousness*. For Vygotsky, the word is an apparatus reflecting the complex relationships and associations of the external world. Therefore, its ontogenesis involves (among other things) a change in word meaning, the links and associations which determine the structure of consciousness also change. It is precisely because of this that the claim about the systematic development of word meaning is a claim about the systematic development of consciousness.

It is not difficult to see the critical nature of this proposition. It provides a new materialistic theory of the ontogenesis of language and consciousness. This theory is an original contribution of Soviet psychology.

MEANING AND SENSE

Before coming to our main theme, we wish to introduce a distinction that will play an important role in our discussion. Along with the concept of "meaning," Soviet psychology relies on the concept of "sense" to analyze the problem of language and consciousness. In classical linguistics, "meaning" and "sense" were almost synonymous. It is only very recently that these two concepts have begun to be differentiated by foreign investigators. Authors such as Halliday (1970, 1973) and Rommetveit (1968, 1974) have begun to distinguish between "referential" meaning on the one hand and "social-communicative" meaning on the other. The distinction between "meaning" and "sense" was introduced in Soviet psychology several decades ago by Vygotsky in his classical work *Thought and Language* (first published in 1934).

By "meaning" ("znachenie"), we understand the system of semantic relations connected with a word. This system has evolved during social history. For example, latent in the word "chernil'nitsa" is the meaning we outlined earlier in Chapter 2. As noted there, the meaning of this word involved dye ("chern-"), instrumentality ("-il"), and receptacles ("-nits-"). Thus, it can be used not only to denote a certain object, but also to analyze this object. It introduces it into a system of objective associations. When we utilize word meanings, we utilize general human experience which reflects the world in varying degrees of completeness and depth. "Meaning" is a stable system of generalizations represented by a word, a system which is the same for everyone.

Along with this concept of meaning we can distinguish another concept, that of "sense" ("symsl"). By "sense" we understand the signification of an individual instance of a word, as opposed to the stable, objective system of relations. Sense is concerned with those connections which interest a user in a given situation. If meaning is an objective reflection of a system of relations and associations, sense is a transformation of meaning, a selection from among all possible meanings of those which interest the person at a given moment.

Let us analyze an example illustrating this distinction. The Russian word "ugol'" (coal, charcoal) has a definite and clear meaning. It involves a black substance, most often having its origin in wood, that is derived from the carbonization of trees. It involves a substance having a definite chemical composition, the chief constituent of which is the element C (carbon). However, the sense of the word "ugol'" can vary greatly for different people in different situations. For the housewife, "ugol'" is associated with something used for heating the samovar or something used for heating the stove. For the scientist, "ugol'" is associated with a subject of study. He/she singles out the aspect and the word meaning concerned with the structure and properties of "ugol'" (carbon). For the artist who wishes to use "ugol'" (charcoal) for making a sketch, it is associated with the means he/she has for outlining a picture. And for the little girl who has smudged her dress with coal, the word "ugol'" carries an unpleasant sense. It is something that has spoiled her dress, something that evokes an affective feeling.

Hence, we see that one and the same word has an historically evolved meaning. In addition, every use of a word has its sense. The latter is concerned with isolating the aspects of this meaning which interest a given person at a given moment. This sense involves the subject's feeling or emotion. That is why modern psychologists have good reason for believing that if referential meaning is the basic element of language, social-communicative meaning or sense constitutes the basic unit of communication. In other words, communication involves the perception of what it is that the speaker wishes to convey and what motivates his/her utterance. Sense is the basic element of the live use of a word by a speaker in a specific concrete situation.

A mature adult can make use of both the meaning and the sense of a word. He/she understands the stable meaning of the word quite well and can also select the necessary system of connections from the given meaning in any particular speech situation. It is not difficult to understand that the Russian word "verevka" (rope, string, cord) has one sense for someone wishing to pack something which he/she has bought and another sense for someone who has fallen into a ditch and wishes to get out by using a rope as a means of rescue. It is only in the case of certain aberrations of the mind (e.g., with schizophrenics) that the ability to choose the proper sense in a situation deteriorates. Thus, if the person who has fallen in the ditch begins to argue about the properties of the rope which has been thrown to him/her (i.e., begins to philosophize rather than act), we are witnessing a deviation from the norm.

So, in addition to a word's meaning, we must be aware of its sense (i.e., that which makes possible the isolation of that aspect of the system of relations which is required at a given moment).

THE ONTOGENESIS OF THE REFERENTIAL FUNCTION

We have already pointed out that a word has object reference on the one hand and meaning on the other. By the time a child is 3½ to 4 years of age, the object reference of words is firmly established. Thus, "house" refers to a very definite thing, "cup" to another, and "Mishka" (teddy bear) to a third. However, this does not mean that the development of word meaning is complete at this age.

Development of the object reference of words occurs over a protracted period. Observations have shown that between the middle of the first year of a child's life and the third, fourth, and fifth year there is dramatic development in the referential function of the word. There are several manifestations of the development of object reference during this early period. First is the child's understanding and use of the word, i.e., we can analyze this development from the perspective of either comprehension or production. Does a child understand the stable, clear-cut, object reference of a word during very early stages in the same way that he/she will understand it later? There are several reasons for believing that a word's object reference develops only gradually; that in the beginning this object reference is dependent on some kind of nonspeech, sympractical factors. In other words, during early stages, a child's understanding of the relation of words to objects depends heavily on situational (sympractical) factors.

If every word had a stable object reference from the very beginning of a child's development, then all the factors of the speech situation which we enumerated earlier (e.g., gestures accompanying the word, intonation with which a word is pronounced) would not play an important role. However, if the object reference of a word develops by passing through the process of gradual emancipation from the direct sympractical situation, then we see how during early stages of ontogenesis the reference of a word changes, depending on the situation in which it is used.

An experiment which provided important information was conducted by Kol'tsova (1958). Kol'tsova studied a child from the age of 6 months to about 2 years. She used a procedure wherein a certain object was named for the child. In the experimental setting, the child typically turned his/her eyes in the direction of the designated object and stretched a hand toward it. Kol'tsova wished to trace the conditions that were necessary for the child to understand the meaning of the word and relate it to the corresponding object or action.

The picture that emerged from this study was far more interesting than might have been expected. In the early stages, the child acquired the object reference of the word only if he/she was placed in a certain position (e.g., in a lying position), if the word was pronounced by a certain person (e.g., by his/her mother), if the word was accompanied by a specific gesture, and if the word was pronounced with a certain intonation. If all these conditions were present, the child turned its gaze toward the object and stretched a hand toward it. If any one of these features was absent, the word lost its object reference and the child did not respond to it. Hence, if a child of 6 or 7 months was lying down and heard his/her mother's voice naming an object, the child responded by turning its gaze toward the object. However, the child failed to respond if any of these conditions were changed (e.g., if the child was in a sitting position).

During the next stage, the child's position (e.g., lying or sitting) was no longer important for retaining the object reference of the word, but the identity of the speaker, the intonation of the voice, and the gesture accompanying the utterance continued to have a decisive influence. If the word "cat" was pronounced by the mother, the child turned his/her gaze toward it. However, if the same word was uttered by the father, the child did not respond in the same way.

At later stages, the identity of the speaker ceased to be an important factor in evoking a response to a word, but the child retained the object reference only when the utterance was accompanied by a pointing gesture or if it was included in a practical setting (especially in a play situation). At this stage, word comprehension is not yet separated from gestures or actions. It is only sometime during the second half of this period, or by the end of the child's second year, that the word is completely emancipated from these attendant conditions and acquires its stable object reference. At this point, the child begins to respond selectively to the named object, irrespective of whether the word is accompanied by a pointing gesture or action. This shows that object reference was determined not only by the phonetic and lexical characteristics of the word, but also by the situation in which it was uttered and the kind of gesture accompanying it. All of this demonstrates that the word does not have a stable object reference from the very beginning of a child's development. Rather, it develops sometime around the middle or end of the second year of a child's life.

Similar results have been obtained by other researchers. We shall review only two of these here. The Leningrad psychologist Fradkina (1955) made the following observation. At the end of the first year and the beginning of the second year, a child was taught to turn his/her face to a portrait of Lenin and point to it when asked, "Where is Lenin?" It seemed that the child had correctly learned the object reference of this name. However, when the portrait was removed from its original position and hung in another place, the child continued to turn his/her gaze toward the original position when asked, "Where is Lenin?" This indicates that the controlling factor here was not what the word meant (its object reference), but the intonation, situation, and gesture.

The second observation was made by French investigator Tappolet (1907). In this study, when a child of the same age was asked, "Ou est la fenetre?" (Where is the window?), he/she turned toward the window. From this, it would seem that the child had developed the object reference of the word "window." However, when Tappolet asked the same question in German (a language the child did not know), while retaining the former intonation, the child again turned to the window. Obviously, the response was not based on an understanding of German, and he/she was not responding to the word itself. Rather, the response was elicited by the intonation and situation in which the word was uttered. These studies show that the object reference goes through a complex course of development and that this development is completed at a much later point than one would expect.

Analogous results were obtained while studying children's speech production. As we know, development of speech production lags behind that of comprehension. However, the sequences involved are almost identical. Several investigators have shown that words have an amorphous meaning in the early stages of a child's development. The diffuse meaning of a word is reflected by the fact that its object reference changes depending on the situation. As was noted earlier, it is only when words take on a morphological structure that they acquire a clearer object reference and meaning. However, even when a child's words acquire a definite morphological structure, they sometimes continue to exhibit an unstable object reference. The object reference may change depending on the sympractical context.

One of the classical German psychologists, Stumpf (1926), reported that his son called a duck "ga-ga." Upon closer examination, however, it turned out that the child used the word "ga-ga" not only for a duck, but also for water in which the duck swam and for a coin with an eagle's image on it. The word was associated with everything related to a bird, to the entire situation in which one might come across a bird.

The Soviet psychologist Bozhovich (personal report) made a similar observation. A young child used the word "kkha" for a cat. This was based on the initial sounds of this word ("koshka"). At first it appeared that the word had acquired a stable object reference. However, upon closer observation it was found that the child used the word "kkha" not only for a cat but for any kind of fur, for scratching, and for a sharp stone (which the child associated with the cat because the cat had scratched him).

Thus, during the early stages of a child's development, the meaning of a word is amorphous. It does not have a stable object reference. This diffuse meaning results in the tendency for a word to refer to various objects which possess one or more features in common with the original referent.

Further investigations have shown that the object reference of a word remains quite diffuse even when the morphological structure of the word begins to take shape. It would appear that for a child one know the words "cat," "duck," and "cup" and can use them appropriately to name objects, that these words should have a clear object reference. However, through careful observation, we often find that this only seems to be the case and that the object reference of the word is still unstable. It may be based on only one feature of an object and thus may be easily transferred to other objects.

Two studies illustrate this, the first was by Soviet psychologist Rozengart-Pupko and was described in her book *Speech and Development of Perception in Childhood* (1948). She identified children who knew certain words by using a procedure whereby the words were included in requests such as, "Give me the cup," "Give me Mishka" (teddy bear), "Give me the duck." If a child picked up the correct object without difficulty, it would seem that he/she understood these words. However, Rozengart-Pupko carried out further procedures to test this conclusion. She continued to make requests, but now the group of items placed before the child, or kept in an adjoining room (from which the child was expected to retrieve the object), did not include the object identified in her speech. There were, however, objects which had one of the features of the named item. In this setting, she found that words which seemed to be well known to the child did not, in fact, have a clear and stable object reference. For example, the experimenter said to the child, "Give me Mishka" (teddy bear) and sent the child to the table which had several items on it, but no teddy bear. Without hesitation, the child brought back a soft glove because this object had one of Mishka's features. When Rozengart-Pupko said to the child, "Give me a birdie," the child again did not hesitate. He/she brought back a porcelain ball with a protruding end which was similar to the beak of a bird. This indicates that at a given stage of a child's development the word does not yet possess a stable object reference. In the early stages of development, a word signifies only a certain feature and does not necessarily signify the coordinated set of features which characterize the object.

Another study was carried out by the brilliant Soviet psychologist Shvachkin (1954). In this study, a child was taught the meaning of the words "boat" and "iron." In order to ensure that the child fully understood the word "boat," certain characteristic features of a boat were demonstrated. For example, the child was shown that a boat sails on water and that it rocks in the water. In the case of the word "iron," the child was shown that it can be used for ironing clothes. After the child demonstrated clear evidence of having learned these words—by saying "This is a boat," in response to being presented with a boat, and saying "And this is an iron," in response to seeing the iron—the crucial phase of the experiment began. It consisted of the experimenter's selecting other objects and either rocking it or moving it along the surface of a table. When the child was asked to identify the object in the first instance (no matter what it really was), he/she said, "a boat." In the second instance, he/she replied, "an iron." That is to say, the word "boat" meant "rocking" for the child, and the word "iron" meant "pressing" or "ironing."

This leads us to the conclusion that however simple the notion of object reference might appear at first glance, it is the product of prolonged development. During early stages, the word is inextricably tied to a situation, a gesture, mimicry or intonation. It is only in the presence of these that it acquires its object reference.

Later, the object reference of the word is gradually freed of these conditions. However, even when it appears that the word has acquired a clear-cut object reference, it preserves a close link with the practical act for a long period and continues to signify not the object, but some feature of the object. Thus, even at this stage, the word has a diffuse, expanded meaning. Since it is still closely tied to the practical act, it easily loses its object reference.

THE DEVELOPMENT OF WORD MEANING

Let us now consider another important question. If the object reference of the word develops in a child during the first two years of life, the question arises as to whether the development of word meaning is complete at this stage. A child of 3 or 3½ years of age knows very well the object reference for expressions such as "cat," "cup," "fish," "rooster," and "window." He/she never confuses one of these things with another. Does this mean, however, that the development of the word as a unit of language and cognition is complete?

That is what had been claimed for many years. For several generations, psychologists considered a word to be a simple sign substituting for an object. Since they assumed that its main function was to refer to an object, it was also assumed that the development of word meaning was completed by the time a child was 3 years old. It was supposed that all subsequent development consisted of vocabulary growth and the development of the morphological and syntactical aspects of the word. This view has been accepted by investigators, beginning with classical psychologists Stern and Stern (1928) and continuing down to modern authors. It has turned out, however, that this assumption is not at all in accordance with reality and that in fact the development of the word does not end by the age of 3 or 4.

It has been found that the further development of the word occurs after it has acquired a clear, stable object reference. This development is no longer concerned with object reference. Rather, it is concerned with the generalizing and analyzing function of the word (i.e., its meaning). Thus, if the word "dog" has the same object reference for a child at the age of 3 years as it does for a child 7 years of age, or a university student, this does not mean that it has the same meaning at each of these stages of development.

This was one of Vygotsky's most important discoveries. He showed that although a word may retain the same object reference at each of several ontogenetic stages, its meaning is constantly being redefined. In addition, Vygotsky (1934) showed that profound psychological changes are associated with this. As word meaning changes, psychological processes also change. That is the essence of his account of word meaning, an account which also concerns the evolution of the capacity of consciousness to reflect the external world.

Let us consider this proposition in a very general way by taking as an example the word "store." Even by the age of 3, this word has a precise object reference. It does not signify a tower, or an animal, or a roof. Rather, it is used to refer to a store, where one can buy something.

However, the question arises as to whether the meaning of the word "store" remains fixed or undergoes changes. It turns out that the meaning of this word undergoes fundamental changes during ontogenesis. During the early stages, the word "store" signifies something pleasant. It is a place where people can obtain delicious sweets or cakes for the child. Thus, the word "store" evokes certain emotional associations in the child. This is as yet not the objective meaning of the word; it is rather the affective sense which the word "store" has for the child. Subsequent development is different. For a child of later preschool or early school age,[6] a store is a place where one goes to buy provisions, where the child is sometimes sent to buy something, or where something is sold. It is situated around the corner. Housewives go there to buy various items. The word "store" no longer simply has an affective meaning for the child. The affective sense gradually becomes secondary or subsidiary. A concrete image of a shop now plays the main role in defining meaning. It is a place where people go and things are sold. When a child of late preschool age hears the word "store," it evokes in him/her an entire concrete situation of a store where people buy provisions.

The word "store" has quite a different meaning for an adult. For example, if we consider the case of an economist, the object reference remains the same, but the word "store" involves several concepts. It involves the economic system of exchange, the formula "money—goods—money," or the form of exchange (capital exchange, cooperative exchange, socialist exchange). In other words, a quite different system of connections arises in conjunction with this word. The meaning of a word does not remain the same; it changes and develops.

In addition to changes in the meaning of a word, there are changes in the psychological processes involved in using it. We saw that in the case of a small child the chief factor in a word's meaning is an affective factor (e.g., the feeling of something pleasant). For the older preschool child or the young school child, the concrete image is particularly important; a stores is a place to buy products and gifts. Finally, for the scholar, the key role is played by the system of logical connections which stand behind the word.

Let us analyze a second example: the word "dog." For a small child, a dog may be something terrible if he/she has been bitten by one, or it may be something quite pleasant if the child has grown up with a dog and is accustomed to playing with it. Thus the word "dog" has an affective sense. This affective sense is the essence of the word's meaning. During the next stage, the word "dog" evokes

---

[6] Soviet children usually begin school at the age of 7.—*J. V. Wertsch*

Scheme of the structure of semantic fields in ontogenesis.

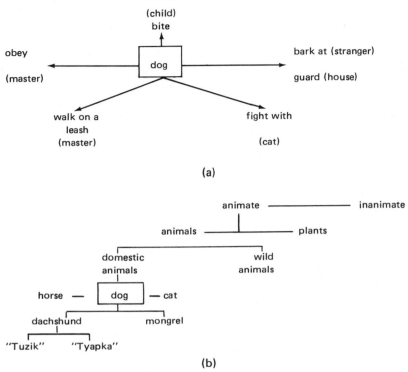

(a)

(b)

the memory of a concrete experience (a dog being fed, a dog guarding the home, a dog keeping thieves away, a dog carrying things, a dog fighting with cats, etc.). In other words, the word "dog" begins to give rise to a whole range of concrete images of situations. For a child who is studying science, and even more so for a college student, a dog is an animal that is included in an entire hierarchy of mutually subordinate concepts.

What we have said above may be illustrated in the two diagrams shown above. The first diagram illustrates a word's meaning structure when a concrete image has replaced affective connotations. Here, word meaning involves actual practical associations or concrete situations. Each element is connected with this word on different grounds. A dog obeys its master, guards the house, bites a child, etc.

The structure of word meaning takes on an entirely different character at later stages. The lower diagram illustrates that the word enters into a system of hierarchically connected and mutually subordinated categories. It acquires, as linguists say, a paradigmatic character. The word's meaning is situated in an hierarchical system of abstract oppositions. Thus, a dashshund is not a mongrel, but they belong to the same category; a dachshund is a dog not a cat; a dog and a cat are animals and not plants; etc. These categories are mutually subordinated in a hierarchy. They form the system of abstract concepts and are distinguished thereby from the concrete situational relations characteristic of words at an earlier stage of development. At the stage of concrete concepts, the key role is played by situational, object-actuated bonds; whereas at the stage of abstract concepts, the key role is played by the verbal and logical hierarchically constructed bonds. We may therefore say that changes in meaning simultaneously involve changes in associated processes.

Thus, following Vygotsky, we would conclude that word meaning develops even after the object reference of a word is stabilized. This fact means that the structure of consciousness also changes. During the earliest stage of ontogenesis, consciousness has an affective character. During the next stage, it begins to assume a concrete character. Words, through which the world is reflected, evoke a system of practically actuated connections. It is only at the final stage that consciousness acquires an abstract verbal-logical character, which differs from the earlier stages both in its meaning structure and in psychological processes, although even at this stage the connections that characterize the previous stages are covertly preserved.

Chapter 4

The Investigation of Concept Development

Up to now we have focused on the development of object reference and meaning of the word during ontogenesis. We have also pointed out that the system of psychological processes associated with the word changes during ontogenesis. During the initial stages, the affective aspect of the word predominates. During the next stage, concrete memory representations play the major role. Finally, during the last stage, the child begins to understand the complex systems of verbal-logical relations of the word.

We shall now address the question of how we can establish the nature of the concrete associations of words, especially in the case of the young child whose mental processes have not yet fully developed and in the case of certain forms of pathology. An answer to this problem is not only of basic theoretical importance. It also has vital practical significance, because if we can identify the system of a word's interconnections for individual adults, for children of varying ages, and for individuals with various forms of pathology, we shall be able to use scientific methods to diagnose development or underdevelopment. That is, we shall be able to solve what is perhaps the most fundamental problem confronting modern psychology in connection with normal and abnormal functioning. If we can develop methods for dealing with this problem, psychology will have acquired methods for analyzing the unique characteristics of human cognitive activity and for ascertaining the level of a child's mental development.

THE METHOD OF CONCEPT DEFINITION

The simplest way to analyze the associations of a word during each stage of development is the well-known method of defining concepts. It consists of carefully studying children's replies to a request to define something. For instance, one might ask a child questions like, "What is a dog?", "What is a table?", "What is a tree?", and "What is milk?"

There are two possible ways of replying to such questions. The first type of answer does not really define the word. Instead, the subject simply identifies some characteristic or function of the given object, or he/she introduces the given object into a concrete situation (e.g., "A dog guards the home.", or "A dog bites.", "A dog barks."; or "A table stands.", "There are writing tables.", "We dine at a table."; or "Milk is delicious.", "Cats like to lap up milk.", "Little children don't like to drink it.").

It is not difficult to see that this type of answer does not provide a real definition of a concept. Rather, the question evokes some concrete features of the object or those situations in which the object appears. This type of answer reflects the fact that for such subjects *concrete associations* of the word play a predominant role. The word elicits some kind of concrete characteristic of a given object, or some concrete situation in which the object may appear.

The second type of answer is fundamentally different from the first. In response to questions like "What is a dog?", "What is a table?", or "What is bread?" one may get answers such as "A dog is an animal.", "A table is a piece of furniture." or "Bread is food." The psychological construction of the answer does not consist of reproducing a concrete situation in which the given object appears. Rather, it relates the object to a category and introduces it into a system of concepts. Thus, this simple method, which has long been used in psychological experiments, can provide very important results. It can identify which subjects mention the concrete situations or features associated with an object instead of defining it. It can also identify subjects who introduce the object into a system of hierarchically structured abstract categories. This means that even this simple practice of having subjects define concepts allows us to lay bare the connections (concrete or verbal-logical) that predominate in a word's associations.

Studies have shown that answers of the first type predominate among preschool children. A preschool child will never reply to the question "What is a dog?" by relating it to the category of animals. He/she will always give a concrete characterization of the dog, name its features, or reproduce a concrete situation in which a dog appears. We can therefore say that for him/her it is the concrete content of the word that predominates. In young schoolchildren (along with answers of the first type), answers of the second type begin to appear. There is still a strong tendency to answer by reproducing a concrete situation (e.g., "A dog bites." or "A dog guards the home."). However, these children begin to utilize quite different operations in formulating their response. They introduce the object into a system of categories, i.e., they begin to provide real definitions of concepts. For example, young schoolchildren begin to answer the queries with replies such as "A dog is an animal.", "A rose is a flower.", "A sofa is a piece of furniture.", etc.

It is worth noting that everyday objects (a dog, milk, a table, a cow) often continue to evoke responses based on the concrete situation in these children. Conversely, what we call "scientific concepts" give rise to the other type of answers. For instance, if we ask a child, "What is America?" he/she will answer, "It is a country."; if we ask "What is a sword?" he/she may answer, "It is a weapon.", etc. It is easy to see that the answers relate the object to a general category or introduces it into a system of concepts. It is precisely because of this that Vygotsky (1934) distinguished between "everyday concepts," which evoke a system of associations based on concrete situations, and "scientific concepts," which relate an object to a system of verbal-logical definitions.[7]

In the case of older schoolchildren, the second type of answer begins to predominate, i.e., the definition of a word begins to be based on the way the word is linked to items in a system of verbal-logical relations. Naturally, such definitions based on a system of abstract categories also predominate among people with higher education. If we were to ask them "What is a dog?", they would hardly answer, "A dog barks." or "A dog guards the home." The overwhelming majority would say, "A dog is an animal." or "A dog is a domestic animal."

This simple method can provide information about the level of a child's mental development as well as about various forms of pathology. Thus, in a mentally retarded child, definitions based on the concrete situation predominate. As a result, the consciousness of such children is concretely based and does not reflect the system of verbal-logical relations into which a word introduces an object.

With schizophrenics, it is just the opposite. Attempts to elicit definitions lead to a quite different type of answer. These subjects may introduce the word into many categories that are quite detached from reality. They base these definitions on extremely general and inconsequential characteristics of the object. For instance, in response to the question "What is an exercise book?" schizophrenics may answer, "It is inorganic matter which gravitates toward the center of the earth." He/she may be incapable of identifying a concretely based definition of this word, and as a result, misuses the purely formal relationship of the word. Very important data in this connection were collected by several researchers who

[7]In particular, see chapter six of Vygotsky's (1934/1962) *Thought and Language.—J. V. Wertsch*

studied the process of definition of concepts by schizophrenic patients (e.g., Zeigarnik, 1962; Polyakov, 1974).

THE METHOD OF COMPARISON AND DIFFERENTIATION

The method of comparison and differentiation consists of giving two words that name objects to a subject and then asking him/her what the two objects have in common. Sometimes, instead of naming the objects, the objects themselves are visually presented. This does not alter the procedure in any essential way. The method is based on the assumption that a subject can arrive at a correct answer by identifying a feature common to both objects, that he/she can relate the two words on the basis of some shared cateogry. Thus, when comparing a cow and a horse, the subject might say that both are animals; when comparing a bed and a soda, he/she might say that both are pieces of furniture; etc. In exactly the same way, it is assumed that subjects who are asked how two things differ can point out that they belong to different categories (for instance, that bread is food, whereas a knife is a tool, etc.).

There are three main categories of word pairs that can be used in the method of comparison and differentiation. The first and simplest consists of giving the subject two words which clearly belong to a single category. For example, a subject might be asked: "What do a dog and a cat have in common?", "What do a lion and a tiger have in common?", or "What do a bicycle and a motorcycle have in common?" (the objects share common features and also belong to a common category). The subject can readily arrive at a categorical answer as follows: "A dog and a cat are both domestic animals.", "A lion and a tiger are wild animals.", and "A bicycle and a motorcycle are means of transportation.", respectively.

The second type of word pair is more complex. It involves two quite dissimilar objects for which it is difficult to find common characteristics. In this case, the objects have more differences than similarities. For instance, a subject might be asked to identify the characteristics shared by a lion and a dog, a crow and a fish, or a pencil and a typewriter. These objects are quite different from each other in concrete terms. The subject, therefore, must make a special effort to abstract their characteristics and relate them to a common category. For instance, a subject might point out that a lion and a dog are animals, a crow and a fish are living organisms, etc.

The third version of this task is still more complex. We shall refer to this version as "comparison and differentiation under conditions of conflict." In this case, a subject is given pairs of objects which have little in common and can more readily be related on the basis of their presence in the same practical situation than on the basis of a single abstract category. For instance, if we were to ask a subject what "rider" and "horse" have in common, the natural answer would be, "The rider rides on the horse." This answer does not relate the words to a category.

Rather, it reproduces a concrete situation. In such cases, it is quite difficult to disengage oneself from this concrete image and say that both the rider and the horse are living organisms.

Thus, the method of comparison and differentiation can involve tests of varying complexity. The complexity of the problem is attributable to the level of difficulty in ignoring the characteristics which differentiate the objects and/or ignoring their concrete co-occurrence. The subject must inhibit these relations and focus on the inclusion of the objects in an abstract category.

What are the types of answers one may expect to find when using this simple test? One type of answer is based on identifying the concrete features common to both objects or pointing out the relationship of the two objects in a concrete situation. For example, in answer to the question "What do a dog and a cat have in common?", one may begin by saying that both have sharp teeth, long tails, etc. In response to the question "What do a motor car and a cart have in common?", one may reply that one can ride in both, both have wheels, etc.

In contrast to this type of concrete answer is an answer which includes the two objects in a concrete practical situation. For instance, one may answer that the common point between a dog and a cat is that the cat can scratch the dog, or that the dog can bite the cat. In this case, the word "common" is understood not as relating the words to an abstract category, but as indicating the possible concrete interaction of the objects. It is quite natural that when the difference between two objects is greater than the similarity, a subject will tend to identify the differentiating features rather than the common ones. For instance, he/she might say, "A dog barks, but a cat meows.", "A cart is pulled by a horse, whereas an automobile moves by itself.", etc.

A second kind of response is fundamentally different. Here the subject disengages himself/herself from the concrete commonalities of the two things and relates them to a common abstract category. As a rule, this involves isolating the shared features and relating the objects to one abstract category. In this case, concrete reproduction of the object does not predominate. Instead, the verbal-logical processing of information is used.

What concrete data can we obtain with the help of this method? Psychologists have pointed out that concrete operations predominate in preschoolers and young schoolchildren. In this connection, we should note that a paradoxical fact has been widely known for many years, but its significance has been understood only recently. The paradox is that when preschoolers or young schoolchildren are asked what a dog and a cat or a bicycle and a motorcycle have in common, they usually point out how they *differ* rather than what they have in common. Psychologists have long known that differentiation develops earlier than generalization, but this fact remained unexplained. The proper explanation is that differentiation is characterized by *concretely based thinking* ("The dog has sharp teeth, the cat has sharp claws." "The cat can climb a tree, but the dog cannot.").

The process of identifying *common* features, however, is not based on concrete thinking. Rather, it involves including an object in an abstract category (the dog and the cat are animals, the bicycle and the motor car are means of transport, etc.). The predominance of differentiation during early ontogenetic stages is a manifestation of the fact that the processing involved relies on concrete description.

The transition from differentiation to generalization reflects a transition from the isolation of features based on a concrete representation to abstract, verbal-logical generalization. Because differentiation predominates over generalization in preschoolers, the second and third types of problem (where there is no immediately obvious similarity between the two objects) is especially difficult for them. In many cases, the early forms of generalization are still interrupted by concrete comparisons of objects or the inclusion of both objects in a concrete practical situation. Thus, if a young schoolchild is asked, "What do a sparrow and a fly have in common?", he/she will answer that the sparrow can swallow the fly; in response to the question, "What do a dog and a cow have in common?", he/she will answer that a dog can bite a cow, etc. That is, generalization is often still beyond his/her capacity. Older schoolchildren characteristically rely more heavily on abstraction. Because of this, they can solve even the most complex conflicting problems in which one must overcome either the influence of an obvious concrete difference or the fact that both objects are part of the same practical situation (e.g., "What do a rider and a horse have in common?"). This improved performance is attributable to the fact that the older schoolchild can disengage himself/herself (although with some effort) from concrete factors.

The importance of this simple test for diagnosing mental retardation is quite obvious. A mentally retarded child cannot solve the problem by abstracting the common feature and including it in a hierarchy of categories. Instead of a response based on abstraction and generalization, he/she will answer either by indicating the difference or by including the objects in a practical situation.

Conversely, in the case of a schizophrenic the opposite is true. There is no reliance on the concrete co-occurrence. Instead, generalization based on some unimportant features is used. For instance, if we ask a schizophrenic what an umbrella and a gun have in common, he/she may answer that both of them are affected by gravity which attracts them to the center of the earth. In response to a question as to what a human and a bird have in common, he/she may answer that both are subject to the universal law of gravity. That is, he/she may perform the operation of generalization on the basis of a feature which has no practical significance, thus completely divorcing his/her reasoning from concrete experience (cf. Zeigarnik, 1969, 1973; Polyakov, 1974).

THE METHOD OF CLASSIFICATION

The method of classification involves much more complex processing than the previous two, but it also provides richer information. It is essentially an extension of the method of comparison and differentiation. It has three basic versions, which we shall consider separately.

The first, simpler version of classification is commonly referred to as the "superfluous fourth." In this case, a subject is given four objects or four drawings. He/she is told to select the three objects that may be designated by the same word and which, consequently, have something in common, and to set aside the remaining, fourth object that does not fall into this cateogry. Thus a subject who is given drawings of a saw, an axe, a spade, and a log should pick out the first three because they belong to the category of "tools" and set aside the fourth, which does not. Such a decision reflects categorical thinking.

In this first variant of the superfluous fourth task, the subject is offered three objects similar in shape and belonging to a common category and a fourth object differing in shape and color and not belonging to the category. For example, he/she might be given four drawings, three of round fruits or vegetables (e.g., an apple, a plum, and an orange) and the fourth of an object quite different in shape as well as in substance (e.g., an umbrella, a window, or a table). It is quite easy to solve such a problem. However, the solution may derive either from the categorical feature (i.e., three drawings are of fruit while the fourth represents some other type of object) or from a visual feature (i.e., three objects are round while the fourth is solid). This is precisely what makes this version of the task easier.

The second version of the superfluous fourth task is more complex. A subject is given three objects belonging to the same category, but differing in their external appearance (shape, color, or size). The fourth object may be similar to one of the three in shape and color, but belongs to a different category. For instance, a subject may be given drawings of a turnip, a carrot, and a tomato, which are all vegetables but differ in shape. The fourth object may be a ball, which, like the tomato, is round but belongs to a different category. In this instance, the subject must ignore the external appearance and single out the three objects belonging to the same category. Naturally, this version is more difficult than the first.

The third version of the superfluous fourth task can be termed the "conflicting" version. In this case, a subject is given three objects (e.g., a saw, an axe, and a spade) belonging to the same category designated by the same word ("tools"). The fourth object (e.g., a log) belongs to a different category of materials, but is commonly part of the same situation as these tools. When asked to separate the three objects having something in common and set aside the fourth, the subject must overcome the concretely based situation. If he/she is unable to do this, the classification will reflect situational, rather than categorical reasoning. For instance, the subject might group the log, the saw, and the axe together because the log must first be sawed and then chopped and say that the spade belongs to another category (e.g., the garden).

Numerous studies based on this method have yielded unambiguous results. These studies have shown that preschoolers and young schoolchildren tend to group objects according to their concrete features or according to their inclusion in a single concrete situation. As a rule, these subjects can sort drawings on the basis of color, shape, or size. Somewhat later, they can group items on the basis of their inclusion in a single concrete situation. Of course, subjects have their own concretely based logic at this stage.

Interesting differences among these young subjects appear if an experimenter proposes an alternative answer based on an abstract category. For example, in the case of the axe, saw, spade, and log, the experimenter might say, "You know, these things may be called tools, but a log is not a tool." Preschoolers will not be able to comprehend this suggestion because their thinking is still bound by concrete factors. Young schoolchildren will grasp something about the suggestion, but they will not consistently follow the principle. They often will slip back to the concretely based principle of grouping objects. On the other hand, in older schoolchildren the predominant process will involve abstract classification. The three appropriate items will be grouped together even in the conflicting version of the task. They find it possible to overcome immediate, concrete impressions.

Once again, mentally retarded children cannot disengage themselves from concrete criteria. As a rule, they select three objects which have a common concrete sensory feature (e.g., direct resemblance in color or shape), or they will try to find the concrete situation in which all three objects can be included. Experimenters' attempts to change this operation into a more abstract categorical plan will not succeed. After these children have been shown a possible categorical solution, they will continue, as before, to carry out the operations by selecting the objects either on the basis of their concrete features or on the basis of their inclusion in a concrete situation. For example, they may group a fork, a knife, and a piece of meat together and exclude a spoon as something that is "not needed." Weighl (1927) was the first to examine the process of classification. He used the German terms "Aufraumen" to refer to concretely based classification and "Ordnen" to refer to categorical classification. Later, the psychological difference between these two types of solutions was investigated by German neurologist Goldstein (1934).

These methods also have yielded important findings about differences in the cognitive processes of people who vary in their socioeconomic living conditions and in their level of schooling. Several studies (e.g., Luria, 1974a; Cole and Scribner, 1974) have demonstrated that people who live in relatively elementary socioeconomic conditions and who are nonliterate tend to classify objects according to their inclusion in a concrete situation. For instance, they may group the axe, the saw, and the log together and explain, "The log should first be sawed and then cut by the axe." They refuse to include the spade in this group and explain, "The spade is not needed here, it is needed for the garden." It is important to note that these subjects can also understand the other, categorical, form of classification, but they consider it to be "unimportant." It is only at a later stage, with the acquisition of literacy and transition to more complex socially organized forms of production, that they can easily master the categorical form of generalization of objects. This supports the notion that advances in cognitive operations arise as a result of advances in socioeconomic and cultural conditions.

A second, more complex version of the classification procedure provides much richer information. This is the procedure of *free classification*. It involves giving a subject several objects or cards with pictures of different objects on them (e.g., animals, plants, cooking utensils, pieces of furniture, vehicles, etc.) The subject is asked to arrange these objects in groups such that each group can be named by one word. After the subject has carried out this task, he/she is asked to name each group and to explain precisely why he/she grouped the cards in the given manner. After carrying out this second assignment, the subject is given the third assignment of decreasing the number of groups. For instance, if he/she has divided the cards into ten groups, he/she is asked to arrange them in only three groups. The experimenter observes how the subject carries out this task and asks him/her once again to name each of the new groups and to explain the criteria on which the regrouping has been carried out.

A subject can arrange the objects on the basis of different sets of criteria. He/she can group them according to external, sensory features (e.g., by placing all red objects in one group and all blue ones in another; by placing all round objects in one group and all angular ones in another). This is the most elementary type of classification. He/she can also group objects together which form part of a single concrete situation (e.g., a group might consist of a loaf of bread, a plate, a fork, a knife, a table, and a chair because they all are associated with dinner; it might consist of a cat, milk, and a mousetrap because a cat drinks milk and catches mice; or it might consist of a dog, a kennel, and meat, because a dog lives in a kennel and eats meat).

Finally, a third method can be used to solve this problem. A subject can identify certain features which he/she considers important, and on the basis of these features he/she can collect different objects into one category, irrespective of whether these objects are part of any concrete situation. In this case, bread, meat, a plate, and a table will never form one group because bread and meat form the group of edible items; plate, fork, and knife made up kitchenware; etc. In this instance, the basis of classification is the operation of abstracting a feature and grouping objects in a certain common category, i.e., classification is based on verbal-logical operations.

Some of those subjects in whom concretely based thinking predominates will begin by considering how to combine objects belonging to different groups into a single concrete situation. They may try to combine a situation involving bread, meat, a fork, knife, plate, and table with a situation designated as dinner. Sometimes they add the person who is eating and the dog which stands near the table waiting for food. They may try to combine a man, a suit, a pair of shoes, and a shirt because the man has to dress himself. In other words, they expand the situation by introducing new objects, each of which plays a role in the situation. This process requires great effort. More often than not, subjects find themselves unable to enlarge the groups, and thus declare that the groups have nothing in common. When asked to label these larger groups with one word, they experience great difficulty because they do not have access to a sufficiently complex lexical item to embrace everything involved.

This process is quite different for subjects who classify objects on the basis of abstract categories. These people not only can carry out the required verbal-logical operations, but also can shift easily from one level in the hierarchy of associations to another. They can move from concrete to general and can label the groups formed with a word denoting the corresponding concept. These more mature subjects can begin by identifying one category, such as domestic animals, and then include another category, such as wild animals, to arrive at the super-ordinate category of animals in general. They can transfer objects into more and more abstract categories.

Thus these subjects utilize a hierarchy of concepts which, to use Vygotsky's term, have a certain "longitude" (from the elementary to more complex). They also have a certain "latitude" because this system includes concretely based items as well as things which never have appeared in subjects' experience. The presence of a logical hierarchy of concepts is the essence of what separates concrete uses of word from verbal-logical uses.

The transition of word meaning to the stage of abstract concepts not only insures an improvement in the processing of information, but also gives rise to a certain freedom in human perceptual processes. This was pointed out by Gelb (1937), who analyzed the psychological changes which result from categorical word meaning. A mentally retarded child can arrange items into groups only on the basis of a sensory characteristic or on the basis of their inclusion in a single concrete situation. I recall the case of a mentally retarded child who was asked to group several pictures. He placed a bottle, a glass, a table and a crayfish together because, "One can place a bottle of beer on the table and eat the crayfish with beer." All attempts to convince him that these objects belonged to different categories failed. On the other hand, a normal schoolchild, who may begin with a similar type of concrete classification, can easily switch to a more complex classification system. To induce this switch, it is sufficient to suggest to him/her that objects can be classified in a different way. For example, an experimenter might identify their essential feature and relate them to a category.

To use Vygotsky's (1978) term, we can say that the first child's "zone of proximal development" is not sufficient to take advantage of adult assistance. He cannot make the transition from concretely based thinking to abstract thinking, whereas the second child's zone of proximal development made this possible. In this second case, an explanation or an example of the abstract use of a word enabled the child to solve the problem. Furthermore, the mentally retarded child experienced great difficulty in using words to describe the grouping of objects that he provided. Therefore, he was not in a position to comprehend the operations he had performed. In various cases he either failed to answer the question as to why he had arranged the objects in these groups, or he simply referred to his concrete situational experience. On the other hand, a normal schoolchild (even in the primary grades) can easily label the groups with a word which has a generalized categorical meaning.

A further difference between mentally retarded children and normal schoolchildren is that the former cannot switch to more inclusive groups when asked to do so. They can break up their original groups into smaller, more concrete ones, but they are usually unsuccessful in their efforts to combine their groups into more abstract, inclusive sets. Normal children can perform this task quite easily. If they are once shown how, they not only can form more inclusive groups, they also can label them with a word. Thus, we have seen that this simple method can provide a great deal of information. That is precisely why it has become one of the most important tools for diagnosing mental retardation.

THE METHOD OF FORMING ARTIFICIAL CONCEPTS

We shall now proceed to the final version of the method of classification, a version seldom used in practice but nevertheless quite important because of the role it has played in Soviet psychology. It enables us to study, in great detail, the process of concept formation. It was first proposed by Ach (1921). Almost 50 years ago, it was modified and used for quite different purposes by Vygotsky (1934) and his student Sakharov. This method not only gave rise to a description of the connections which are represented by a word, it also made it possible to describe the psychological processes connected with a word at various developmental stages. One of Vygotsky's main reasons for using it was that it allowed an investigator to study children independently of differences in individual experience.

This method involves giving a subject several geometrical figures of various shapes, colors, and sizes. Among these items, for example, is a small, flat, red triangle; a small, flat, green triangle; a small, flat, red square; a small yellow cube; a small cylinder; a large red triangle; a large green triangle; and some three-dimensional figures, such as red and green pyramids and red, green, and blue cubes, etc. Thus, the objects to be classified differ in shape, color, dimension, and volume. Each item was labeled with a certain artificial word. When a subject picks up one of the figures, he/she can see on its previously concealed bottom an artificial word such as "ras," "mor," or "pak."

The main feature of this method is that the artificial word designates a new concept which did not previously exist in the child's experience. The artificial word applied to a set of items (e.g., all small and flat items, or all small and tall items, or all large and flat items, or all large and tall items). Under these conditions, subject cannot use an existing concept, but must form a new one.

When carrying out this study, adult subjects were informed that the word had a meaning. When the study was carried out with children, subjects were told that the word had a meaning in Papuan. Subjects were told that they must discover the meaning of the word by selecting objects they thought could be designated by it and turning them over to see if they had the appropriate label. A subject might begin by selecting and inverting a figure labeled "ras." At this point, he/she could only guess the meaning of the word. Next, he/she would choose a second figure, read its label, and make a new guess. Of course, during these successive choices, a child might come across different artificial words as well as the same one he/she had seen earlier.

With the progressive selection of figures, certain hypotheses begin to appear. For instance, a child might pose the hypothesis that all cylinders are labeled "ras." Following this hypothesis, he/she would invert a cylinder of another size, but if this did not have the label "ras" that hypothesis was not supported and he/she had to make a fresh assumption. For instance, a child might test the hypothesis that the word "ras" designates either all red objects (color) or all triangles (shape). On this basis, he/she would select and invert another object. If this hypothesis was not supported, then a third hypothesis had to be formed, such as the artificial word designated a dimensional feature. He/she could then test whether this hypothesis was supported. The difficulty created by this procedure for the subject was that the artificial words designated complex, rather than simple concepts. For instance, the word "pak" designated all objects that were both large and flat, and the word "ras" designated all figures that were both large and tall, irrespective of their color, shape, etc. Every artificial word used by Vygotsky had a complex meaning which did not exist before being introduced into the experiment.

By carefully conducting this experiment, Vygotsky was able to analyze how subjects utilized information from successive choices to arrive at the concept. This elaborate procedure has yielded extremely rich information. It has been found that normal, mature subjects create a sequence of hypotheses, coordinate these hypotheses with the facts, and reject some and substitute other hypotheses for them. In this way, an experimenter can observe how a new abstract concept gradually takes shape.

In the case of subjects who operate on the basis of a system of hierarchically organized concepts, it is possible to follow the formation of an abstract concept quite clearly. The sequence of logical operations occurs within the framework of categorical systems. Quite the opposite was observed in the case of subjects who did not operate on the basis of hierarchically organized conceptual systems.

The most retarded subjects were found to be quite incapable of even approaching a solution. As a rule, when asked to find all the objects designated by the arbitrary term "gatsun," they simply grouped all the objects in one heap without trying to analyze these basic features. Vygotsky (1934) called this stage "the stage of unorganized heaps" or the "chaotic stage." It has also been termed the "syncretic phase." During this stage, there are no firm principles underlying the grouping of objects.

During the next phase, a quite different picture emerges. Subjects include the items in a definite category based on a particular feature, but this feature does not remain constant. A subject might begin with a small red triangle (labeled "ras") and a small green circle, using the criterion of size. Then he/she might proceed by adding a tall red pyramid (on the basis of color), a large green triangle (on the basis of shape), etc. As a result, the items in the group were chosen on the basis of a "complex" rather than on the basis of a stable generalized concept. In a complex each object is included on the basis of a feature it shares with at least one other object in the group, but the critical feature may change with the selection of each object rather than remaining constant throughout. In addition to the terms "thinking in complexes" or "situational thinking," Vygotsky sometimes described the group as a "family" on the basis of the fact that members of a family are included in it on different premises. For example, in X's family, there is a father, a mother, a brother, a sister, a son, a nephew, etc. Vygotsky characterized this stage by pointing out that the subjects selected objects not on the basis of a single stable feature, but on the basis of a variety of features.

Sometimes the sequence of choices comprised what Vygotsky termed a "chain complex." For instance, if a subject discovered that a green triangle was designated by the desired artificial word, he/she might first choose a green circle because it is green, then a small red triangle because a previous item was triangular, then a small square because the previous item was small, etc. In this case, every object can enter into the group, and a stable abstract concept cannot be formed. Subjects respond not by including the objects in a common category, but by linking them together into a chain in accordance with changing features.

Classification of objects on the basis of categories reflects a higher, more logical process. In this case, the strategy of looking for the solution is psychologically quite different. The subject tries to discover the true concept designated by the artificial word. He/she bases his/her selection on a stable combination of features, thus evolving a new abstract category. Naturally, the processes observed during this type of performance are quite different from those mentioned earlier. The strategy reveals that the operations are performed on a verbal-logical plane and that the word has acquired a new stable, abstract meaning.

The method of forming artificial concepts had limited practical significance and is too complicated to become a quick diagnostic test. However, it has an enormous theoretical and historical significance. It was by following this method that Vygotsky (1934) arrived at the conclusion that the word conceals different systems of relations during different ontogenetic stages. Subsequently, other psychologists have used these methods. For example, Bruner and his colleagues (Bruner, Goodnow, and Austin, 1957) used them for the study of concept formation, and Hull (1930) used the method of "artificial words" in a different way in an effort to trace the process of complex habit formation.

THE STUDY OF THE CONSCIOUS UNDERSTANDING OF THE LEXICAL COMPOSITION OF LANGUAGE

It is a well-known fact that the processes involved in consciously understanding the lexical composition of the words in a language present a special and quite important problem. We know that a child acquires the words of a language at a relatively early age. We also know that an entire period in the ontogenesis of speech is characterized by the great attention the child pays to words and by creative word building [described in detail in Chukovskii's (1958) widely read book]. It is an extremely important process in language development.

This does not mean, however, that a child consciously understands the lexical composition of speech without going through a period of development. Observations have shown that during early stages children cannot consciously understand words as isolated units of language and that they easily confuse words with the things they denote. Observations have also shown that the process of becoming consciously aware of the various lexical forms of language is extremely complex and that this process follows an interesting path. This may escape our attention during ordinary observation, but it reveals itself with great vividness when special analytic techniques are used.

The method which enables us to recognize these facts and to follow the dramatic course of a child's conscious understanding of the lexical composition of language was first proposed by Vygotsky (1934). We have also used this method in some of our earlier research (Luria and Yudovich, 1956), and it has been further elaborated by Karpova (1967). Let us now turn to some of the results obtained from these studies.

If a child of 3 to 5 years, who has already mastered elementary counting, is given two isolated words (e.g., "table" and "chair") and is asked how many words were spoken, he/she will answer, without any difficulty, "two." However, if we turn from concrete nouns to verbs or adjectives and give a child such combinations as "sobaka bezhit" (dog-runs) or "limon-kislyi" (lemon sour), he/she will no longer be able to give the correct answer. Often, he/she will say, "Obviously, it is one word—"sobaka" or "limon." This indicates that substantive words (nouns) occupy a special place and are consciously understood before words denoting actions or qualities.

This emerges even more clearly if the construction given to the child includes several objects. For instance, if asked how many words there are in the sentence "There are 12 chairs in the room.", a child of the above-mentioned age group will reply, without hesitation, "12.", obviously confusing the number of objects named with the number of words used to express this phrase. We have even come across cases where a child, when asked how many words there are in the sentence "Kolya finished all the cakes.", answered, "None, he ate them all!" The same difficulty in abstracting a word from the object it denotes and comprehending the verbal composition of speech is observed in a child when he/she is asked to count the number of words in a more complex sentence. Thus, in response to the question "How many words are there in the sentence daddy and mummy have gone to the woods?", a child might answer, "Two—daddy and mummy." In certain cases, he/she might add, ". . . And woods!" Thus, words denoting actions (and properties) are used by children easily in practice, but they do not yet consciously separate them as words.

Young children face even greater difficulty distinguishing auxiliary words (e.g., prepositions and conjunctions) in a sentence. A child who is able to pick out nouns (and sometimes verbs) from a sentence, such as "Petya has gone to the woods with his father.", may be quite unable to distinguish and consciously understand such auxiliary words as "with" and "to." Children may develop the ability to identify these auxiliary words through special training techniques, but as Karpova (1967) has pointed out, even in this the process is by no means simple. The child who has learned to isolate the prepositions "v" (in) and "na" (on) may begin to isolate corresponding morphemes in words. Thus they may say with assurance that "vstat'" (get up) and "nakryt'" (cover) are two words ("v+stat'" and "na+kryt'") and make the same error in writing these words. In these cases, the child must be taught to take the next step in abstraction and learn to distinguish auxiliary words from elements of complex words which resemble them.

A similar process can be observed at a later stage of development when shoolchildren are asked to identify parts of speech. Teachers have long known that if a noun denotes a concrete object and is given in its citation (zero) form (i.e., nominative case singular), children identify it without difficulty as a noun. However, if children are given nouns which do not denote concrete objects, but states or actions, the task of determining the grammatical class to which they belong becomes noticeably more difficult. The child who has just said, without hesitation, that "table," "house," and "window" are nouns begins to hesitate when faced with such words as "sleep" or "rest." When confronted with words such as "beg" (race),[8] he/she may confidently answer that it is a verb.

---

[8]The Russian word "beg" is the citation form for the noun "run" or "race" (i.e., a sporting event). The verb "to run" ("begat'") is clearly distinguished by morphological means in Russian.—*J. V. Wertsch*

The elementary schoolchild faces the same difficulties when the noun is used not in the nominative case but in an oblique case, imparting to it a shade of action. For instance, if a child is given the word "lopatoi" (instrumental case of "lopata"—spade), "piloi" (instrumental case of "pila"—saw), "ptichku" (accusative case of "ptichka"—birdie), or "sobake" (dative or prepositional case of "sobaka"—dog), he/she may begin to hesitate and either be wholly unable to characterize words in such forms or take them to be verbs. Something similar occurs when children are confronted with verbs. Verbs which clearly express actions (such as "begat' "—to run), "khodit' "—to walk, and "rubit' "—to chop) are characterized correctly by elementary schoolchildren. However, children begin to waver when asked to characterize verbs expressing passive states, such as "spat' " (to sleep), "otdykhat' " (to rest), "bolet' " (to be ill). They are often unable to place these in a clear grammatical class.

These facts have not yet been investigated in detail. A careful analysis of them needs to be made. However, both the first set of facts (concerned with difficulties in isolating words from word constructions and the order in which a child comprehends nouns, verbs, adjectives, and auxiliary words) and the second set of observations (showing the close unity between the morphology and semantics of words) are matters of utmost interest and call for careful psychological and linguistic investigation.

Chapter 5
The Objective Study of Semantic Fields

In the previous chapters, we have argued that the word has a complex semantic structure. On the one hand, it has an object reference because it can be used to refer to objects, actions, or properties. On the other hand, it analyzes and generalizes referents and relates them to a category. Following Vygotsky, we have used the term "word meaning" for this second function. We have also shown that the object reference and the meaning of the word undergo significant changes during ontogenesis.

However, as already noted, this does not exhaust our analysis of the word's psychological structure. Each word evokes a complex system of associations and thus becomes the center of a semantic network. It actuates specific semantic fields which play a significant role in the psychological analysis of the word and its functions. In this connection, the question naturally arises as to whether it is possible to undertake a rigorous psychological investigation of semantic fields. Can one identify the associations evoked by a word and analyze both the probability with which these associations will occur and the components of meaning structure involved? Psychologists have been attempting to answer this question for many years. Let us turn to a brief review of some of these attempts.

THE USE OF ASSOCIATIVE METHODS IN EVALUATING
SEMANTIC FIELDS

Perhaps the most widely known method used to investigate semantic fields is the association experiment. Subjects are given a list of words and asked to respond to each with the first word that comes to mind. Studies of this problem have shown that such associations are almost never random. They can be divided into at least two large groups on the basis of whether an "external" or "internal" association is involved.

External associations usually have been understood as associations by contiguity. In this case, the word evokes some component of the concrete situation in which the referent of the first word appears. Such associations as "house"–"roof," "dog"–"tail," "cat"–"mouse" are examples of external associations.

Internal associations are usually understood to be associations evoked by the inclusion of a word in a certain category. Associations such as "dog"–"animal," "chair"–"furniture," and "oak"–"tree" are examples of this type of association. In classical psychology, these were called "association by similarity" or "association by contrast."

Many investigators have tried to examine the ease with which these links can be evoked and the probability of their occurrence. In connection with the first problem, researchers often use response time (the time required to produce an associated word). This method showed that more complex forms of association require a longer response time than the simpler forms. This method also enabled us to trace the development of verbal associations in ontogenesis (cf. Luria, 1930) and it has been used to examine the affective inhibition caused by some words (cf. Jung, 1906, 1910; Luria, 1932).

A second issue is the probability with which a certain word will be elicited when a subject is presented with a word. This is usually studied by counting the frequency a word occurs in response to a given word. Perhaps the first such study was that of Kent and Rosanoff (1910). In some of our own early research (Luria, 1930), we examined the dependence of the response frequency on the subject's personal background. We demonstrated that associations in the speech system of a rural child were more permanent than those in the speech system of an urban child or a homeless child with far more diverse life experiences. In recent years, response probability has been studied in detail by several American investigators (e.g., Deese, 1962). This widely used method obviously can play an important role in the detailed study of semantic fields.

THE USE OF SCALES TO MEASURE SEMANTIC FIELDS

A second technique that allows one to analyze semantic relations has been developed by the well-known American psychologist Osgood (1964; also Osgood,

Suci, and Tannenbaum, 1957). Osgood utilized a method giving subjects a word (or a person's name) and asking them to place the word on a scale or continuum ranging between two opposite qualities (e.g., strong—weak, good—bad, bitter—sweet). Subjects are asked to indicate the point on the scale occupied by the item. Naturally on the "sour—sweet" scale the word "lemon" occupies an extreme position near the first term. On this same scale, the word "sugar" occupies the opposite position, and the words "apple," "plum," and "pear" occupy intermediate points.

The Osgood method undoubtedly introduces certain new dimensions into the study of semantic fields. However, his critics (Carroll, 1964; Weinreich, 1958) correctly pointed out that this method is rather limited, since it allows subjects to arrange the connotative meanings of the word in accordance with only one or two artificially selected scales. The importance of this method is also limited by its heavy reliance on subjective judgment and by the fact that the "semantic differential" developed by Osgood is concerned with the affective meaning of the word.

THE CHARACTERIZATION OF SEMANTIC FIELDS

From what we have seen so far, it is obvious that a semantic field is quite complex and requires the development of objective psychological methods. In order to deal with this problem, let us return to an analysis of the concept of a semantic field.

As already noted, to a naive observer it may appear that a word possesses a single permanent meaning. However, a more careful analysis shows that this is far from being the case. If a word had only a single constant meaning, humans could not point to the different aspects of an object or analyze it and isolate certain associations from among all possible ones. If a word had a constant meaning, there would be no possibility for observing the transition from its "denotative" meaning to the specific connections which emerge at a particular moment. That is to say, there would be no possibility for analyzing the relationship between meaning and sense.

This hypothesis about the polysemantic nature of the relationships that lie behind a word calls for a more detailed discussion. In connection with any word there exists a system of phonetic, situational, and conceptual connections. For instance, the word "koshka" (cat) evokes phonetically similar connections, such as "koshka" (cat), "kroshka" (crumb), "kryshka" (lid), "kruzhka" (mug), and "okoshko" (dimunitive of window). This word may also evoke situational connections, such as "milk," "mousetrap," and "fur." Finally, the word "koshka" (cat) may evoke certain conceptual connections, such as "domestic animal" (as opposed to wild animals) or "living being" (as opposed to inanimate objects). The same can be said of the word "skripka" (violin). The word "skripka" may suggest connections similar in sound, such as "skrepka" (paper clip), or situational connections, such as "bow," "music stand," "orchestra," or "concert." Finally, it may suggest a system of conceptually associated words, denoting things belonging to the same category, such as "musical instrument," "instruments in general." Since the word "skripka" has such conceptual connections, it will enter the same category as "balalaika," "guitar," "mandolin," "cello," and "piano."

The various connections are not always equally powerful. In a normal adult, phonetic associations are almost always inhibited since these interfere with cognition. Hardly anyone would think of the words "kroshka" (crumb) or "kryshka" (lid) when he/she hears the word "koshka" (cat), or think of "skrepka" (paper clip) when hearing the word "skripka" (violin). We move away from phonetic associations because it is then possible for semantic associations to dominate. Normally, it is the meaning bonds, both situational and semantic, which dominate. It is therefore natural that the word "koshka" (cat) is likely to elicit either the situation "catching mice" or the semantic association "dog," or "domestic animals"; and the word "skripka" (violin) is likely to elicit either situational associations, such as "bow" or "concert," or categorical semantic associations, such as "musical instrument." In all such situations, there is a selection of the necessary meaning from among the many possibilities which occur with varying degrees of probability.

However, in special states of consciousness, this selectivity disappears and phonetic associations begin to occur with the same probability as associations based on meaning. Among these states of consciousness are the inhibiting or "phasic" states of the cerebral cortex which were studied by Pavlov. These occur during the transition from the state of wakefulness to sleep, in conditions of severe fatigue, and in certain other pathological conditions of the brain.

Pavlov demonstrated that when the cerebral cortex is in its normal state it works in accordance with the "law of strength." This means that strong (or important) stimuli elicit strong responses and weak (or nonessential) stimuli elicit weak responses. It is only through the law of strength that the selective work of the cerebral cortex can take place, that the cortex can highlight important features and inhibit the nonessential ones, thus ensuring the steady operation of complex functional systems. It is precisely these conditions that are disrupted when the cerebral cortex is in a phasic state. These conditions are characterized by the fact that the law of strength ceases to operate. Furthermore, during the first stage of phasic conditions, all stimuli (strong and weak) begin to elicit an equally strong response. When there is increased inhibition, a "paradoxical" or even an "ultraparadoxical" phase arises. In this phase, weak or nonessential stimuli elicit stronger responses than strong stimuli, or the strong stimuli elicit inhibitory processes.

Naturally, when the cortex is in such an inhibitory state, all types of associations begin to appear with equal probability (or the weak associations begin to appear even more actively than the strong ones), selectivity in the operation of the cerebral cortex disappears, and the probability of occurrence of phonetic, situational, and connotative alternatives become equal. This is what happens in oneroid states, when a person is almost, but not quite asleep or in conditions of extreme fatigue. In these cases, the inhibited phonetic associations of a word begin to surface, and selectivity is disturbed.

A striking example of this confusion of types of association while in an oneroid state may be found in Tolstoy's *War and Peace*. Tolstoy was a great master at describing the subconscious conditions in humans. In this passage, Nikolai Rostov dozes off and different images begin to float in the mind. He looks at a knoll and sees some sort of white spots.

> On this knoll was a white patch Rostov could not understand; was it a moonlit clearing in the wood or the remains of snow or white houses? "It must be snow . . . . that spot, a spot—une tache," Rostov mused, "But that's not a tache . . . . Natasha . . . . sister, black eyes . . . . Na . . . . tashka . . . . Natashku, tashku voz'mi" (take the tashka[9]) . . . . No tashku nastupit' (advance!) tupit' na . . . . kogo? (advance, on whom?). The hussars. Hussars and moustaches. Along the Tverskaya Street rode the hussar with moustaches . . . . I was thinking of him too, just opposite Gur'ev's house . . . Old Gur'ev . . . But that's not important. The important thing is not to forget the important thing I was thinking of. Yes, Na-tashku, nas-tupit', yes, yes, that's fine."

This is a brilliant description of the disturbance in the selectivity of associations that can occur in a tired person in a drowsy state. Let us analyze these associations. First there is "It must be snow . . . . that spot."; next, the French word for "spot"— *une tache*. After the word *tache*, we have words that are phonetically similar to the French word—"Na-natasha, Na-tashka, Na-tashku." Following this come other phonetically similar items: "tashku voz'mi" (take a sabre belt worn by Hussars); "nastupit" (to step on or to advance—an association from "portupei"—sabre belt, not sword, "tupit' nas" (to cut us down—again the play of these phonetic associations); "kogo?" (whom—"gusarov" (hussars), "a gusary (hussars) usy" (moustaches—phonetic associations), etc. It is easy to see that in a drowsy state associations may occur in a person's mind that never occur in a wakeful state. In a drowsy state, we observe an equalization of all possible associations—phonetic, situational, and connotative.

Thus the word represents a potential network of multidimensional associations. Normally, the phonetic associations are inhibited and other, semantic associations dominate. The entire process acquires a selective character. In certain states of consciousness (e.g., in conditions of drowsiness or fatigue, or during the search for half forgotten words), this selectivity is disturbed, the strength of various

[9]A pouch worn by hussars on the belt.—*J. V. Wertsch*

associations is equalized, and the choice of the necessary word from among many possible ones becomes difficult.

OBJECTIVE METHODS FOR INVESTIGATING THE MULTI-DIMENSIONAL ASSOCIATIONS OF A WORD

In order to investigate a word's associations, one needs a set of objective psychological methods. We have already mentioned some of these methods above (comparison, differentiation, and classification).

As already noted, associations to a given word can vary quite widely. Sometimes, a certain word suggests a characteristic feature of the object that it designates (e.g., "dog"—"barks," "cat"—"meows," etc.). Sometimes, though seldom in normal cases, a word may occur that is phonetically similar with the given word; e.g., in response to "koshka" (cat), one may find "kroshka" (crumb) or "kryshka" (lid). Also, in some cases, a response may be based on situational factors (e.g., "cat"—"milk") or semantic links (e.g., "cat"—"animal"). As we have said, simple associative experiments make it possible to determine which type of association occurs most readily and which predominates.

Another variant of this method involves *free association*. In this case, a subject is given a word and is asked to say any words that may enter his/her mind without trying to inhibit any items. The subject is asked to continue producing free associations until the experimenter asks him/her to stop. This method of free associations was used by Freud. He showed that the flow of associations that come to mind in such cases may be determined by cognitive, situational, or conceptual processes or by affective processes (sometimes by hidden inclinations or feelings). It is easy to see that this method can also play an important role in analyzing the dynamics of semantic fields.

However, all of the methods mentioned so far provide only indirect evidence for the analysis of semantic fields. That is why it is so important to devise an objective method for investigating semantic fields. The first attempts at developing such a method can be seen in the early works of Riess (1940) and Razran (1949), later continued by Shvarts (1948, 1954), and finally, a version of this method was utilized by Vinogradova (1956), Vinogradova and Eisler (1959), and Luria and Vinogradova (1959, 1971). All of these authors used techniques based on conditioned-reflex methodology. This allowed them to use indices which reflect the structure of semantic fields objectively, either through motor responses or vascular responses induced by conditioned reflexes.

Our review here will be limited to semantic association data from experiments carried out in our laboratory. Vinogradova devised a special technique based on the orienting reflex in order to study semantic fields. This technique is based on the fact that each new stimulus (including a verbal stimulus) gives rise to a reflex which is manifested in a series of motor, electrophysiological and autonomic indicators (e.g., constriction of blood vessels in the fingers and expansion of blood vessels in the brain). As Sokolov (1958, 1959) demonstrated, this constitutes the well-known symptom of heightened attention and is a nonspecific orienting reflex. A different picture emerges in the case of specific indicators. Thus, painful stimuli cause the blood vessels in the hand and head to become constricted, and with the stimulus of warmth both types of blood vessels expand. It is precisely these patterns that distinguish specific (unconditioned) vascular responses from the class of orienting responses. That is what makes it possible to use these indicators in the study of semantic fields.

In order to carry out this type of investigation, a subject is given several different types of words. A natural orienting response occurs in connection with each of these. It is manifested in the changes in blood vessels we mentioned earlier. The presentation of various types of words continues until the subject becomes habituated to them. Habituation is manifested by the extinction of the orienting response.

It is at this stage the actual experiment begins. In one set of conditions, the subject is instructed to press a button upon hearing a test word (such as "koshka"—cat). In other conditions, when subject hears a test word (such as "skripka"—violin), a painful stimulus (e.g., an electric shock) is administered to his/her arm. Our observations have shown that both of these procedures produce very interesting results. In the first case, when subject must press a button in response to the word "koshka" (cat), we observed not only movement of the right hand but also vascular responses in the left hand and temple. The blood vessels of the left hand constrict and those of the head dilate. This indicates that the test word has attained a situational meaning and is beginning to evoke an involuntary vascular orienting response. In the case of the word "skripka" (violin), which was reinforced by pain, the blood vessels of the hand as well as those of the head are constricted. In other words, a specific response to pain emerges.

Given this set of conditions, we can now proceed to the essence of the experiment. This concerns the question of what other words will cause similar responses, i.e., what other words will elicit the orienting response in the first instance and the response to pain in the second. In order to answer this, we presented several additional words to the subject. These were divided into three categories. First, we included *neutral words* such as "okno" (window), "lampa" (lamp), and "tetrad'" (notebook). These words bear no relation to the test word. Second, we included words which are *phonetically* similar to the text word. Thus, when "koshka" (cat) was the test word, we used the words "kroshka" (crumb), "kryshka" (lid), "kruzhka" (mug), and "okoshko" (diminutive of window). Third, we included words on the basis of their *meaning* association with the test word. Thus, we used words with situational associations—such as "kotenok" (kitten), "mysh'" (mouse), and "moloko" (milk)—in the first case, and "smychok" (bow) and "kontsert" (concert) in the second case. We also used words which have categorical association with the test word, e.g., "zhivotnoe" (animal) and "sobaka" (dog) in the first case and "mandolina" (mandolin), "fortepiano" (piano), and "muzyka" (music) in the second case. The experimenter who presented these words carefully observed whether they caused the involuntary responses enumerated above.

This study provided extremely interesting results. We found that as a rule neutral words (i.e., words which bore no relationship to the test words) evoked no response. In contrast, words related to the test word produced an involuntary vascular orienting response. In the first condition, when subjects were to press a button in response to the word "koshka" (cat), they showed no voluntary motor response to the neutral stimuli. However, some of the words which were close to the test word evoked an involuntary orienting response. It is precisely this that enabled us to provide an objective demonstration that certain words are in the semantic field of the text word "koshka" (cat).

In the second condition, when a test word such as "skripka" (violin) was rein-forced by a painful stimulus, we found that other words, which had never been reinforced by a painful stimulus, begin to evoke either an orienting response or a specific pain response.

Hence, it was found that all of the words which were presented to the subject could be divided into three groups. First, the neutral words did not enter into the semantic field evoked by the test word and did not elicit any vascular (pain or orienting) responses. Words of the second group were in the semantic field evoked by the test word and elicited a specific response, such as pressure by the hand or a specific vascular response to pain. The third group of words consisted of items which enter into the semantic field evoked by the test word, but to a lesser degree. These words elicit neither direct motor responses nor specific vascular responses to pain. However, they do elicit involuntary vascular orienting responses.

We found that words which are phonetically connected with the test word do not elicit any response. This meant that phonetic associations are normally inhibited. They do not enter into any relationship with the test word. On the other hand, words which are semantically close to the test word evoked either a specific or a nonspecific orienting response. With normal subjects, the word "myshka" (mouse) or "sobaka" (dog) evoked a response similar to that evoked by test word "koshka" (cat), and the word "mandolina" (mandolin) evoked a response similar to that evoked by test word "skripka" (violin).

Finally, the study showed that there is a third group of words which also form part of the semantic field evoked by the test word, but occupy a secondary posi-tion in this field. These words are located on the "periphery." For example, in the condition in which the test word is "skripka" (violin), neither "struna" (string) nor "fortepiano" (piano) triggered a specific response to pain, but they do evoke an orienting response. We therefore have an objective criterion for establishing the degree of proximity of a word to the test word.

Our methodology provides us with an important means for examining the semantic fields evoked by words. Our objective method allows us to do this without questioning the subject. We have also seen that this method enables us to identify whether the phonetic, the situational, or the connotative aspects in a subject's system of associations predominates.

As we have shown, words phonetically similar to a test word do not evoke any response in a normal adult subject. This is also true of normal schoolchildren. Such words, therefore, do not enter into the semantic field evoked by the test word. On the other hand, words semantically close to the test word evoke autonomic specific or orienting responses of varying intensities. A quite different picture emerges in the case of mentally retarded children. In the case of children who are severely retarded (imbeciles), words semantically close evoke no autonomic responses, but phonetically similar ones give rise to the constriction of blood vessels in the hand and dilation of blood vessels in the brain.

The most interesting data emerged in the case of children with mild mental retardation. In their case, we found that both semantically similar and phonetically similar words evoked orienting responses to the same degree. This indicates that a mentally retarded child understands words in a way different from a normal child and that the system of association evoked in him/her by words is different from that evoked in the normal schoolchild. At the same time, it indicates that with such children words can evoke associations both on the semantic level and on the phonetic level.

The results of the experiments we have described reveal another set of very important facts. They show that the semantic fields are not identical in different children. Rather, they vary significantly depending upon various conditions, especially fatigue. When we examined mildly retarded children while they were fresh and alert, semantic associations predominated over phonetic ones. However, when we carried out our experiment with a child who had already completed five classes in the schoolday and was therefore tired, phonetic associations predominated.

Finally, our investigations led to another interesting conclusion that is very important both for linguistics and for the psychology of language. We found that it is possible to control the system of associations by introducing the given word into a new context. If the test word was "skripka" (violin), the word "truba" (pipe, trumpet, chimney) may or may not evoke a response, depending upon the context in which it is used. If subject is given the series of words "skripka"— (violin—the test word), "violonchel" (cello), "kontrabas" (double bass), "forte-piano" (piano), "fagot" (bassoon), "truba" (trumpet), the word "truba" is understood as a musical instrument and elicits responses similar to those elicited by the test word. However, if after test word "skripka" subject is given a new set of words— "dom" (house), "stena" (wall), "pechka" (stove), "krysha" (roof), and "truba" (chimney)—the word "truba" is understood in a different semantic context and does not elicit the same responses as the test word. Consequently, it is possible to control the perception of a word by introducing it into different contexts.

It thus becomes clear that this is a valuable method for objectively analyzing a word's systems of associations and for deciding which of these associations predominate. One can use this method for diagnosing a child's level of development, for examining associations depending upon fatigue and exhaustion, and finally for studying the regulation of a word's associations by introducing it into various contexts.

Another result of our studies of this phenomenon has great significance for psycholinguistics. We have found that this method makes it possible to measure objectively the degree of proximity of various elements in a semantic field. Experiments conducted by Khomskaya and her colleagues (Artem'eva, 1963; Pestova, 1958) bear on this issue. They found that autonomic responses may vary as a function of the semantic relationships among words. For example, if a subject is given test word "zdanie" (building), which has been reinforced by a painful stimulus, and then, in the context of other, irrelevant items is given words such as "stroenie" (construction), "pomeshchenie" (lodging), "dom" (house), "izba" (cottage), "yurta" (yurt—Mongolian dwelling), as well as "muzei" (museum), "teatr" (theater), "krysha" (roof), and "kryl'tso" (porch), quite dissimilar autonomic responses occur. For a normal subject, the words "construction," "lodging," and "house" elicit a specific autonomic response to pain similar to the one elicited by the test word. On the other hand, words such as "yurt," "museum," "theater," "cottage," "roof," and "porch," which are semantically removed from the test word, elicit a clear nonspecific orienting response. Finally, the word "znanie" (knowledge), which is phonetically similar to the test word, evokes no response at all.

Having broached the issue of how word meaning changes when the word enters into a new series of semantic items (i.e., into a new context), we now arrive at two questions. The first question concerns the possibility of strengthening and widening a word's semantic field. That is, we are concerned with the experimental creation of a stable concept and with the issue of whether this concept can be reconstructed or replaced by another.

Experiments carried out by Vinogradova and Eisler (1959) provide an answer to this question. In the studies described earlier, the painful stimulus accompanied only one word, such as "skripka" (violin) which elicited a semantic field. In the experiments we are now going to discuss, the situation was changed. After a test word, such as "repa" (turnip), had begun to trigger clear autonomic responses, another word from the same category also began to be accompanied by a painful stimulus. For example, if we used the word "svekla" (beet), clear orienting responses began to be elicited by an entire *class* of words belonging to the category of vegetables.

This experiment shows that there exists the possibility of eliciting an experimental concept, which is the result of the "categorical generalization" that occurs spontaneously in the subject. It is not difficult to understand that such a spontaneous categorical generalization is of considerable interest and that it opens up new possibilities for the objective study of the process of concept formation as well as of the structure of semantic systems.

A second, related question concerns the possibility of experimentally altering a concept that has been just created by replacing it with another. To answer this question, Vinogradova and Eisler (1959) conducted the following experiment. While carrying out the experimental procedure, and without any warning, new words began to be reinforced. Instead of the words "ogurtsy" (cucumbers) and "repa" (turnip), which were related to the category of vegetables and had been eliciting clear cateogircal generalization, other words began to be accompanied by painful stimuli. For example, one might choose "pushka" (cannon). This procedure produced very interesting results. After a few reinforcements of the new word "cannon," the earlier words from the category of vegetables stopped evoking specific or orienting autonomic responses. However, such responses now began to be elicited by a new group of words which denoted weapons.

This study demonstrates that we can experimentally alter semantic fields by replacing one semantic field with another. However, as later experiments have shown, this possibility is limited. If we change the conditions several times in the course of an experiment by first reinforcing the category of fruits and then weapons, subjects may not follow this change in an organized manner. Difficulties may arise due to such changes which lead to an "affective failure." This is often manifested by a complete disorganization of vascular responses and the appearance of "respiratory waves" which characterize an affective state.

These results are, of course, of great importance for psychology. They show that the observation of autonomic responses which are evoked by a test word enables us not only to identify semantic fields, but also to study their structure and dynamics.

Until now, we have been concerned with the involuntary actualization of semantic fields which can occur without the subject realizing their existence. The question arises, however, as to whether humans can consciously control semantic fields. If they can, then what are the aspects of the dynamic organization of the semantic fields that can be consciously controlled?

In order to answer this question, Khomskaya (1952) and her colleagues carried out a study. Unlike the study described earlier, where subjects were given test words without any special instructions, in this study subjects operated under certain consciously accepted conditions. Our concern was with the extent to which these conditions were able to change the character of the involuntary autonomic responses.

This study showed that a consciously accepted change in the situation can alter the structure of an involuntarily constructed semantic field in a very specific way. When a subject was told that there would be an electric shock when a word close to the word "zdanie" (building) occurred, the range of words evoking orienting responses expanded considerably. This was reflected in the average curve of autonomic responses. Specific (painful) autonomic responses continued to be evoked by the same words which caused them in the previous experiment, but an entire series of new words also began to elicit nonspecific orienting responses.

Let us now turn to the issue of the extent to which we can *destroy* semantic fields that have been elicited by a test word. Experiments conducted under Khomskaya have shown that the process of destroying earlier semantic fields with the help of generalized verbal instructions is not so simple as would appear. The simple instruction that "A shock will occur only in connection with the word 'building.'" did not cause complete cessation of the atonomic responses formed earlier. Subjects continued to respond as they had to the words in the earlier semantic field.

Autonomic responses to all the words ceased only when subjects were told that we were completely canceling the conditions of the experiment ("There will be no more shock."). The autonomic responses continued only in response to the word (building) which had been presented earlier. It continued to elicit specific (pain) and nonspecific (orienting) responses.

The use of methods which enable one to trace the formation of a semantic field around a given test word makes it possible to open up a new approach to the problems of semantics. Such methods enable the investigator to trace the formation of semantic fields and to study their structure and dynamics.

These experiments represent only the first step of research in this area. Still required is an objective study of the semantic fields of different classes of words. It will also be interesting to characterize the properties of the semantic fields during various ontogenetic stages, to examine their dependence on various forms of life experience (e.g., professional experience), and to study how these semantic fields are involved in the utterance of words which denote objects, actions, or properties. Lastly, it would be interesting to analyze the changes in the structure and dynamics of semantic fields during different pathological conditions of the brain. All these problems still await a solution. There can be no doubt that they will challenge more than one generation of investigators.

RECALL AND THE PSYCHOLOGICAL ANALYSIS OF THE NOMINATIVE FUNCTION OF SPEECH

All that we have said up to this point helps us deal with the important problem of the mechanisms of word recall and the nominative function of speech. If each word gives rise to a semantic field and is embedded in an entire network of involuntarily occurring associations, then it is not difficult to understand that the recall of a word or the naming of an object is quite complex. It is not simply the process of finding the specific monosemantic label which designates an object. Rather, there is every reason to believe that both the recall of a word and the naming of an object involve a process of selecting a word from a complex network of associations and that both recall and naming are much more complicated than is generally believed.

We know that there are at least two factors that determine the facility with which a word can be recalled or an object can be named. One of these factors is the frequency with which the word occurs and the context in which it used. We know that frequently used words can be recalled with much greater ease than words occurring relatively infrequently and that when trying to recall a word even a normal person may go to the stable context in which the word is most often used. When one encounters difficulties in recalling an infrequent word, such as "mikrotom" (microtome), one often begins to experience difficulties because other words emerge involuntarily. The words that come to the surface of memory are morphologically similar. For example, one might come across "mikroskop" (microscope) or "mikrokosm" (microcosm). These difficulties can often be overcome by placing the required word in its context (e.g., "I am cutting thin sections with a microtome.").

A second factor that influences the ease with which a word or name of an object can be recalled is the inclusion of the word in a specific category. Words belonging to a specific category are recalled more easily than those lacking such categorical nature. For example, one often experience great difficulty in remembering surnames. These do no have any generalized character and are part of a general, diffuse semantic field. When a person attempts to recall a name, either an entire network of words somehow connected with the real name or a group of morphologically similar words arises. As an example of the first case, we may cite Chekhov's famous story, "A Horse Name."[10] In this story, an entire series of semantically connected words, such as "Zherebtsov," "Kobylin," and "Telegin," occurs when the main character tries to recall the surname "Ovsov."

As an example of the second case, we may cite an instance when attempts to recall the surname of Georgian primitivist *Pirosmanishvili* gave rise to such morphologically similar names as *Prangishvili* and *Passanauri*. These are similar to the surname because of their two-member character, their being Georgian, and their

[10]The reference is to the humorous story by Anton Chekhov in which the main character, who is suffering from an excruciating toothache but is afraid of getting his tooth extracted, is told that in a village nearby there lives a man who can cure such cases. However, the person who gives him this information is unable to recollect the surname of the man and says that "it is connected with a horse." Various names connected with horses are tried in vain. Ultimately, after the desperate man has got his painful tooth removed by a dentist, he learns that the man's name was "Ovsov"—connected with the Russian word *Ovvos*, which means "oats". The names given here are connected with the Russian words *zherebets* (stallion), *kobyla* (mare), and *telega* (cart).—*J. V. Wertsch*

initial sound. It is interesting that this surname could finally be recalled only when it was subjected to an artificial semantic analysis: "pir" (fire, pyrotechnics), "-osman" (a Turk), and the typical Georgian surname ending "-shvili."

These examples clearly show that word recall usually involves a process of selecting an item from a network of involuntarily occurring meanings and that difficulties are connected not so much with poor memory as with a surfeit of associations. In this connection, we should note the findings of two American psychologists, Brown and McNeill (1966), in an article entitled "The tip of the tongue phenomenon." In their study, they examined cases in which subjects were trying to recall some name (of an instrument or a town) and were on the verge of getting it (i.e., it was "on the tip of their tongue"). However, some quite different words began to occur. These words were connected with the desired word in their phonological, morphological, situational, or conceptual properties.

We have already noted that difficulties in word finding may reflect special states of the cerebral cortex (e.g., inhibitory or phasic conditions). These states result in the equal occurrence of strong (or important) and weak (or insignificant) traces, disrupting the cortical selectivity necessary for the selection of a word from all the possible choices. We have pointed out that this type of disturbance may occur during states of extreme fatigue. We observed a similar disturbance in selectivity in cases of mental retardation.

Finally, such a difficulty in word recall may occur when a pathological process causes a partial, localized inhibition in the cortex. Such partial phasic conditions can be observed both in physiological and psychological studies. Electrophysiological research has shown that the slow waves which characterize pathological condition may not occur with equal intensity throughout the cortex. Rather, they may be manifested in the affected zone while in the other zones no slow waves are observed. Such localized or partial debilitation of the cortex can be established psychologically by a variety of methods used in neuropsychology. In particular, these methods can be used to study the associations of such patients during attempts to find a word. An example will help clarify this point.

If we ask a person who is in the hospital because of a cardiac or gastrointestinal ailment where he/she is, that person will answer, without the slightest difficulty, "I am in a hospital." In this case, the word "hospital" is selected quite easily. However, matters are quite different if the same question is asked of a patient whose left parietal and temporal regions of the cerebral cortex are affected, resulting in a disturbance in the selectivity of speech processes. Such a patient experiences the same difficulties in word finding as those described by the investigators of the "tip of the tongue" phenomenon or those we experience when trying to recall a poorly learned word. In one case, when the clinician asked a patient, "Kak vy zaboleli? Gde vy seichas nakhodites'?" (How did you become ill? Where are you now?), the patient answered, "Zabol . . . , Zabyl . . . zalel . . . Zabolel . . . " That is, the patient experiences great difficulty finding the word he wants. It is very difficult to separate it from the uncontrollable phonetic alternatives that begin to occur to him. "Well I was working . . . then . . . suddenly . . . well, there wasn't anything wrong in particular when I forgot (zabyl) . . . no, I didn't forget, I . . . fell backward (zapal), no, that isn't it, I didn't fall backward, I fell down (upal) . . . and then . . . I found myself in this, what do you call it . . . police force (v militsiyu)?" (Clinician: "V militsiyu?") "No, no, not in the police force (v militsiyu)! (Clinician: "V shkolu?"—In a school?) No, no, not in a school . . . Well, here, in this . . . well, where people are given help . . . " (Clinician: "V bol'nitsu?— In a hospital?) "Yes, yes, yes, that's it, . . . in a hospital ("v bol'nitsu")."

Why is it that when searching for the word "bol'nitsa" (hospital) the word "militsiya" (police force) occurred to this patient? This can be explained by two factors. First, the "militsiya" is also a public institution. There are policemen and those who are taken into the police force, and there are patients and doctors in a hospital ("bol'nitsa"). Secondly, both of these words end with the sound *ts* ("bol'ni*ts*a, mili*ts*iya"), and the patient confuses these. We also have a similar semantic structure in the case of a school. We have teachers and pupils (whereas in a hospital there are doctors and patients). Then situational guesses came to his mind, "where people are given help." And when the word "bol'nitsa" (hospital) is suggested to him he grasps it, "Yes, yes, yes, that's it . . . in a hospital."

In this instance, word recall has lost its selectivity. Instead of selecting a word on the basis of its semantic character, we see all kinds of words surfacing with equal probability on the basis of phonetic, situational, and conceptual similarity. That is why this type of speech disorder (called amnesic aphasia) should be explained differently from textbook situations. Textbooks often account for this form of disorder in terms of a memory defect. It is often said that such patients have too few memory traces. However, as we have shown, there are far stronger reasons for explaining this phenomenon by a surfeit of memory traces. These traces surface in the patient's memory not selectively but with equal probability, making the selection of a word much more difficult.

SUMMARY

In summary, the following points have been made. The word is by no means a simple, indivisible signifier of an object, action, or property. It does not possess a unitary, permanent meaning. The word always involves multiple systems of associations. The systems include phonetic, situational, and conceptual associations. Meaning connections (situational or conceptual) normally play the predominant role, but this may change depending on the task confronting a subject. When meaning associations predominate, phonetic connections are inhibited. This selectivity may be lost in pathological conditions of the brain. In such cases, it may be replaced by the equally probable appearance of any kind of association. This disrupts the selectivity needed in normal speech.

There are several methods by which we can examine the loss of selectivity. Important among these is the method of objective investigation of semantic fields described above. The physiological basis of selectivity is the law of strength which states that strong and significant stimuli or their traces elicit strong responses and weak or insignificant stimuli or their traces elicit weak responses. In pathological states of the cortex (inhibiting or phasic conditions), the law of strength no longer operates. The result is either that all stimuli are equalized and their traces surface with equal probability or weak stimuli cause an even stronger response than the strong ones. This inhibitory or phasic condition occurs in the general population (e.g., in states of drowsiness), and it may occur in a special population as in the case of a focal brain damage. In the latter case, the loss of selectivity may be manifested in a particular sphere.

Chapter 6

The Development of the Role of Speech in Mental Processes: the Regulative Function of Speech and Its Development

Up to now, we have analyzed the role of speech in reflecting the external world and in processing and retaining information. But speech is not only an instrument of cognition; it also serves to regulate the flow of mental processes. This regulative function of speech has been studied in connection with the following two questions: (a) How does speech influence perception? (b) What kind of regulative role does it have in organizing volitional acts?

In connection with the first question, one area of research has been concerned with the degree to which language plays an organizing role in the process of color perception. The well-known American linguist Sapir (1927, 1944), and later Whorf (1956), advanced the thesis that the set of words available in a language to denote color is not simply a linguistic phenomenon, but also has an important influence on the process of color perception. The Sapir-Whorf hypothesis has a certain amount of attraction. It proposes that language does not exist as an isolated phenomenon, but can influence the flow of mental processes.

However, many studies that were motivated by the Sapir-Whorf hypothesis have shown that it could be accepted only with certain important reservations. The color terms in a language undoubtedly determine the process of *classification* in some way. Elsewhere (Luria, 1974a), we have tried to show that people who

87

possess varying categorical designations of colors also classify these colors differently. All of the available studies do not, however, lead to the conclusion that the perception of the world is entirely determined by linguistic forms. Criticism of the Sapir-Whorf hypothesis—by authors such as Lenneberg (1953) and Lenneberg and Roberts (1956)—has shown that the relationship between language and perception is more complex and indirect than was previously assumed. A detailed treatment of this question would take us far beyond the limits of our present subject, however, and we shall therefore proceed to the second question, one that has motivated much of our own research, i.e., the question of the role of speech in the voluntary act.

THE PROBLEM OF THE VOLUNTARY ACT

The structure of the voluntary act has remained for centuries one of the most complex problems of psychology. The problem is as follows. It is quite apparent that in addition to performing instinctive reflex acts, we can carry out conscious, voluntary acts. Humans can prepare a plan and carry it out. They may wish to raise their hand and they do so. This is self-evident. The main difficulty for psychologists has been to find a scientific explanation for it.

Some psychologists have been perfectly willing to accept the existence of voluntary acts. These acts are manifested in all kinds of behavior—movement, memory, and thinking. However, they have usually failed to provide a viable explanation of these voluntary acts. They have limited themselves to saying that the voluntary act is a result of voluntary effort, that at the root of this act there lies some spiritual force. This spiritual force was called by some (e.g., Wundt) "apperception." Others give it the Latin name of "Fiat" ("Let it be done.") and viewed it as an indication of the part played by spiritual forces in the organization of our behavior. French psychologist Revault d' Allonnes (1923) proposed that volitional acts are founded on certain "internal schemes" which take on external manifestation in the voluntary act. All of these writers belonged to idealist schools of psychology. This was the dominant school for several decades, stretching from the 19th century to the first quarter of the 20th century.

Naturally, such a position, which describes the voluntary act but refuses to explain it deterministically, was not acceptable to scientific psychology. Therefore, another, opposing school developed based on mechanistic explanation. However, it relied on a form of reductionism which held that complex psychological processes can be reduced to elementary processes. Psychologists from this school simply rejected the very concept of the voluntary act by reducing all behavior to conditioned reflexes or habits.

Refusal to recognize that volitional acts exist was characteristic of a large number of psychologists who accepted mechanistic explanations. Among them were psychologists who superficially accepted Pavlov's theory of conditioned reflexes and applied this theory to higher psychological processes. They tried to understand all acts of conscious activity, including voluntary acts, as conditioned reflexes. American behaviorists were also part of this school. They viewed all behavior as either innate responses (instincts) or as acquired responses (habits). They argued that the voluntary act is in fact a habit and, as such, is essentially no different from more elementary forms of behavior.

Obviously, such an outlook ignores the concept of voluntary action and therefore is as unacceptable as the idealist position which acknowledges the existence of free volitional acts but refuses to explain them.

Scientific psychology must retain the problem of volitional acts. At the same time, however, it must subject human voluntary activity to a scientific analysis and find ways of producing a deterministic explanation for it. As we have already stated, the difficulty here is that in order to deal with this problem in a genuinely scientific way, we must stop looking for the sources of voluntary activity in deterministic biological factors or in spiritual factors. Instead, we must go beyond the limits of the individual organism and examine how volitional processes are formed for the child in his/her concrete contacts with adults. This was the basic position adopted by Vygotsky (1934, 1956, 1960). It proved to be a turning point in the development of scientific psychology.

Vygotsky's basic idea, which he developed in a series of lectures on language and consciousness, can be stated as follows. Whan a child is born, he/she is physically separated from the mother but remains connected with her biologically. Later, when the mother stops breast-feeding the child, he/she is separated biologically, but remains psychologically dependent on her. The mother communicates with the child and gives him/her instructions with the help of speech. For example, she draws his/her attention to objects in the environment (e.g., "Take the ball.", "Lift your arm.", "Where is the doll?" etc.), and the child carries out these spoken instructions. What is the mother doing when she gives the child these verbal instructions? As we have already said, she is drawing his/her attention to something, she is singling out one thing from among many. With her speech, she organizes the child's motor acts. Thus the child's motor act often begins with the mother's speech and is completed with his/her own movement.

Vygotsky pointed out that initially the voluntary act is shared by two people. It begins with the verbal command of the mother and ends with the child's act. It is only at the next stage of development that the child learns to speak and can begin to given spoken commands to himself/herself. This occurs first externally, in the form of overt speech, and later internally, through inner speech.

Therefore, the source of the volitional act is the child's communication with adults. The child at first submits to the spoken commands of the adult. As a result, during subsequent stages of development, he/she is in a position to transform this "interpsychological" activity into his/her own inner, "intrapsychological" process of self-regulation. The essence of the voluntary act, therefore, lies in the fact that like all other acts, this volitional act also has its own origins and developmental transitions. These origins are to be found in the social forms of behavior.

A careful analysis reveals that the ontogenesis of voluntary action begins with the practical act that the child performs in response to the command of an adult. At the next stage, he/she begins to use his/her own external speech, at first in conjunction with the act, and later preceding it (cf. Bühler and Hetzer, 1928). Finally, during later stages, this external speech is "internalized." It becomes inner speech, which takes over the function of regulating behavior. This process has been carefully studied by Gal'perin (1959, 1976) and his colleagues. Thus the function that originally was shared by two people—the mother and the child—comes to be carried out by the child himself/herself.

All of this means that investigators should stop searching for the origins of volitional activity inside the brain or in "spiritual life" and should turn to the relationship between children and adults. This requires an analysis of the basic forms of children's activity and their verbal communication with adults. Clearly, this hypothesis is basic to modern scientific psychology. It views complex ontogenetic processes not as resulting from biological development, but from social forms of human activity. Along with the cognitive function of the word and its function as a means of communication, there is a directive function. The word not only reflects reality, it also regulates behavior.

THE GENESIS OF THE REGULATIVE FUNCTION OF ADULTS' SPEECH TO CHILDREN

We have already said that the source of self-regulative speech is the process whereby the child submits to adults' speech. The speech of the adult, often accompanied by pointing gestures, brings about essential changes in the organization of the mental activity of the child. Labeling by the mother and her pointing gesture focus the child's attention. These communicative behaviors single out an object from several equally attractive things in the environment. Consequently, the child's attention ceases to obey the rules of natural patterned reflexes and begins to be subordinated to the adult's speech. This is what makes the origins of this new type of act in the child social rather than biological. When Vygotsky (1960) formulated this hypothesis, he did not have enough data to document all the successive stages of development of the regulative function of the word. It was unclear whether the child's ability to submit to adult's spoken commands arose suddenly or over a period of time. If the second hypothesis were true, the next research task would be to identify the stages through which this development passes.

The stages in the formation of capacity to submit to adults' verbal commands have been examined in children from 1 to 3 years of age by Luria and Polyakova

(1959). As a result of their study, we now have sufficient data to trace this process in much greater detail than was possible earlier. Before presenting these findings, let us review some earlier research on this topic. Psychologists have documented that an adult's speech attracts a child's attention even at a very early age. Bronstein, who belonged to Orbell's school, showed that if a mother begins to whisper something to her child while breast-feeding him/her, the child instantly stops sucking. Similar observations have recently been analyzed by the eminent American psychologist, Bruner (1973). Thus, even at a very early age, the mother's speech results in an orienting response in the child that inhibits instinctive processes. This indicates that although the mother's speech is not a particularly strong stimulus from a biological or physical perspective, it can become a strong social stimulus. It gives rise to a stable orienting response and inhibits more elementary instinctive responses.

The real birth of the regulative function of speech occurs later when the mother directs a command to the child and when the child's responses assume a specific character, e.g., when the child's gaze switches to a cup when the mother says to the child, "Where is the cup?". At this stage, the spoken instruction does not simply evoke a general orienting response and inhibit other ongoing responses. It oftens elicits a specific response.

At first it might appear that the child's response to the spoken command of the adult develops quite suddenly and immediately assumes a stable form. However, observations by Luria and Polyakova (1959) and Luria and Subbotskii (1975) showed that the adult's speech, which focuses the child's attention or regulates his/her action, does not immediately attain these powers. Rather, the formation of this directive function of adult speech goes through a rather long and dramatic development.

We conducted several studies in order to trace this development. Our first finding was that already at the beginning of the second year of life (12 to 14 months), children produce an orienting response to commands such as "Give me the ball.", "Lift your hand.", or "Where is the cup?". They turn their gaze toward the named object or reach for it. It appears that adults' speech is already functioning to regulate children's activity. However, this response pattern appears only under the simplest of conditions. In fact, adults' speech has not yet attained the stable capacity to regulate children's behavior.

This can be demonstrated simply by making the situation more complex. For example, consider some of the factors in a situation in which we placed several toy objects, such as a fish, a chicken, a cat, and a cup, in front of a child who is familiar with all these things and is equally attracted to each of them. In this setting, the experimenter said to the child, "Pick up the fish." when the fish was placed farther from the child than the cat or the cup, or the fish was not as bright in color as the chicken or the cup. Thus, in order to select the appropriate object, the child had to overcome the influence of location (i.e., the objects placed nearer) and the general brightness and attractiveness of objects. We found that a typical response consists of the child's first gazing at the appropriate object and reaching out toward it, but then becoming distracted by another object. For instance, while reaching for the appropriate object, he/she may come across the closer object, the one which is brighter, or the one which happens to be more interesting. In such cases, the child picked up one of these rather than the item named by the adult, i.e., the object which evoked an orienting response. This indicates that at this stage the child begins to submit to the spoken command of the adult, but while carrying out the command he/she is interrupted by other objects that evoke a direct orienting response.

We have found that it is possible to strengthen the regulative function of speech at this stage, but this requires highlighting the appropriate object. For example, the experimenter might say to the child, "Give me the fish." and then lift the fish, shake it, tap on it, or point at it with his finger. If the adult speech is reinforced with some action connected with the object, then this object assumes a particular force and the child can carry out the task.

We should also note, however, that an additional factor may prevent a child from carrying out the adult's spoken command at this stage. This factor is the inertia of the child's action. Two examples will illustrate this. Let us first consider the case of a small child of 14 or 16 months who is given the task of placing rings on a rod to build a toy pyramid. He/she is told, "Put on the ring!", "Put it on!", "Put it on!" every time a ring is placed on the rod. Then, in the same tone of voice, he/she is told, "Take it off!" "Take it off!". We know, on the basis of independent procedures, that the child understands the words "Put it on!" and "Take it off!". However, if a child has repeatedly been given the command "Put it on!", "Put it on!", "Put it on!" and then in the same tone of voice given the command "Take it off!", he/she often will continue putting the rings on and sometimes will do this even more energetically than before. Even if the command "Take it off!" is given in a loud voice, the child may continue more energetically than before to put on the rings. The inertia of his/her own action prevents him/her from carrying out the command.

Our second observation comes from the study by Luria and Polyakova (1959). In this case, a goblet and a cup were placed before the child. A coin was dropped into the goblet while the child was watching, and the experimenter said, "Now, come on, find the coin!". The child, who was quite interested in this game, began to search for the coin that had been dropped into the goblet in front of his/her eyes by reaching out for the goblet and taking the coin. In this case, the child was able to carry out the adult's command quite well. If this command was repeated five or six times, the child always responded appropriately by reaching toward the goblet. However, if the coin was then dropped into the cup (again, while the child is observing) and the child was told, "Now the coin is in the cup, find it!", he/she often continued reaching for the goblet. Even if the child understood the instructions, the inertia of the previous action was so powerful that he/she was unable to overcome it.

We observed this phenomenon in children up to about 18 months; after that, it began to disappear. By 2½ years of age, they were able to overcome this inertia of the previous act and carry out the command correctly. By this time, the regulative influence of the word was quite well established. However, its development was not yet complete, as an ensuing study showed.

In this, case we used the same procedure except for the fact that the experimenter restrained the child's hand for 10 or 15 seconds before allowing him/her to carry out the instructions. We found that when the act was delayed in this way, the regulative role of speech was weakened. Children who could carry out the command when allowed to act immediately again fell victim to the stereotyped inertia we mentioned earlier. This happened even when children were over 2 years of age. They continued to reach for the goblet even though they had just been told that the coin was in the cup and they had just seen it being dropped there.

Some control studies shed additional light on these phenomena. All of the experiments described so far were carried out in settings where the adults' spoken command was reinforced by visual experience; i.e., the coin was dropped into the goblet in front of the child's eyes and only then was the command given. Studies based on these procedures do not fully confirm the presence of regulation through speech. In order to document the role of speech in regulating the child's action, we shall now proceed to a third experiment. In this case, the overall setting and procedure were the same as in the previous study. The goblet and the cup were placed in front of the child; however, the child could not see the coin being dropped into the goblet or cup. The objects were shielded by a screen. The spoken command was, "The coin is in the goblet; find it!" or "The coin is in the cup; find it!". Here the child could no longer rely on his/her own experience and therefore had to depend on the experimenter's speech.

We found that children of 2 or 2½ years of age who could carry out this task appropriately when reinforced by visual experience could not do so when they had to rely solely on verbal commands. Without visual reinforcement, their performance was extremely unstable. Even when allowed to respond immediately, children of this age either reverted to an orienting response and reached for both the objects or were overpowered by the inertia of previous responses if they have executed several trials. It is only around the third year of life that children become capable of obeying this "pure" spoken command, first when allowed to act immediately and later when asked to carry it out after some delay. Thus we see that a small child cannot initially carry out an adult's verbal directive and that the development path of the ability is long and complex. It matures only during the third and fourth years of children's lives.

However, this is not the final stage in the development of children's capacity to obey adults' verbal commands. This is illustrated by the findings from one more study we conducted on this topic. In the study just described, we argued that the child's difficulty in obeying the adult's verbal commands was based on the fact that the verbal command had to overcome either the immediate influence of an orienting response or the child's inertia from a preceding act.

The following study points out an additional factor that can prevent a child from obeying an adult's instructions. In this study, the adult's verbal command conflicted with the child's visual experience. In order to respond appropriately, the child had to overcome this experience. In one task, the experimenter demonstrated a certain movement to the child and then asked him/her to repeat it. For instance, if the experimenter held up his/her fist, the child was to do likewise; or, if the experimenter held up his/her finger, the child was to do likewise. This simple version of the task was carried out easily by the child. We should note that here the child not only had a verbal command but also a visual pattern to imitate.

However, in order to test the real force of the verbal directive, we must separate the verbal instruction and the visual experience. For this purpose, we changed the instruction to another, "conflicting," version. We told the child, "When I raise my fist you are to raise your finger." We found that children of up to 3 years of age who can carry out the direct, nonconflicting directive without difficulty are not able to carry out the command in conflicting conditions. Although they could understand and repeat the verbal command quite well, they often did just the opposite and substituted the imitative movement. Thus, in response to a raised fist, they might first hesitatingly show their finger; but then they would substitute their fist, i.e., imitate the experimenter's movement. The spoken command gives rise to a conditioned response for a very short time. This response is then immediately overcome by the influence of the action. It is only when children are approximately 3½ years old that this interference of the spoken command disappears and the adult's verbal directions begin to be carried out properly.

Another study of this problem has also been carried out by Subbotskii. In this study, the experimenter picked up two objects (e.g., a pencil and a pair of eyeglasses) while two other objects were placed in front of the child (e.g., a toy fish and a rooster). The experimenter told the child, "When I pick up the pencil, you pick up the fish, and when I pick up the eyeglasses, you pick up the rooster." After several repetitions, the child could carry out these instructions quite well, demonstrating that the connection among the agreed upon meanings had been established quite firmly. However, if the procedure is changed so that the experimenter picks up a fish and a rooster and also gives the child a fish and a rooster and then says to the child, "When I pick up the fish, you pick up the rooster, and when I pick up the rooster you pick up the fish.", children could not carry out this instruction.

These findings indicate that children's difficulties often do not stem from a failure to learn the agreed upon mean of the command and establish the required connection. Rather, their difficulty can arise because of direct visual experience. The emancipation from the influence of direct experience and the consolidation of the regulative power of adult speech become firmly established only when the child is approximately 3½ years old. It is interesting to note that this is also the age when the anterior parts of the brair mature. These represent the cerebral apparatus that ensure obedience to verbal instructions. We shall discuss this in greater detail later.

In all the studies described so far, the child was asked to carry out a single action. The picture that emerged when an adult's verbal instruction required the child to carry out several successive actions is quite different. In order to study this phenomenon, we gave the child the task of carrying out a *series* of actions mentioned in a verbal instruction. We could then observe how a child could obey not just one directive but a series of successive directives.

This study has several variations. In one, we gave the child red and white checkers and asked him/her to arrange them in accordance with a rule provided by the experimenter. For example, the child might be shown a row of white checkers and be asked to continue this row. This is the simplest instruction because it consists of repeating elements already in the series. It can be made more complex by alternating white and red checkers. This program consists of a more complex series of directives which may be formulated as follows: "Put down a white checker. Then don't put down a white checker. Put down a red one, then don't put down another red one. Put down a white one.", etc. This program involves two shifting elements and is therefore more complicated. We shall term such a program a "symmetrical program" (white, red, white, red). We can further complicate the task by providing an *asymmetrical* program. Such an asymmetrical program could be as follows: "Put down two white checkers, one red checker, two white checkers, one red checker," etc.

In the case of any program, one may conduct the study in two versions (cf. Lebedinskii, 1966). In the first version, a visual example is used and the verbal instruction consists only of asking the child to continue the series. In the second version, verbal instruction alone is used. Thus, we can tell the child, without showing him/her anything, "Here are some checkers for you. Make a row by putting down a white checker, then another white one, then another white one." Or we can say, "Put down the pieces in a row, but in the following way—a white checker, then a red one, then a white one, then a red one." Or, in the third instance, we can say, "Put down the pieces in the following way—one red checker, then two white ones, one red one, two white ones." In this version, the child has no visual support from an example and thus has to follow a complex process which has been formulated in speech.

In the second condition in our study, we complicated the task by using yet another type of activity. Instead of being given ready-made objects which were simply to be placed in some order, the child was asked to draw figures (e.g., "a series of circles" or "a circle, a cross, a circle, a cross," or, finally, "a circle, another circle, a cross, a circle, another circle, a cross"). We can easily see that here we have the same programs. However, in the former cases, the child simply had to arrange the checkers, whereas in the latter he/she had to perform the more complex acts of drawing, each of which consists of a special program. In order to draw a cross, the acts should be programmed as, "Draw a vertical line, draw a horizontal line across the vertical line," etc. This experiment too could be carried out either using a visual example or with purely verbal instructions.

Let us turn to the results obtained in these studies which were carried out by Lebedinskii (1966) and later by Luria and Subbotskii (1975). It was found that a child of about 3 years of age, who can carry out single actions when given verbal instructions, was not able to perform any complex program of actions on the basis of oral instruction. Furthermore, children at this age slip very easily into an inert stereotype. For instance, when arranging checkers which alternate in color, a child of this age would be likely to put down a white piece, then a red one, then again a red one, then a red one once more. That is, the child cannot switch repeatedly and smoothly from red to white. Children of the next age group (around 3½ years of age) can carry out this symmetrical program successfully, but they are completely incapable of carrying out an asymmetrical program, such as using two white checkers, then a red one, then two white ones, etc. Instead, they are likely to use a symmetrical program, such as two white pieces, two red ones, two white ones, etc. In this way they simplify the program given to them.

The second type of activity—drawing—turned out to be even more difficult for young children. Lebedinskii (1966) and Luria and Subbotskii (1975) found once again that a child of 3 cannot as yet carry out a series of actions. The performance of a program is cut short by the child's use of an inert stereotype, into which he/she easily slips. Thus, when a child can carry out a simple symmetrical program of actions (around 4 years of age), he/she will often continue to have difficulty carrying out an asymmetrical program. He/she may slip into inert repetition of one figure or the realization of a simpler, symmetrical program, such as the consecutive alternation of one cross and one circle. It is only when a child is 4 or 4½ years old that it becomes possible for him/her to carry out every program.

All of these studies show that the subordination of an act to verbal instruction is by no means simple and does not emerge suddenly. Volitional acts, subordinated to the oral instruction of an adult, develop gradually. We now know approximately what the stages are that this process passes through and when it is completed. On the whole, it can be said that the process is complete by the time the child is 3 to 3½ years old.

THE PSYCHOPHYSIOLOGICAL FOUNDATIONS OF THE REGULATIVE FUNCTION OF SPEECH

So far we have *described* the stages of the formation of the regulative function of speech. However, we have not come anywhere nearer to an *explanation* of these stages, and we have not said anything about the physiological mechanisms that make possible the regulative function of adults' speech. Moreover, we have not begun to analyze the extent to which the *child's own speech* can exert a regulative influence on his/her motor responses. To answer these questions, we must proceed to some studies in which we not only observed the results, but also the process of the formation of the actions carried out by children.

The best and the simplest method for doing this involves measuring a child's movements while carrying out adults' instructions. For this purpose we carried out the following study. A child was given a small rubber bulb that was connected to a recording apparatus. Each time the child squeezed the bulb, the pressure registered on a revolving drum. Initially, the child was given a very simple command (e.g., "Squeeze the bulb!"). Then the experiment proceeded to investigate how the child carried out more complex commands, such as a simple response to a signal or the response of selecting between two possible signals.

A series of these studies have been conducted with children, beginning with 2-year-olds (sometimes even 20-month-olds), and ending with children of about 3 years of age. The simplest procedure consists of the immediate execution of an adult's verbal command, such as "Press!" "Press!" "Press!". Yakouleva's experiments have shown that a child of 20 months, 22 months, or 2 years of age is already able to do this. However, an adult's command, which can set this movement in motion, cannot stop it once it has begun. When given the signal "Press!", a 2-year-old squeezes the bulb and squeezes it again on the second, identical signal. After that, however, his/her own movement takes over and he/she is not able to stop. Thus, when the child is told to press, a wave of movement occurs, and if we then tell him/her to stop, this wave continues even more strongly. Indeed, a very emphatic command by the adult, such as "Press *only* when I tell you!" or "When I don't ask you to press, don't press!", does not lead to the desired result. Quite often it even intensifies the child's uncontrolled movements. During this phase, the adult's verbal command can elicit an impulse but it cannot inhibit this impulse. The stimulating function of speech arises earlier than its inhibiting function. This has been demonstrated using a second procedure.

This second procedure involves replacing the simple command "Press!", "Press!" with a "conditional" verbal command. In this case, a small light in front of the child is turned on and he/she is told: "When the light is on, press, but don't press when it is off!". A 2-year-old child, who can easily obey the direct command, masters the more complex conditional command only with difficulty. In the case of a 2½-year-old, even if he/she can memorize and repeat the verbal command, the practical execution of it is very difficult. When the light comes on, the child often looks at it (a simple orienting response) and maybe squeezes the bulb. However, if the child begins to squeeze the bulb, he/she often does so when no longer looking at the light. A child of this age is not yet able to coordinate an orienting response to the light with a motor response. It is only around the age of 3 years that a child begins to acquire the ability to coordinate the conditioning signal and his/her movement. However, at this stage, the coordination is still extremely unstable. The flash of the light often initiates a movement which the child seems unable to control. If the child is asked not to press the bulb when the light does not flash, he/she begins to sqeeze it still more vigorously.

Therefore, at this stage the verbal command evokes a nonspecific response. The louder the command to halt, the harder the child squeezes the bulb. These facts indicate that the child reacts not to the meaning of the command but to the external force of the instruction, to the voice of the experimenter. When given in a loud voice, the adult's inhibiting command begins to play the opposite role—that of a stimulus. The more the adult raises his/her voice, the harder the child squeezes the bulb. His/her attention is fixed on the sound of the voice, not on the meaning of the command.

The same phenomenon can be noted when the task is made still more complex by requiring a selective response rather than a simple one. In this version of the task, the child sometimes sees a red light flash and sometimes sees a green one. The command is: "When you see the red light, press, and when you see the green light, don't press!". The verbal instruction is learned, and after some time a child who is over 2½ years of age can successfully memorize and repeat the verbal command. However, this does not mean that he/she can carry it out. In response to the red (positive) light, he/she often squeezes the bulb; but he/she also often squeezes it in response to the green light. Sometimes a child of this age will suddenly remember the instructions and correct his/her mistake, but more often than not he/she is unable to cope with the task and does not correct himself/herself at all. Thus, grasping the differentiating command in words does not necessarily mean a differentiated form of response.

These results indicate that a child of this age is still not able to give a selective repsonse to an adult's command. The process set in motion by the command is governed by the child's inertia which prevents him/her from carrying out the inhibiting part of the command. This inertia sometimes consists of uncontrolled stimulation such that when the child squeezes the bulb upon seeing the red (positive) signal, he/she also squeezes it upon seeing the green (inhibiting) signal. On other occasions, inertia is manifested in the inhibiting process. Thus, if we reinforce the inhibiting significance of the green light, inertia is manifested in the inhibition of all responses. The child does not squeeze even when he/she sees the red flash. It is precisely this inadequate mobility of nervous processes that obstructs the occurrence of a differentially selective response.

Let us now turn to the question of whether we can reinforce the performance of the verbal command by involving the speech of the child. With this question, we enter into the second issue in our study. This is the central aspect of our inquiry. We are concerned here with whether the speech of the child can play a regulative role in controlling his/her behavior. If it can, what are the stages in the formation of this very complex process? In order to answer these questions, we carried out yet another variant of our study. In this case, the child is taught not to respond immediately to a verbal command with a motor act. Instead, he/she was supposed to respond with an appropriate utterance. In response to the red light, he/she was to say, "Yes!" (i.e., he/she was to squeeze the bulb). In response to the green, he/she was to say, "No!" (i.e., he/she must not squeeze it). Young children performed this task with only minimal degree of success. We found that for children of the younger group (i.e., 2 years 4 months) even these verbal responses showed certain signs of inertia. For example, they often said "Yes!" or "No!" irrespective of the color of the flash. In the case of 3-year-olds, however, this inertia in verbal processes disappeared, and the children were able to respond correctly to the signals with the necessary verbal responses.

The question now arises as to whether the child's own speech can play a regulative role. To answer this question, we carried out a study in which the presentation of the two signals (red and green) with their corresponding functions (stimulation and inhibition) was continued and the instructions remained the same as before. The child was to say, "Yes!" and squeeze the bulb when shown the red light and say "No!" and refrain from squeezing it when the green light appeared. In this way, we attempted to join both links (speech and motor) of the child's response into one "functional system." In this functional system, the verbal response played a regulative role, reinforcing the adult's verbal command. During the first stages of development, children often produced incorrect verbal responses. Their speech still suffered from inertia. During the next stage, they began to produce the correct verbal responses (i.e., "Yes!" or "No!"). However, when we joined speech and motor responses, children often answered correctly, but produced a motor response in all cases. At this stage, we see a very interesting paradoxical phenomenon. While saying "No!" or "Don't squeeze!", the child often did not stop. He/she might even continue to squeeze the bulb harder, intensifying his/her motor response. In this case, he/she was responding not to the meaning, but to the "impulsive" effect of his/her own verbal command. Thus, his/her verbal response did not regulate his/her motor response. In a child of this age, a functional system in which the verbal response regulates the motor response did not exist.

It is only during the third stage, around the age of 3 years, that a different picture emerged. At this age, the child's motor response, when not reinforced by his/her own speech, still was often governed by inertia. However, we only had to introduce the reinforcement of speech to find that the child's own speech could organize his/her movements. When the red light flashed, the child said "Yes!" and squeezed the bulb. When the green light came on, he/she said "No!" and refrained from squeezing it. It is only at this age that the child began to subordinate his/her movements not to the impulsive aspect of a verbal response but to the meaning of the word. He/she did not intensify his/her motor response after an inhibiting command, but inhibited it.

This method of investigating the regulative function of speech has great diagnostic significance. It not only reveals the physiological mechanisms involved, but also enables us to examine the directive function of speech in cases of mental deficiency. In this connection, we investigated older children (8, 10, and 12 years of age) who were either mentally retarded or had a cerebro-asthenic syndrome. Thus, all of these children suffered from nonspecific (e.g., food) intoxication and as a result were retarded in their development, although they need not have been mentally retarded. Our investigation of the regulative function of speech enabled us to differentiate between children who were mentally retarded and those in whom mental retardation was only apparent. A severely mentally retarded child (an imbecile) of 10 to 12 years of age could memorize the verbal instruction which told him/her that in response to a red light he/she was to squeeze the bulb and that in response to a green light he/she was not to squeeze it. However, when such children began to carry out this command, they squeezed the bulb when any light flashed. Even if we reinforced this command, imbeciles did not carry it out correctly. He/she either continued to squeeze the bulb in response to all signals or inhibited the response to all signals. The first impulse to emerge had so much inertia he/she could not halt the movement once begun or initiate it if not begun. Even if we brought the child's own speech into action, we did not get the desired result. A selective response based on the meaning of the child's speech did not emerge. Instead, there was a direct impulsive response.

We see quite a different picture with children who appear to be mentally retarded but in fact are only enfeebled. These children fall into two categories. In the first group were impulsive children who, after responding appropriately once or twice to the red signal, squeezed the bulb in response to the green (inhibitory) signal. The second group was comprised of inhibited children. Here we see the opposite phenomenon. If they once did not squeeze in response to the green (inhibitory) signal, they also did not squeeze in response to the red (positive) signal.

However, these children were basically different from the children described earlier. This became apparent when we proceeded to the task in which we combined verbal and motor responses. Recall that in this case they had to say "Squeeze!" and squeeze when given the red signal, and say "Don't squeeze!" and refrain from squeezing when given the green signal. We found that their speech retained its regulative role and thus led to appropriate motor responses.

This directed us to an important conclusion about diagnostic procedures. Many physiologists think that the decisive factor for diagnosis is the preponderance of stimulating or inhibitory processes (i.e., the presence or absence of inertia). In fact, however, this is not the case. It is true that there are both inhibited and impulsive children, but the decisive factor here concerns the system in which maximum mobility is manifested. Is it the speech system or the motor system? With this in mind, the diagnostic criterion becomes the relationship between the neurodynamics of the speech system and the neurodynamics of the motor system. In other words, the crucial concern is whether or not the child's speech which accompanies motor behavior can regulate this behavior by overcoming inertia.

In the case of mentally retarded children, speech does not play a regulative role; but with children with a cerebro-asthenic syndrome who only seem to be mentally retarded, the more mobile speech can play a regulative role. This psycho-physiological fact opens up possibilities for the study of laws which account for the regulative role of speech. It also provides the experimenter with a reliable and objective diagnostic tool for detecting the degree of mobility of nervous processes in mentally retarded children.

It now remains for us to pose a final important question, for which we have as yet only a preliminary answer. This question concerns the precise description of the mechanisms which make the directive function of speech possible. The first, and so far only, attempt to approach this problem has been made by Khomskaya (1958). Her method is based on a detailed examination of motor response latencies. Khomskaya discovered that in impulsive children with a cerebro-asthenic syndrome the motor response latency to positive stimuli gradually decreased, after which even inhibitory signals began to elicit positive motor responses. However, the latency of speech responses demonstrated much greater stability. This is precisely why the combination of speech and motor responses leads to their stabilization and to the disappearance of positive responses to inhibitory signals.

On the other hand, in the case of children with a cerebro-asthenic syndrome of the inhibitory (torpid) type, Khomskaya found that successive presentation of positive signals led to increasing motor response latencies. As a result, motor responses to positive signals began to be retarded, and then disappeared altogether. The inclusion of a child's own speech responses, something which has considerably more stable latent periods, changes this picture. The motor responses "move up" to the more stable latent periods of speech responses. This accounts for the fact that the motor responses to positive signals begin to occur. These data represent only the first attempts to understand how the regulative function of the child's own speech develops. However, even these observations show the significant results may be obtained by following this line of inquiry.

For many years, the investigation of the directive function of speech did not attract the attention of researchers to the degree that it should have. It was only after the appearance of several summarizing works (e.g., Luria, 1959, 1961; Luria and Yudovich, 1956) that a substantial interest in this problem emerged. In various countries, several studies have been carried out which partially confirmed and elaborated our observations and sometimes questioned the validity of some of the data described above (Beiswenger, 1968; Bronckart, 1970; Jarvis, 1968; Johnson, 1976; Shubert, 1969; Wozniak, 1972).

All this gives us reason to hope that the regulative function of speech will attract the attention of investigators in the future.

Chapter 7

Inner Speech and the Cerebral Organization of the Regulative Function of Speech

We have traced the path of the first stages in the development of the regulative function of speech, as a result of which children can subordinate their action to the spoken commands of the adult. During these early stages of ontogenesis, the volitional act begins with the speech of the mother and concludes with the child's action, i.e., it is carried out on the interpsychological plane of functioning. This early functioning marks only the beginning of the child's ability to subordinate his/her behavior to adults' verbal commands. During the next stage, functioning that had been distributed between two people (mother and child) gradually changes its structure by becoming intrapsychological and internalized—this functioning begins to regulate the child's behavior through the speech of the child himself/ herself. At first, this self-regulation is realized through the child's expanded external speech. Then this speech gradually turns inward and becomes converted into inner speech.

The development of the independent volitional act is possible because of these processes, and essentially involves subordination of the child's behavior, no longer to adult speech, but to his/her own speech. Our present task is to follow this second stage in the formation of the volitional act, i.e., we shall attempt to analyze how the inner speech of the child, with its regulative function, develops.

THE FORMATION AND STRUCTURE OF INNER SPEECH

For a long time, "inner speech" was understood as speech without an observable motor component. It was understood as speech to oneself which retained the general structure of external speech, but whose function was not clear. However, both of these assumptions have been undermined by observations made by Vygotsky as far back as the end of the 1920s. As a result, the concept of inner speech has undergone a fundamental change.

A particular type of study used by Vygotsky (1934) served as a starting point in his analysis of the development and function of inner speech. In this well-known experiment, a child 3 to 5 years of age was given a simple concrete task, such as tracing a picture. While the child was carrying out this task, the experimenter would unobtrusively create some impediment. For example, the experimenter might remove the thumb tack securing the paper on which the child was tracing the outline of a picture, or the experimenter might give the child a pencil that would be likely to break during the activity. Accordingly, the child would be faced with a difficulty preventing him/her from solving the task in a simple direct way.

Vygotsky's main observation was that when children encountered such impediments in this setting, they first would make some attempts to solve the problem in the practical sphere and then would transfer these attempts to the verbal sphere, i.e., they would begin to speak. It appeared that the speech was not addressed to anyone in the immediate environment. The children continued to speak even when there was no other person in the room. Sometimes, children would turn for help to the experimenter. Sometimes, they would only express the difficulty confronting them by describing aloud the situation and asking themselves how to solve the problem. In this situation, typical utterances were, "What's to be done?", "Look, the paper has come off!", "The task's gone!", "The pencil's broken.", "How am I going to fasten the paper?", "Where am I going to find a pencil?", etc.

Children tended first to *describe* the setting and to state the difficulty. Then they would begin to *plan* a possible solution—they would begin to exercise their imaginations and to struggle with the problem on the plane of speech that they could not solve on the practical plane. In this setting, Vygotsky observed speech that sometimes was not addressed to anyone else. This type of speech had been noticed and described before Vygotsky began his research on the topic. The most important example is found in Piaget's (1955) account of "egocentric speech," i.e., speech not addressed to others. Such speech has no communicative function and is addressed to the speaker himself/herself.

At first, this speech appears in a very expanded form. During the following stage of ontogenesis, it gradually becomes more and more abbreviated, finally turning into whispered speech, in which children describe haltingly the difficult situation they find themselves in. In the next stage (after another year or two), external speech disappears altogether. Only by watching the child's lip movements can one surmise that this speech had turned "inward," had become abbreviated and "internalized" or transformed into what might be termed "inner speech."

Several years after completing his initial set of studies, Vygotsky's observations were corroborated by other studies. Among those were the extremely important investigations of Sokolov [for a complete description, see Sokolov's (1968) volume on inner speech and thinking]. By means of electrodes placed on children's larynxes or lips, Sokolov and others were able to show that when children are thinking about how to overcome a difficulty, it is possible to register weak electromyographic responses in their speech organs. This indicates that egocentric speech does not simply disappear, but turns into unobservable inner speech.

Egocentric speech data have long called for an explanation. According to the great Swiss psychologist Piaget (1955), during early years the child is an autistic creature, a little hermit, who lives by himself/herself and has little contact with the outside world. That is why young children's speech is autistic or egocentric. It is addressed neither to same-aged children nor to adults. In Piaget's view, children's behavior only gradually becomes socialized. Within this process, their behavior and speech are socialized. One of the outcomes is that speech gradually becomes a means of communication. Proceeding from this assumption, Piaget considered egocentric speech to be a reflection of the children's autism or egocentrism, and explained the disappearance of egocentric speech as a consequence of the socialization of children's behavior.

Vygotsky proceeded from a quite contrary hypothesis, arguing against the assumption that the earliest stages of children's development are autistic. According to him, children are from the very beginning social beings. During the prenatal period, they are connected with their mother physically. Then after birth, the bond continues to be a biological one through breast-feeding, but it is also a social bond. This social relationship, later reflected in the mother's speech to the child and the child's execution of her commands, characterizes ontogenesis from its very beginning. This leads to the conclusion that the evolution of children's speech is not a matter of egocentric or autistic speech becoming social speech. The developmentmental progression is quite different. It is founded on the fact that children use social speech from the beginning, both for communicating with others and for solving problems. They address adults and ask them for help. In those cases where they receive no assistance, they begin to analyze the situation by themselves through speech. Finally, with the help of speech, they begin to plan their action. In this way, according to Vygotsky (1934), speech begins to take on an intellectual function as well as a behavioral regulative function. That is why egocentric speech, which initially is overt and expanded, gradually becomes abbreviated and is eventually transformed into inner speech. The progression does not consist of the dissolution or disappearance of autistic speech. Rather, it reflects the formation of new types of mental activity. Inner speech retains all of the analytic, planning, and regulative functions found in external speech; it continues to fulfill the same intellectual role originally performed by the adult's speech addressed to the child and later carried out by the expanded speech of the child himself/herself.

During the last few decades, Vygotsky's ideas have been further elaborated in the studies of Gal'perin and his colleagues (1959, 1976). These investigators have shown that any mental act begins as an expanded material action. In other words, it begins as an action based on the expanded external manipulation of objects. Later the subject begins to use speech, and action passes on to the stage of expanded speech. Subsequently, that external speech becomes abbreviated and turns into inner speech. At this stage, inner speech begins to play a role in the organization of the complex type of activity which Gal'perin terms a "cognitive action." This type of action is manifested in the use of inner schemes to carry out tasks such as doing mathematics "tables" or forming concepts. It is this cognitive action which is created through speech. The speech was initially expanded and later became abbreviated.

This approach enables us to deal with the extremely important problem of the inner structure and origin of the volitional act. A volitional act is not initially a mental act, nor is it a simple habit. Rather, it is mediated by speech. By this we mean not just external speech as a means of communication, but also the child's own regulative forms of speech. A typical form of such regulative speech is the inner speech which orginates in external speech but evolves into a novel psychological formation. It can be seen that this points to a completely new solution to one of the major complex problems of psychology. It enables us to approach the voluntary and mental act in a materialistic way, as a process which is social in its origin and structure, and which possesses novel conscious and voluntary functions.

Turning to the problem of the structure of inner speech, it is quite incorrect to view inner speech simply as speech addressed to oneself. That is how psychologists thought of this phenomenon for many decades. One often comes across the assertion that inner speech is the same thing as external speech except for the fact that it has no overt behavioral form, that it is "talking to oneself" with speech that has the same lexical, syntactic, and semiotic rules as external speech. This is an erroneous view, because talking to oneself this way would have no functional significance. It would involve performing double the amount of work that seems necessary. Mental acts, such as decision making and identifying the correct solution to a problem, occur much faster, often in a fraction of a second. In such a short period of time, it is impossible to produce for oneself a complete sentence, much less a complete discussion. Inner speech, with its directive or planning role, has an altogether different, abbreviated structure.

This structure can be traced by studying the course of external speech as it gradually is converted into inner speech. Let us analyze children's speech in settings where they confront a difficulty. At first, their planning speech has a completely expanded and overt character ("But the paper is slipping, what can I do so it doesn't slip? Where can I get a thumb tack? Maybe I should lick the paper and wet it so that it won't slip?"). Then this speech gradually undergoes a fundamental change. It becomes abbreviated and fragmentary. What remains, in an overt whispered form, are mere fragments of the former complete phrases ("but the paper . . . it's slipping . . . what can I do? . . . Where can I get a tack? . . . . "). Later this speech becomes even more abbreviated ("paper, tack, how can I?").

In carefully tracking the structure of speech in its transition from external to inner speech, two simultaneous changes are observed. First, it evolves from audible to whispered to inner speech. Secondly, it becomes abbreviated; it changes from expanded speech into fragmentary, condensed speech. Both of these trends indicate that inner speech possesses a structure quite different from that of external speech. It undergoes a complicated and dramatic transformation.

Another important characteristic of inner speech is that it begins to take on a purely "predicative" character, a reflection of the fact that when using inner speech to solve a problem the problem-solver knows very well what the speech is about. The nominative function of speech, that function of picking out something to be talked about, or, to use a term from modern linguistics, the "theme"[11] is already included in inner speech and hence does not have to be specially signaled. This fact leads us to the second semantic function of inner speech—its capacity to point to something new. It must indicate what is to be said about the given theme, what new information is to be added, and which action is to be carried out. Linguists refer to this aspect of speech as the "rheme."

These notions can also be described in everyday terminology. Since inner speech operates between the general intention to solve a problem and its concrete solution, it operates without a subject and simply indicates what is to be carried out, what the direction of the action should be. Hence, while it is abbreviated and amorphous in structure, it always preserves its predicative function. It is possible to expand the predicative form which designates only the plan of the next utterance or the plan of the next action because the origin of inner speech is expanded external speech. Thus inner speech can be transformed into expanded speech. For example, if I am going to a lecture to speak about the mechanism of inner speech, I

[11] Luria's use of the terms "theme" and "rheme" is based on Mel'chuk's (1974) terms "tema" and "rema." In the mid-1970s, Luria (e.g., 1975a) began to utilize linguistic notions such as Mel'chuk's idea of theme and rheme in order to be more precise about the issues raised by Vygotsky (1934) in his analysis of psychological subject and predicate. In Western literature, Chafe's (1974, 1976) notion of given and new information may have the most similarity with what Luria had in mind when he spoke of theme and rheme.—*J. V. Wertsch*

carry only an abbreviated outline of the lecture in my mind. Items such as "inner speech," "egocentrism," and "predicativity"—items which do not name the theme but indicate what I want to say about it (in other words, predicative items)—are precisely what enable me to go on to produce the external utterance. Accordingly, on the basis of inner speech, the lecturer can expand a scant outline into an entire lecture.

The role of inner speech in speech production has been examined by investigators such as Katsnel'son (1972), A. A. Leont'ev (1969, 1974), Sokolov (1968), and Akhutina (1975). We shall return later to the question of how inner speech functions in the production and comprehension of utterences. For the present, we confine ourselves to examining how inner speech regulates children's actions.

THE CEREBRAL ORGANIZATION OF THE REGULATIVE
FUNCTION OF SPEECH

Psychology perhaps has never had to deal with a more difficult problem than identifying the cerebral mechanisms that underlie human volitional acts. That is why it has not begun to arrive at a solution and why we still have only the most elementary data about this problem. Let us first consider the relatively limited facts at our disposal.

It would be incorrect to assume that the cerebral mechanisms involved in the regulative functions of speech are the same as those involved in the processing of sound or meaning in communicative speech. We know that the temporal lobe in the left hemisphere is concerned with phonemic perception. This zone, first described by Wernicke (1874), enables us to identify phonemes in the flow of speech. It is thus the basic cerebral mechanism of phonemic perception and organization. These capacities in the superior regions of the left temporal lobe are connected by U-shaped links, both with the lower regions of the post-central (kinesthetic) area of the cortex and the lower regions of the premotor (kinetic) zone of the cortex, providing it with a unique potential for ensuring the phonemic organization of speech. We also know that if this region of the cortex is damaged, the patient ceases to distinguish phonemes.

It is also known that mechanisms responsible for articulatory processes play an important role in speech processing. These mechanisms ensure correct pronunciation of phonemes and facilitate their comprehension. The cerebral apparatuses responsible for the formation of articulemes are located in the post-central zones of the speech cortex, the cortical regions of the motor analyzer. Damage to these regions of the brain is known to cause motor aphasia, a syndrome manifested by a disturbance of articulemes (see Luria, 1947, 1962, 1970, 1975a). However, this by no means indicates that phonemically defective speech loses its directive functions. Studies have shown that the inner speech of such patients remains relatively intact and that a patient whose perception of speech and phonemes is badly affected (in other words, a patient suffering from sensory or motor aphasia) may continue to regulate actions that are either self-initiated or are assigned by others. Of course the latter is true only if the patient can understand a command. This means that the posterior temporal or post-central regions of the left hemisphere, which play a decisive role in the phonemic organization of speech, do not play the same role in the processing of inner speech and, consequently, in the regulation of the volitional act.

Studies have shown that the understanding of complex logical-grammatical construction requires participation of other regions of the left hemisphere as well. In particular, the parieto-occipital regions are important in this regard. Precisely these zones of the cortex ensure spatial orientation and the transformation of successively received information into simultaneous schemes. Our observations over many years have shown that lesions in these zones of the cortex do not interfere with the perception of speech sounds. However, lesions in this area lead to other types of serious processing deficits. In particular, they result in distortions in word meaning and in visual processes that are important for the comprehension of complex logical-grammatical structures (cf. Luria, 1962, 1970, 1971, 1975a). We have described these phenomena in many studies and have shown that patients with damage to the parieto-occipital regions of the brain have a great deal of difficulty understanding such logical-grammatical structures as "father's brother" or "brother's father," "a cross under a circle," and "circle under a cross." Such patients find it necessary to spend a long period of time trying to sort out the logical connections that we grasp immediately.

Our research has shown that even in such cases patients do not suffer any impairment of the regulative function of speech. They not only do not lose the capacity to organize volitional acts, but also continue to work assiduously to overcome this handicap. This is possible precisely because their inner speech, with its predicative, sense-forming function, remains largely unimpaired. On the basis of inner speech, such patients are able to convert simultaneous schemes into a series of successive acts and thereby substitute complex, sequential decoding for direct perception of logico-grammatical structures. Thus the inferior parietal regions of the left hemisphere, which play a decisive role in ensuring the comprehension of complex logico-grammatical structures and complex forms of information processing, do not have the same significance for inner speech and its directive function.

All of these facts leave us with the problem of identifying cerebral mechanisms that underlie the regulative function of speech (and hence the complex forms of volitional acts which depend on inner speech). These mechanisms seem to be located in the anterior cortical regions, particularly in the left hemisphere. The morphological structure of the anterior cerebral cortex is quite different from that of the posterior regions. Whereas the posterior regions are characterized by transverse lines and are well equipped to receive and process incoming information, the structure of the anterior regions of the cortex is characterized by vertical lines. This is a structure characteristic of motor cortex areas responsible for the organization of all efferent motor acts which unfold over time. Furthermore, it is known that the anterior regions of the hemisphere fall into two large zones.

The first, immediately adjacent to the motor zones of the cortex, contains what are known as the "premotor" regions of the cortex. This zone makes possible the integration of separate movements into integrated kinetic melodies. Impairment of this cortical zone does not lead to paralysis or paresis, but gives rise to a disturbance in the smooth transition from one movement to another and the integration of these movements into a single, smoothly executed motor program. This is reflected in the handwriting of such patients. When writing, their movement loses its smoothness and disintegrates into a series of individual, isolated motor impulses. The transition from one of these impulses to another requires great effort.

Problems are also manifested in the flow of speech. The grammatical structure undergoes a marked change. Whereas the grammatical structure of fluent expanded speech includes predicative elements along with nominative elements, the external expanded speech of a patient with a lesion in the lower regions of the premotor area of the left hemisphere often becomes abrupt and loses its fluent kinetic character. In certain cases, this speech retains only nominative elements (nouns), which sometimes acquire a predicative meaning, while the special predicative elements (verbs) disappear altogether. When asked to relate the events of their lives, such patients confine their narrations to one type of signs. For example, when narrating the history of their injuries they might say: "battle . . . . . . gunfire . . . . . . bullet . . . . . . injury . . . . . . pain . . . . . . ," etc. The most interesting fact for us here is that this disturbance of the predicative aspect of external speech gives rise to a distortion of inner speech which is unable to provide fluency to speech utterances. There is, therefore, reason to believe that when these cortical zones are damaged, inner speech with its predicative function suffers considerably more than external, expanded speech.

The second large anterior region, which is situated above the premotor region, comprises the "prefrontal" lobes of the cortex. They are much more complex structurally than the premotor regions. The second and third layers predominate here, (i.e., the layers of associative neurons), and the role of this region in realizing isolated movements, if it exists at all, is much less important. Thus, damage to the frontal lobes, especially in the left hemisphere, does not lead to any motor damage, to paralysis or paresis. The movements and the external speech of a patient who has suffered massive damage to the frontal lobes remain intact. There is no disturbance such as the telegraphic style seen in motor aphasia. However, frontal lobe lesions impair the inner dynamics of systematic, organized volitional action in general and speech activity in particular. A patient suffering from such impairment still can easily carry out elementary, habitual movements, e.g., greeting a doctor and answering routine questions. However, if he/she is required to execute complex verbal or nonverbal programs that involve genuine volition (and thus are inevitably based on inner speech), we immediately find a massive pathology not seen in patients with lesions in other cortical regions.

Impairments in the volitional behavior of these patients occurs even at the level of the motives that govern behavior. They can lie in bed motionless for long periods, and despite the fact that they experience biological needs (e.g., hunger, thirst, etc), may never express them through requests. Such a patient does not ask those near him/her to assist in satisfying these or any other needs. Their voluntarily organized behavior is even more seriously impaired. They execute habitual acts without difficulty. For instance, they can sign their name and use a spoon, fork, or knife appropriately. Often they also can carry out such tasks as tying their dressing gown or even putting it on. However, if such patients are asked to execute a novel task or a familiar, but complex, internal program (i.e., if they must depend on inner speech and on the internal plane of action), they are quite helpless.

During the war, we observed many patients for whom complex purposeful activity was impossible and was replaced either by primitive or perseverative actions. I remember the case of a woman who would go to the public baths, remain there for 2 hours, and come out dirty because she perseverated by scrubbing herself in the same place. I also remember a patient who was to travel from a suburb of Moscow to the center of the city, but boarded a train going in the opposite direction. His mistake did not occur because he was unable to orient himself in space. Rather, it occurred because the train aroused an impulsive response to board it. In another case, a patient with severe frontal lobe damage was lying in bed when his glance fell on a call button for nurses. He pressed the button, but when a nurse came, he looked at her helplessly, not knowing what to say because there was no motive behind his action and because the act was purely impulsive. And I cannot help recalling yet another patient with severe frontal lobe damage who began occupational therapy after the war. He was instructed to plane a piece of wood. He planed a board down completely and continued to plane the work bench, being unable to stop at the appropriate point and control his stereotyped movements. Finally, there was the case of a patient with a frontal lobe lesion who was discharged from a long stay in a military hospital in order to go home. Instead of going home, however, he traveled to the town mentioned by the man in front of him in line. He accompanied this man and got off at a station 40 kilometers from his home, exhibiting a complete lack of purposeful action. Thus, disturbance of behavior caused by damage to the frontal lobes involves impairment of complex, voluntarily organized programmed acts.

Experimental research has provided additional facts of exceptional interests. It turns out that damage to the frontal lobes leads to impairment of precisely those forms of action that are organized with the help of one's own external and/or inner speech. As we saw earlier, these forms of action become established in a child at 3 to 4 years of age.

In one study, patients who have suffered damage to the frontal lobes are asked to repeat certain movements made by an experimenter. They are asked to raise their fist when the experimenter raises a fist, a finger when the experimenter raises a finger, etc. Such patients perform this task without difficulty, but if the procedure is then modified so the patient is required to raise a finger when a fist is raised, a fist when a finger is raised, etc. (i.e., to subordinate their actions to spoken instructions that are contrary to the pattern shown to them), the result is quite different. They can repeat the spoken instructions without difficulty, but are unable to follow them in their action. When shown a fist, they might say, "Now I have to show my finger," but raise their fist nonetheless. Such studies graphically illustrate that damage to the frontal lobes results in impairment of the regulative function of speech, while leaving its external forms unaffected.

We get even clearer results when a frontal lobe patient is asked to raise his/her hand slowly in response to a loud knock, and rapidly in response to a soft one. In this case, the patient again is often capable of remembering the spoken command. However, if the command goes against what he/she sees, the command loses its regulative power. Instead of carrying out actions in accordance with the command, he/she often becomes subordinated to the action of the experimenter (i.e., in response to a soft knock, he/she raises a hand slowly and in response to a loud one, rapidly).

The same pheonmenon was observed in a third set of experiments carried out by Khomskaya (1972). She found that frontal lobe patients experienced difficulty in pressing an object once in response to two knocks and twice in response to one knock. In this instance, too, the patient retained the spoken command quite well, but could not carry it out. Instead, his/her movements were geared directly to the movements demonstrated.

It is very interesting that if we ask such patients to use their own speech to regulate actions, we find that speech has lost its directive role. For example, a patient might be asked to raise a finger in response to the experimenter's raised fist and to say at the same time, "Fist—so I must raise my finger." In response to a raised finger, he/she might be instructed to raise a fist and say at the same time "Finger—so I must raise my fist." However, while such patients may retain and repeat the spoken instructions, they often execute actions that are in conflict with their own overt speech. In the more serious cases, even the retention and repetition of the spoken command turns out to be beyond the patient's ability. He/she even fails to repeat the spoken commands correctly, substituting for them an inert speech stereotype.

Hence, the fact that the frontal lobe region is of decisive importance for ensuring the regulative function of external and inner speech, and therefore for the organization of the volitional act, has already been shown and is demonstrated by the fact that while impairment of the frontal lobes leaves elementary movements unimpaired, it causes drastic disturbances in voluntary programmed actions. Precisely this supports the assumption that the frontal lobe region, which is connected intimately with the mechanism of inner speech, is crucial for organizing voluntary acts.

All these facts and many others have been described in detail elsewhere (Luria and Khomskaya, 1966; Luria, 1962, 1970, 1974b; Khomskaya, 1972; Pribram and Luria, 1973). It should be noted that although we cannot dispute the hypothesis we have just enunciated—that the frontal lobes participate intimately in effecting voluntary acts—the physical mechanisms underlying this phenomenon are still far from clear. One may surmise that only a whole generation of new psychological and electrophysiological research will reveal the secret of the mechanism of frontal lobe functioning—one of the most complex problems of neuropsychology.

Chapter 8
The Syntactic and Semantic Structure of the Sentence

Heretofore, we have been dealing with the basic element of language—the word. The role of the word in the processing of information and the formation of concepts has been discussed and the preceding two chapters have examined the regulatory function of the word.

We shall now turn to the psychological analysis of the entire utterances. First we shall take up the sentence as the basic unit of speech and discuss how sentences are used in communication. Then we shall analyze the psychological structure of an extended complex text.

THE PROBLEM OF LANGUAGE UNITS

To repeat, the word is the basic element of language. However, several psychologists and linguists have argued that the basic unit of speech, and perhaps the basic unit of language, is not the individual word, but the entire utterance. In its simplest form, this is the sentence.

By combining an isolated word (e.g., "table," "dog," "coal," "suffering") which designates an object or state with another word (e.g., "run," "sleep," "go," "red," "green," "bitter") which designates an action or quality, we introduce the words into a system of relationships. An individual word does not designate a complete judgment or thought. When a person utters "table," "sun," or "eyeglasses," he/she only names an object and includes it in a system of definite semantic relationships. He/she has not yet formulated any *thought*. On the other hand, even such simple sentences as "The house burns.", "The dog barks.", or "Doubt is useful." do more than designate an object. They express an idea or inform us of an event. It is precisely this that has led many psychologists and linguists (e.g., Humboldt, 1905, 1907; de Saussure, 1922; and the Russian linguist Potebnya, 1888) to argue that it is not the word but the *sentence* which constitutes the basic unit of living speech. As we shall see, simply naming something, without formulating a thought or idea, is quite artificial, whereas the expression of a complete thought or the formulation of an idea is the basic unit of communication. Thus, we may assert that *if the word is the element of language, the sentence is the unit of living speech.*

The assertion about the primacy of the utterance or sentence is supported by the history of language itself, or rather by its protohistory. As previously noted, during the first stage of its protohistory, language consisted of sounds or "words" which acquired their meaning only in the context of an action or situation. These words had a sympractical character. If a word designated an object, then this word, accompanied by a specific intonation or gesture and uttered in a particular situation, began to designate an entire idea, leading to the formation of an entire one-word sentence.

In this case, only one part of the sentence (the subject) is expressed while the second part (the predicate) remains in the gesture or in the practical act. In other instances, we may observe the reverse. In other words, a pointing gesture designates an object and serves as the subject, while the word serves to formulate the action.

It is only during the later stages of language development that the verb takes on the function earlier carried out by an action or gesture. At that point, the second component in the utterance is replaced by a synsemantic connection (i.e., a connection based on the relationship between two words) and the unit of living speech is no longer the isolated word, but the entire sentence.

This development can be traced more easily in the evolution of children's speech. Even the individual words with which children begin to speak are in fact "one-word sentences." During early stages of development, these words are intertwined with the situation in which they occur. The word "doll" uttered by a child in fact means, "Give me the doll." or "I want the doll."

THE PSYCHOLOGICAL PROBLEM OF THE SENTENCE AS AN UTTERANCE UNIT

What makes the transition from the single word to the sentence possible? Psychologists and linguists have attempted to answer this question in a variety of ways.

In the past, when psychology was based on the traditions of associationism, it limited itself to the general claim that the sentence is only a series of individual words. According to this approach, a word elicits associations, which in turn cause other words to surface. When these words are linked together, they form a sentence.

However, it is easy to see how fruitless those attempts must have been when trying to understand the relationship between an utterance and the denotative and connotative meanings of the individual words. Neither the designation or generalization of objects, actions, and properties nor the occurrence of semantic fields can lead to the appearance of an interconnected utterance.

Instead, the sentence must be viewed as a *serially organized system* which is related to the types of processes identified by Lashley (1951). He was the first to outline the problem of "serially organized forms of behavior" or "complex dynamic structures." Certain Gestalt psychologists (e.g., Ehrenfels) who thought that it was possible to analyze a musical melody as a dynamic whole also studied this problem. As members of the Würzburg School of psychology pointed out, general intentions or purposes probably provide the foundation for dynamic formations which generate an entire idea.

Such hypotheses, however, simply outline the nature of the dynamic structures giving rise to the sentence, and do not provide a concrete explanation for how they operate. It was a long time before the first steps could be taken toward understanding how the entire sentence is produced.

As noted earlier, some words must be viewed as elements of a more complex group. When taken by themselves, they give one a feeling of incompleteness. The word "kill" necessarily involves another word which answers the question "whom?" ("a fox," "a wolf," "a man"). The word "lend" involves words which answer the questions "what?", "from whom?", "to whom?", and "for how long?".

The phenomenon of the inevitable occurrence of accompanying words has been studied by several investigators, both in classical and in contemporary linguistics, under the term "word valency." The number of relevant words that must accompany a word in order to make a linguistic (syntactic) whole has been studied by investigators such as Apresyan (1974), Carroll (1955, 1964), Fillmore (1968, 1971), and Mel'chuk (1974).

There is reason to believe that similar elementary syntactic relationships (syntagmas) emerge in ontogenesis as soon as a word, which first is tightly connected with the child's practical action (i.e., its sympractical context), begins to acquire independent existence. That is, these syntactic relationships emerge when the sympractical context is replaced by the synsemantic context (Bühler, 1934). It seems that the appearance of the syntagmas, which convert a "single-word sentence" of a small child into a chain of two words and later several words (cf. Brown, 1973; Halliday, 1975), originates in sympractical speech. These early syntagmas have the structure "desire—name" or "name—action." Sometimes this type of relationship takes on more complex forms, such as "name—action—object," and thus requires more complex syntagmas. This represents the transfer of activity-based relationships to the level of speech.

It is quite evident that the origin and psychological structure of such syntagmas is not simply the transfer of practical activity to the plane of speech, but also involves the psychological structures required for categorizing a designated object and involves the use of semantic fields which are elicited by the word. Thus, we see that there are two quite different principles in the organization of verbal meanings: One concerns concepts called the paradigmatic principle, and the other gives rise to an utterance called the syntagmatic principle (Jakobson, 1971).

Let us briefly consider how these two principles of organization differ from one another. The paradigmatic organization of language is concerned with the way that a given element of language is included in a system of oppositions or hierarchical system of codes. For instance, every sound is in opposition to another. The sound "b" and "d" differ from "p" and "t" respectively by virtue of being voiced. These sounds are part of the system of consonants and are thus in opposition to vowels. All such sounds in a language form the phonemic organization of that language. This organization is a system of hierarchically constructed relationships.

The same general principles apply to the lexicon. The word "dog" is in opposition to the words "cat," "cow," and "horse." On the other hand, when taken together, all of these words form a group of items designating domestic animals. They, in turn, are in opposition with wild animals. Furthermore, both domestic and wild animals fall within a still higher category—that of animals in general, and animals in general contrast with plants. Finally, both animals and plants enter into a still more complex group of living objects which contrast with nonliving objects.

It is this principle of opposition and organization in a hierarchical system of relations which lies at the foundation of concept formation. Not only the phonemic and lexical elements of the word are structured in accordance with this principle, it also organizes the morphological and semantic forms of the word. Nouns contrast with verbs, verbs contrast with adjectives, and abstract words with concrete words. Each of these groups constitutes a hierarchy, and this is what forms a concept. The first principle of a word's linguistic organization is the paradigmatic organization of the system of codes.

The organization of an utterance or sentence is based on a completely different principle. When we move from the word to the sentence, we move to a new principle of linguistic organization. This is known as the syntagmatic principle. According to this principle, what organizes an utterance is not a hierarchy of oppositions, but the transition from one word to another. If we consider a very simple sentence, such as "The house burns." or "The dog barks.", we are not placing the word "house" in opposition to the word "burns" or the word "dog" in opposition to the word "barks." That is, we are not concerned here with a hierarchy of elements or paradigmatic opposition. Rather, we are concerned with the transition from one element to another.

We know that children do not master sentences of all levels of complexity simultaneously. Rather, they progress gradually from simple to more complex sentences over a long period of development. This process has been studied by many psychologists. It has been found that in the early stages of development a child can use only individual words. For example, when shown a picture, he/she may use the isolated words "dog" and "boy" to describe it. This does not indicate a stage in the development of perception, but a stage in the development of language.

In developed speech, we are dealing not with isolated words, but with series of words. The organizing principle behind these series is not based on how words enter into a hierarchy of relations, i.e., it is not based on the paradigmatic principle. Rather, their organization is based on how words enter into a system of syntagmatic chains which constitute units of sentences. Such word groups which express events or thoughts are made up of individual syntactic elements. In the simplest instances, these word groups are limited to a subject and predicate (e.g., "The house burns."). In more complex cases, they include a subject, predicate, and object ("The boy hit the dog.", "The girl drinks tea."). In still more complex instances, they form quite complicated sentences which are capable of expressing practically any thought. Our main point here is that the expression of a thought in words is determined not so much by the principle of opposition and hierarchical organization as it is by the principle of successive syntagmatic linkages.

An important fact here is that syntagmatic linkages are more natural forms of speech than the paradigmatic system of oppositions. We may even say that the paradigmatic system of oppositions is not so much a unit of speech as a logical unit of language. It is precisely this fact that makes the syntagmatic relationships between the noun and the verb especially significant for the production of an utterance.

I shall take the liberty of illustrating this with an example from one of my own experiments which was conducted almost 50 years ago, but whose real significance I have been able to understand only recently. In this research (Luria, 1927), we studied the formation of relationships between words in a child's speech at different developmental stages. For this purpose, we gave children words—like "sun," "window," and "dog"—and asked them to reply by uttering the first word that occurred to them. This was a classical association experiment. In analyzing our results, we took into account both the nature of the relationship (ranging from simple to complex) and the response times (the time needed by the child to produce a response word). It turned out that the children's responses could be divided into two classes. We called them "associative" and "predicative" at the time we did the study. Some children tended to use associative responses. Thus, in response to "dog" they said "cat," in response to "sun" they said "moon," in response to "roof" they said "chimney," etc. Other children responded to the word presented to them with a verb or adjective: In response to "dog" they said "bark," in response to "girl" they said "cries," in response to "house" they said "burns," etc. These latter answers were what we termed predicative, rather than associative combinations.

Perhaps most significant, however, were the following two facts. We found that young children (from 5 to 7 years of age) relied primarily or completely on predicative responses. They rarely produced an associative response. Associative responses began to appear only with adolescent or adult subjects. Predicative responses, which are syntagmatic units of speech and constitute the prototype of the sentence, appeared earlier than associative responses.

Furthermore, we found that response times for predicative responses were much shorter than those for associative responses. Whereas children's response times for predicative responses fell within a very narrow range (e.g., means ranging from 1.4 to 1.6 seconds), the associative response times had a much wider range. Both of these facts support the notion that associative responses are not the first ones to appear, as most psychologists still think. Rather, predicative responses appear first.

This leads to the conclusion that paradigmatic (associative) responses are quite different from syntagmatic responses. They are more artificial. Syntagmatic (predicative) responses involve not only a different psychological structure, but also belong to a different form of speech activity. It is linked with the child's natural, practical activity, i.e., with more natural forms of speech processes.

THE STRUCTURAL ANALYSIS OF THE SENTENCE

The question naturally arises as to how syntagmatic relationships are formed. Investigators such as Howes (1954, 1957; Howes and Osgood, 1954) have argued that the main factor determining the use of a particular word in the presence of another is the frequency with which the word appears in speech. In their opinion, syntagmatic relationships may be viewed as a unique example of Markovian chains in which each link is entirely determined by the preceding one. However, such explanations have little foundation. The production of a sentence is based on principles which are quite different from the mechanical laws for joining words on the basis of frequency.

Every sentence has an integrated, coherent structure. It is this semantic coherence, rather than the mechanical application of patterns of probability, which lies at the root of sentence production. It is very likely that we need to reverse the way that this problem is normally formulated. Instead of moving from individual words to a sentence, we must begin with the initial idea or intention and trace how it is changed into a system of words that form a sentence.

We have already noted that the syntagmatic organization of an utterance can vary in its complexity. In the simplest cases, it is limited to two words—a noun and a verb—e.g., sentences such as "Dom gorit." (The house burns.), "Sobaka laet." (The dog barks.), and "Devochka bol'na." (The girl is sick.).[12] In somewhat more complex instances, this subject-predicate structure is preserved, but each of these components is divided into additional groups. For example, consider the sentences "The boy hit the dog." and "The girl drinks tea." In these instances, we see that in addition to the subject (S) and the predicate (P), there is also an object (O) toward which the action is directed. Therefore the sentence has a somewhat more complex character (S→P→O).

However, this does not exhaust the possibilities for sentential syntactic structures. Quite often, constructions have an even more complex form. These complex sentences are characterized by the fact that each of the constituents comprises an entire complex group. This can be seen in the sentences "The large glade is overgrown with thick grass.", "The beautiful deer ran quickly across the thick forest.", and "When I heard a loud knock on the door at night, I got very frightened." In these constructions, each constituent is no longer a single element, but a complete group. In contemporary linguistics, these groups are often identified as the subject or noun group (noun phrase, "NP") and the verb group or predicate (verb phrase, "VP"). Each of these groups, in turn, can be divided into additional subordinate constituents.

Complex syntactic constructions such as these involve not only a distinct meaning, but also grammatical structure which is specific to the language involved. Many linguists have devoted their attention to the study of grammatical structure. Although it is often difficult in the course of normal observations to separate grammatical structure from content, these linguists have focused on this structure independently of the meaning of the words which are involved in it. Shcherba (1957), the famous Russian linguist, outlined a grammatical system consisting of artificial, meaningless words while preserving the grammatical forms of these words (word order, suffixes, and inflections). He showed that notwithstanding the utter meaninglessness of each word in the sentence, the general sense of the construction could still be understood. By analyzing such sentences, he demonstrated the independence of grammatical form from content in Russian.

A similar idea about the independence of syntactic structures later became the point of departure for the work of Chomsky (1957, 1965), the well-known American linguist. Chomsky made an important contribution to the study of grammatical structure and was one of the founders of contemporary transformational generative grammar. According to him, it is possible to determine whether

---

[12]These examples reflect the fact that Russian has no definite or indefinite article. Also, the copula is rarely used in the present tense. Therefore, the number of words in surface structure Russian does not coincide with that found in English.—*J. V. Wertsch*

or not a sentence is grammatical without regard to its semantic acceptibility. To illustrate this, he pointed out that the sentence "Colorless green ideas sleep furiously." is grammatical even though it is semantically anomolous. Chomsky's approach made it possible to make progress in the formal syntactic analysis of sentences without becoming bogged down in semantic problems. He demonstrated that it is possible to isolate the complex syntactic structures which constitute the basic scheme of sentences.

In the sentence just given it is easy to identify the subject group (NP), the predicate group (VP), and the subordinate structures that enter into each group. Chomsky called these regular grammatical structures of language "surface syntactic structures" and pointed out that these structures are specific to each language. Of particular importance is the fact that such surface syntactic structures may be expressed in quite different ways in a language. The sentence "Nicholas doubted the correctness of the scientific hypothesis suggested to him." may be expressed by using any one of several alternatives. Consider, for example, "Nicholas was not certain of the grounds of the scientific hypothesis suggested to him.", "Nicholas expressed his doubts that the scientific hypothesis suggested to him corresponded with facts.", and "Nicholas did not consider the scientific hypothesis suggested to him to be correct." These examples demonstrate that the number of sentential alternatives for expressing the same idea can be quite large. One linguist who has studied syntactic variability went so far as to say that the number of sentences one may come across in a living language is considerably larger than the number of seconds in a person's life.

In addition, there is a second issue which poses an important problem for psychology and linguistics. While the examples above show that one and the same idea can be expressed by many different sentences, there are instances when one sentence can be interpreted in different ways. The Russian sentence "Kolya poshel k Ole s Mishei." (literally: Kolya went to Olya's with Misha) may mean that "Kolya went to see Olya, who lived with Misha." or "Kolya and Misha went to visit Olya." The Russian sentence "Muzhu izmenyat' nel'zya." (literally: husband to be unfaithful must not) also has a twofold meaning. It can mean "A husband must not be unfaithful to his wife." or "A wife must not be unfaithful to her husband.". The two interpretations in both examples above serve to convert an ambiguous sentence into an unambiguous one. In order to disentangle the two meanings, the listener must utilize various markers, such as stress and pauses.

Two closely related questions arise in connection with these issues. First, can a child of 3 or 4 years of age master the complex grammatical structures of his/her mother tongue in the relatively short period of 6 to 8 months? Second, what are the mechanisms that make it possible to recognize ambiguity in a sentence? Chomsky made an important contribution to the discussion of these problems. He hypothesized that behind the innumerable surface syntactic structures (which differ among languages) there are deep syntactic structures which reflect the formal patterns of expressing an idea. This hypothesis revolutionized linguistics. According to this approach, the number of these deep structures is quite small. This is what enables a child to master these deep syntactic structures and to extract surface syntactic structures from them in such a short time.

Chomsky also argued that sentence ambiguity reflects the fact that two sentences may have identical surface syntactic structures even though their deep syntactic structures differ. Thus, if we can provide an objective description of these deep structures, we can describe the differences that lie hidden in the surface structure. Since Chomsky's analysis included rules which *generate* deep syntactic structures and rules which *transform* these deep structures into surface structures, it has been labeled a "transformational generative" grammar. His investigation of deep structures and their conversion to surface structures consisted of identifying the components in syntactic structure and describing the relatively small number of transformations which a given construction may undergo.

The transformation described by Chomsky (1957) and others who shared his views (e.g., Miller, 1962; Fodor and Bever, 1965) included rules for transforming kernel sentences. For example, these rules make it possible to transform a simple, active, declarative sentence such as "Peter obtained a plum." into other forms: the passive ("A plum was obtained by Peter."), the negative declarative ("Peter did not obtain a plum."), the negative passive ("A plum was not obtained by Peter."), the active interrogative ("Did Peter obtain a plum?"), or the passive interrogative ("Was a plum obtained by Peter?").

In addition to these possible transformations, Chomsky was able to specify some unacceptable transformations that would result in ungrammatical sentences (such as *"A plum received Peter." and *"Did a plum receive Peter?").[13]

The description of the kernel grammatical structures and the relatively small number of rules that govern their transformation constituted the foundation of transformational generative linguistics. In turn, this made it possible to develop a scientific description of the process of sentence production and to explain how a child is able to master the basic, grammatical forms of language in a very short time.

We shall not address Chomsky's rather unconvincing hypothesis that the incredibly short time required by children to master the basic syntactic structures of language may be attributed to the fact that they possess innate linguistic structures which are simply mobilized when they communicate with adults. This is the "nativist hypothesis" which was proposed by Chomsky and his colleagues (e.g., McNeill, 1970) in their critique of the "empirical" theories of behaviorists. The weakness of the nativist hypothesis springs from the fact that language is formed through the child's actual relationships with reality. These involve the

---

[13] An asterisk placed before a construction indicates that it is ungrammatical. –*J. V. Wertsch*

concrete actions of the child. Such actions invariably include the active subject (e.g., shifting of gaze and orientation) and objects. The interaction between these create the foundation for the future relationship of "subject—predicate—object" found in the kernel structures of language. Because this view has been developed elsewhere by Bruner (1975) and others (also see Luria, 1975a), we shall not examine it in detail here.

Chomsky's description of the relationship between surface and deep syntactic structures has important implications for the study of language acquisition and language comprehension. Investigators such as Miller (1967) have argued that sentence comprehension involves transition from surface to deep syntactic structure. Of great importance here is the fact that the relationship between surface and deep structure is far from always being the same. In some sentences, the relationship between them is straightforward, and the change from surface to deep structure does not call for particularly complex operations. This happens in simple sentences like "The house burns." or "The boy hit the dog." In these cases, the model S—P or S—P—O applies equally to both levels of syntactic structure.

However, in other sentences, this relationship is much less direct. In those cases, the transition from surface to deep structure requires special operations. This is particularly obvious in the case of ambiguous sentences such as those we examined earlier which surface structures may be similar or even identical, but the deep structures are different.

As an example, take the two sentences examined in detail both by Chomsky and Khomskaya (1958). Khomskaya analyzed the process whereby children comprehend the sentences "Petya predlozhil yabloko." (Peter offered an apple.) and "Petya poprosil yabloko." (Peter requested an apple.). These two sentences appear to have identical structures. However, their deep syntactic structures turn out to be quite different. In the first sentence, the subject (Peter) is clearly an agent, and this is represented in the surface structure in a direct way. The semantic structure of this sentence is revealed by reading from left to right. The second sentence, however, involves another person who is not explicitly named. It can be rephrased as "Petya poprosil, chtoby *kto-nibud'* dal emu yabloko." (Peter requested that *someone* give him an apple.). That is, it must be comprehended from right to left (someone will give Peter an apple which he is expecting). This clearly emerges from the deep syntactic structure of the second sentence.

The same can be said of the other sentences cited earlier. Analysis of the deep structure of a single surface structure may reveal two different meanings. This is the case in the Russian sentence "Muzhu izmenyat' nel'zya." (A husband must not be unfaithful to his wife; or, A wife must not be unfaithful to her husband.). This relationship between deep and surface structure has been examined by Chomsky in the case of certain English sentences. These sentences exemplify the problem especially clearly since English does not rely heavily on inflections which indicate a word's syntactic role in a sentence. For example, "They are flying planes." may mean either that some people are flying places or that the planes themselves are flying. Where the surface structures of sentences are identical, the difference in their meaning is revealed only by analyzing their deep syntactic structure.

Thus we see that Chomsky's transformational generative grammar represents an important step forward. It made possible a scientific approach to the study of sentence meanings, and it represented a more serious attempt to analyze the grammatical structures of the sentence than the earlier approaches found in classical descriptive linguistics.

Chomsky's approach also provided a foundation for the study of the issues in producing and comprehending (or, "encoding" and "decoding") sentences. This was not available in earlier classical (descriptive) linguistics. In this connection, we should note that the transformational generative grammar formulated by Chomsky and his colleagues led to a large number of psychological experiments (e.g., Bever, Fodor, and Weksel, 1965; Fodor and Bever, 1965; Fodor, Bever, and Garrett, 1968b; Fodor and Garrett, 1967; Goldman-Eisler, 1964, 1968; Miller, 1965; Miller and Isard, 1963). Many of these studies made use of methods which enabled the investigators to provide a closer analysis of the grammatical units used in understanding complex sentences. These experiments also provided insight into the grammatical units used in sentence comprehension and the psychological problems presented by different sentence constructions (e.g., simple declarative, passive, interrogative, affirmative and negative forms). Miller (1962) and his colleagues and Morton (1964) have been able to devise an entire scale of constructions which successively approximates a correct grammar of English. It allowed them to join pairs, triplets, and larger groups of words that approximate formalized grammatical structures. This represented an important step in developing objective measures of the degrees of difficulty of various syntactic structures.

A CRITIQUE OF THE FORMAL-SYNTACTIC ANALYSIS OF THE SENTENCE AND GENERATIVE SEMANTICS

Unquestionably, the development of an analysis of the relationship between surface and deep syntactic structures was of decisive importance for linguistics. Progress in this area made it possible to pose many questions which earlier had not been asked at all or had seemed to elude an answer. However, this does not mean that this approach was accepted by everyone or that the idea of deep syntactic structures provided a satisfactory explanation of sentence production.

Soon after the publication of Chomsky's basic works (Chomsky, 1957, 1965), several investigators in the U.S. (e.g., Fillmore, 1968, 1971, 1972; Lakoff, 1970, 1971, 1972; McCawley, 1968, 1972), in Germany (e.g., Bierwisch, 1969), and in Hungary (e.g., Kiefer, 1969) raised serious questions about the relationship between deep syntactic structures and logical structures. They argued that at the deep level syntactic structures approximate semantic structures and that a purely formalized study of these structures without regard to meaning is fruitless. Some linguists (e.g., McCawley, 1968) even argued that deep syntactical structures do not exist and that linguistic analysis should be concerned with semantic structures. This response to Chomsky's approach began immediately after the publication of his works and appears to have been quite strong. The discussion which arose served a valuable purpose in that the problem of the semantic analysis the sentence was emphasized for the first time. This happened primarily in "generative semantics."

There is no doubt that the sentence is a single closed system and that coherence is its basic characteristic. What is the semantic structure of the sentence and what are the factors that enable us to derive the surface structure of a sentence from its basic semantic structure? Linguists such as Bellert (1972) have pointed out that there are two basic types of sentences—"free" and "bound" sentences. The first category includes sentences such as "The sun shines." and "The dog barks." These sentences can exist independently of a logical context. The second category includes cases in which the meaning goes beyond the limits of the given sentence.

Some investigators have been even more categorical and have expressed the opinion that no sentences exist "out of context." They have argued that it is impossible to study sentences "in vacuo" (e.g., Rommetveit, 1968, 1974). The factors that determine the semantic structure of bound phrases and sentences may be linguistic as well as an extralinguistic.

Further analysis shows that one can isolate the main "theme," which identifies what is being talked about, and the "rheme," which identifies what is being said or what new information is contained in the predicate. Some investigators (Fillmore, 1972) prefer to analyze sentences in terms of the *topic* (similar to the theme) and the *focus* (that which emerges in the forefront and engages one's attention).

Special linguistic devices are associated with these semantic structures of language. These devices serve to specify the sense of the sentence. They are used to identify its topic and focus, distinguish its theme and rheme. Among them are stress, intonation, and pauses. Goldman-Eisler (1964, 1968) carried out research in connection with this last device. By using some or all of these devices speakers can overrule the potential polysemy of sentences.

However, the semantic organization of a message is not limited to lexical and prosodic devices. In addition, we must consider the issue which linguists often denote by the term "presupposition" (e.g., Bierwisch, 1969; Fillmore, 1968, 1971, 1972; Kiefer, 1972; Rommetveit, 1968, 1974). Presupposition is concerned with the selectivity with which an interlocutor approaches a speech situation. Presupposition sometimes is based on the semantic functions of individual words which form part of a sentence. Thus the use of "widower" indicates that the individual in question had been married. In other cases, presupposition involves extralinguistic factors. It may be concerned with the general context in which the sentence appears or with the speaker's motives. We can illustrate this by considering the sentence, "The light is on." Depending on the speaker's intentions, this may mean "It's nice that after the repairs in our apartment the light is on again." or "You forgot to turn off the light again." In these cases, an analysis of the utterance must go beyond the formal syntactic structure of the sentence and identify the semantic factors which determine its real meaning (and sometimes also its sense).

These problems, which have been tackled in linguistics rather inadequately, have been examined in much more detail in Soviet psychology where Vygotsky (1934) proposed the concept of "sense" as contrasted with "meaning." We shall return to the important studies which Stanislavsky and his students carried out on this question. These studies reveal the unusual richness of the method that humans use to overcome the limits of the linguistic organization of text and proceed to the perception of the inner sense of an utterance.

Chapter 9
Complex Utterance Forms: Paradigmatic Components in Syntagmatic Structures

THEORETICAL FOUNDATIONS

Up to this point, we have discussed the structural analysis of the sentence and have examined the notion that in addition to surface syntactic structures, which differ among languages, there are universal deep syntactic structures which reflect the basic logic of sentence construction. We have also pointed out the limits of formal grammatical analyses of the sentence and have touched on the basic hypotheses of modern generative semantics and other movements which attempt to deal with the semantic structure of sentences.

All of this brings us to the major concern of this chapter—the psychological construction of real speech utterances. That is, we shall be concerned with the factors that determine the difficulty in understanding complex sentences. This problem again raises the issue of the syntagmatic and paradigmatic organization of the sentence at various levels.

We know that most actual speech consists of simple, syntagmatic groups. Thus we can describe various events with the help of simple utterances like "The girl sleeps.", "The boy is ill.", and "The doy barks." As noted earlier, the greater

129

part of the actual speech consists of such simple syntagmas, i.e., simply statements expressing a thought or an event. Using the terminology of Svedelius (1897), we can call such a simple syntagma a *communication of an event* (or a message about an event). Such syntagmas can serve as isolated statements. They can also be united to form chains of serially organized utterances. For example, consider the following segment of text from Lermontov: "The lone white sail gleams in the mist of the blue sea. What does it seek in a far-off land? What has it left behind on its native shores?" It is easy to see that this message involves a series of events and experiences expressed in a single chain of simple sentences and that it has a simple syntagmatically organized character throughout. Perhaps the clearest examples of these simple forms may be found in ancient texts. For instance, in the language of the Bible we see "And He came, and He saw, and He did", etc., where communication about successive events is conveyed by individual statements, linked by the conjunction "and."

All these examples express events in a quite simple way. They are all in the form of simple statements joined together. In each, the surface and deep syntagmatic structures appear to be similar to a degree. Therefore their comprehension does not require any significant transformation of the grammatical units used. These syntagmatic structures, consisting of sequences of simple syntactic forms expressing events, are examples of "parataxis." The simplest form of parataxis is simple joining of individual sentences by means of the conjunction "and."

Let us turn now to a more complex form of communication which is clearly distinguished from the communication of events. This second form involves more complex syntagmatic organization. Svedelius (1897) terms this the *communication of relationships*. Whereas the communication of events can be expressed concretely (i.e., the contents can be reflected in a series of images), the communication of relationships cannot be expressed in this way, because the communication of relationships involves units of complex codes of language that serve as a means for abstract logical thinking.

The communication of relationships differs from the communication of events in grammatical construction as well as content. Communication of relationships, as a rule, involves comprehension of units which require transformations that convert this form of communication into simpler communications of events and therefore provide concrete support, facilitating comprehension. In the communication of relationships, the mere juxtaposition of individual elements of a message (parataxis) is no longer adequate. Other, more complex types of grammatical structure are needed, which allows one to develop an entire hierarchy of mutually subordinate components customarily called *hypotaxis*. These structures allow governance of some groups of words by others. This means that complex types of speech communication differ from the simple type both in form and content.

FUNDAMENTAL WAYS OF EXPRESSING RELATIONSHIPS

With some qualifications, we can say that syntagmatic and paradigmatic organization differ not only in their grammatical structure, but also in their origin. Syntagmatic forms of an utterance are most clearly seen in the communication of events. Paradigmatic forms of an utterance, on the other hand, are manifested most clearly in the communication of relationships. These forms involve complex codes and the transformation of successive links of an utterance into patterns.

Of course this division of the two systems of speech processes is only theoretical. In actual practice, syntagmatic and paradigmatic organizational principles are both involved in complex utterances. However, the distinction between the two is very useful in the study of the psychology of speech, linguistics, and the study of localized brain lesions (e.g., Luria, 1975a, 1975b).

Let us reformulate the general idea that in addition to their syntagmatic linkages, certain structures involve paradigmatic organization, i.e., they require the transformation of serially constructed elements into abstract simultaneous patterns. Thus, both the production and comprehension of connected speech involves specific difficulties the psychologist must take into account. Some speech structures are extremely difficult to understand, and their comprehension requires intermediate transformations. The psychologist's task is to help speakers avoid the use of such complex structures, describe methods which may facilitate the comprehension of these complex syntactical structures and the processes by which they are learned.

Our description of complex paradigmatic structures shall begin by considering the linguistic devices that make possible the formulation of relationships. We shall deal both with the structure and the genesis of these devices. Our discussion will be concerned only with the paradigmatic structure of Russian, while keeping in mind that analogous structures in other languages (for instance, English) may make use of other grammatical means.

Our analysis will deal with four devices used to codify paradigmatic relationships in Russian: inflections, auxiliary words, word order, and comparative constructions.

Inflections

The first device we shall examine in Russian is inflections. In our account, we shall be primarily concerned with noun suffixes, which are a basic means for expressing relationships.

There are two forms of morphological case markers or inflections that enable a speaker to join nouns to express events or relationships. First, there are simple syntagmatic inflections. For instance, in "Ya vizhu sobaku." (I see a dog.), "Ya" (I) is the subject and hence is in the nominative case, and "sobaku" (dog) is the direct object and therefore is in the accusative case. In "Drovosek rubit toporom."

(The woodcutter chops with an axe.), "Drovosek" (woodcutter) is in the nominative case, and "toporom" (axe) is in the instrumental case. In "Pozhar nachalsya v dome." (The fire started in the house.), "Pozhar (fire) is in the nominative case and "dome" (house) is in the prepositional case.

In these examples, noun inflections which designate the nominative, accusative, instrumental, and prepositional cases are simple means of government. The subject governs the predicate and the object, and the inflections determine the correlation of two elements, subordinating the object to the subject. If we consider a sentence which contains a subject, a predicate, and an object, we see that the subject is in the nominative case and the object is in an oblique case. Only in a few cases does the relationship between the sympractical and the logical structure of the sentence change. For example, in so-called passive constructions such as "Mal'chik ukushen sokakoi." (The boy is bitten by a dog.), the logical subject (that which performs the act) is in the instrumental case, while the logical object of the action (which in its meaning has the function of the oblique case) is in the nominative case. However, even in this instance, the mode of inflection governs this oblique case. Examples of languages using constructions where the center is shifted from the noun to the verb can be found in Greek, Northern Caucasian languages, and in ancient languages (Ivanov, 1969).

Keep in mind that only in a few developed languages can we find a complete system of devices for indicating the relationships between subject and object. There exist, for example, certain languages (sometimes called "paleo-Asiatic" languages) in which there are just two cases—the direct and the oblique. The direct case indicates the subject, the oblique indicates any object, without specifying the relationship between object and subject, and one must guess the concrete relationship between subject and object. The real meaning in oblique cases can be understood from the situation in which the utterance occurs, i.e., from the sympractical context. In Russian, which is a very developed language, matters stand quite differently. Russian has an entire series of differentiated cases, and each case inflection indicates a definite relationship of subject to object. These forms may be used to communicate events or relationships.

There are forms, however, that are used only in the communication of relationships. One form appears in constructions such as "Sokrat—chelovek." (Socrates is a human being.) or "Ivanov—student." (Ivanov is a student.). These forms are not simply comprised of two words placed next to each other as if they were two subjects. In Russian, the verb "est'" (to be) is assumed. This is not a communication of an event. Rather, it is the communication of a relationship. This may be demonstrated by the fact that whereas it is easy to portray concretely the content of the phrase "Mal'chik udaril sobaku." (The boy hit the dog.) or "Devochka p'et chai." (The girl drinks tea.), it is not possible to provide a concrete representation of the sentence "Sokrat—chelovek." or "Ivanov—student." If we were to portray, side by side, "Socrates" and "a human being" and "Ivanov" and "a student," this would not constitute an expression of the relationship which is expressed by such constructions.

The point is that the linguistic and psychological structures involved in the communication of relationships are quite different from those involved in the communication of events. In the communication of relationships, one object (or person) is related to another or one object (or person) is represented as being in the class of another. Therefore, the structure "Sokrat—chelovek" or "Ivanov—student" is not a simple syntagmatic structure. It is a complex paradigmatic structure because it is *hierarchically* organized. Socrates, like Ivanov and Petrov, belongs to the common category of "human beings," which is contrasted with other categories of living beings. Therefore this construction is a communication of relationships.

Other forms of syntagmatic linking are even more complex semantically and hence psychologically, and accordingly cannot be understood directly. For example, consider two types of constructions in the genitive case. On the one hand, "kusok khleba" (a piece of bread) is an example of the partitive genitive. On the other hand, "brat ottsa" (brother of father) is an example of the attributive genitive. The partitive genitive does not express the two concepts "khleb" (bread) and "kusok" (piece). Rather, it expresses a very simple relationship between an object (bread) and a part (piece). In contrast, the attributive genitive is a much more complex construction. It does not express two isolated objects. Rather, it designates a third object, not mentioned in the given construction (in this case, "uncle"). It should be noted that the attributive genitive appeared in the Russian language much later than the partitive genitive. Since the genitive involves intermediate transformations, it is psychologically complex.

This complexity is not apparent when we observe the actual speech of a normal person. However, many studies (e.g., Luria, 1946, 1947, 1962, 1975a) of localized brain lesions have demonstrated the relative complexity of attributive genitive constructions. Patients with certain types of speech disturbances continue to understand partitive genitive constructions—such as "kusok khleba" (a piece of bread)—fairly well, but they are quite incapable of understanding attributive genitive constructions—such as "brat ottsa" (brother of father).

Various analyses have enabled us to unravel several factors that lie at the root of these difficulties with the attributive genitive. First, this type of word combination involves clearly expressed hierarchical, paradigmatic components. "Brat ottsa" is not a combination expressing two nouns; it does not mean "brat" + "otets" (brother + father). Rather, it expresses the *relationship* of the brother to the father. The second noun being in the genitive case (i.e., "ottsa") means that it designates a property which semantically takes on the function of an adjective rather than designating an object. Therefore, however simple this construction may appear, it is actually quite complex. The word in the genitive case ("ottsa") acts as an adjective and the two words "brat ottsa" really designate one object and not two. This object is not explicitly indicated in the given construction.

Thus the construction is not used to identify "brother" or "father." Rather, it indicates "uncle," the meaning of which can be understood only after we have grasped the relationship between the nouns.

Another difficulty that arises here is that this construction is a "reversible" one. One can speak of "brat ottsa" (brother of father), or one can change the order of the two nouns and speak of "otets brata" (father of brother). This change means that one is no longer speaking of an uncle. Instead one is speaking of one's own father (father of brother = father).

Matters are quite different in the case of nonreversible constructions. We can say "kusok khleba" (a piece of bread) or "nozhka stola" (a leg of a table), but we cannot say "khleb kuska" (a bread of a piece) or "stol nozhki" (a table of a leg). Obviously this nonreversibility provides additional semantic support and therefore facilitates comprehension. By rearranging the elements of one and the same pair of words, we can give a construction a new meaning.

It should also be pointed out that the attributive genitive, which in fact carries the meaning of an adjective, runs counter to the word order that is normal in Russian. Usually an adjective precedes a noun, as in "sytyi chelovek" (a satiated person) or "krasivyi tsvetok" (a beautiful flower). Therefore, in order to understand the real meaning of the attributive genitive, several psychological operations or transformations are required. First, one must ignore the normal substantive meaning of the second noun ("ottsa") and give it the meaning of an adjective. For this, it is necessary to change the order of words (since in Russian the adjective normally precedes the noun); one must mentally rearrange the order of the two items and also identify the semantic pattern involved. One must understand that "brat ottsa" (brother of father) means "uncle," while "otets brata" (father of father) means one's own father. In other words, in order to decode this communication of relationships, it is necessary to perform a very complex chain of abstract operations.

It is quite natural that one may rely on auxiliary means or auxiliary methods to decode this construction. For example, one may rely on additional markers. Thus, instead of "brat ottsa" (brother of father), we may use "brat *moego* ottsa" (brother of *my* father) to clarify that this means "uncle." In order to understand "otets brata" (father of brother), one may introduce an additional marker, as in "otets *moego* brata" (father of *my* brother)—precisely what many people do when they wish to understand the logical sense of this construction.

Sometimes a *change in the word order* is used as an auxiliary device. Thus, in colloquial speech the construction "brat ottsa" (brother of father) is never used. Instead, the construction "moego ottsa brat" (my father's brother) is used, in order to place the attributive sense (i.e., the sense of adjective) in the first position. This device corresponds with the normal practice of putting an adjective before a noun in Russian.

Thus the mental operations required to understand this seemingly simple construction may be carried out with the help of auxiliary supports (e.g., demonstrative pronouns and the rearrangement of word order). Such devices enable us to avoid the conflict that may arise due to the use of the adjective in an unusual position in Russian.

It is interesting to note that complex constructions appear in the history of a language three to four centuries after the simpler ones, explaining why in ancient Russian chronicles such forms of the attributive genitive as "brat ottsa" (brother of father) do not appear. In those chronicles, one does not come across the construction "brat ottsa" (brother of father) or "deti boyar" (children of boyars), but one does see the construction "boyare deti," (boyars' children). That is, the Old Russian construction avoids the conflict which arises in the genitive attributive by using simple paratactic proximity of individual nouns. Interestingly, when complex constructions occur, they always occur with additional indicators. Thus, in "moego ottsa brat" (my father's brother), in addition to "moego" (my), there is a change in the word order. The noun in the genitive case, which plays the role of an adjective, is placed in the normal adjective position.

It is also worthy to note that in old forms of any language (e.g., Old Church Slavonic) there is often a tendency to avoid subordination and to replace the "hypotactic" construction of the attributive genitive with simpler "paratactic" constructions expressed by the conjunction "a" (and, but) or "i" (and). So, in the language of the Bible and in colloquial language, instead of the construction "krotost' tsarya Davida" (the gentleness of King David), the construction used is "uvidel tsarya Davida i vsyu krotost' ego" (saw King David and all the gentleness of his). The genitive case is replaced by the conjunction "i" (and) and the hypotactic form by the paratactic.

In contemporary colloquial language, one can find a strong tendency to avoid these complex way of expressing relationships. For instance, instead of "nomer telefona" (number of a telephone, i.e., "telephone" is in the genitive case—*J.V.W.*), we hear "telefon nomer" (telephone number, i.e., "telephone" is in the nominative case instead of the genitive). Instead of "den' rozhdeniya" (day of birth), we hear "den' rozhdenie" (day birth—i.e., "birth" is in the nominative case instead of the genitive—*J.V.W.*). Complex constructions are avoided in colloquial speech. Speakers substitute simpler constructions which do not require the complex processing of information.

Auxiliary Words

Auxiliary words constitute a second device for communicating relationships. Prepositions are one class of auxiliary words. Of course, prepositions can also be involved in the communication of events, as is evident from the contrast between "Ya vyshel iz lesa." (I came out of the forest.) and "Ya poshel v les." (I went into the forest.). For an example of how prepositions can express relationships, consider "Ya delayu vyvod iz etoi posylki." (I derive a conclusion from this premise.), in which the preposition "iz" (from) acquires the meaning of a logical relationship. Or consider "Ya veryu v silu mass." (I believe in the power of the masses.), where the meaning of the preposition "v" (in) is logical rather than spatial.

There are special forms of prepositions that express spatial, temporal, and causal relationships. This class of auxiliary words is of enormous importance. It comprises a device that makes language into a tool of thinking. Consider the examples "krug pod kvadratom" (a circle under a cross) or "kvadrat pod krugom" (a cross under a circle), "leto pered vesnoi" (summer before spring) or "vesna pered letom" (summer before spring), or "Ya pozovtrakal pered tem, kak prochel gazetu." (I had a breakfast before reading the newspaper.). Finally, consider the following auxiliary words serving to link sentences: "Ya poshel v kino, nesmotrya na to, chto u menya ne bylo bileta." (I went to the cinema despite the fact that I had no ticket.) or "Ya poshel v kino, khotya u menya ne bylo bileta." (I went to the cinema although I had not ticket.).

In all of these examples, auxiliary words place the events in a certain relationship. They may express relationships based on space, time, causality, or even more complex factors. By utilizing various formal analytic notions (e.g., conjunction, disjunction, inclusion, etc.), modern mathematical logic has made it possible to classify or formalize the relationships that can be expressed by these auxiliary words. A common feature of all of these cases is that auxiliary words express more than a simple chain of events; they also designate specific interrelationships, reflecting the fact that these words are a means of communicating relationships rather than events.

This problem is further complicated because some prepositions may be used in several different ways. For instance, the prepositions "v," "na," and "iz" have dozens of meanings in Russian. This is obvious if we consider the sentences "Ya polozhil knigu na stol." (I put a book on a table.); "Ya nadeyus' na svoego druga." (I am depending on my friend.); "Ya vynul knizhku iz portfelya." (I took a book out of a briefcase.); "Ya sdelal vyvod iz etoi posylki." (I derived a conclusion from this premise.). Since the auxiliary words have many possible meanings, one must always select a particular meaning in a given speech situation.

In addition, two more conditions influence the comprehensibility of such constructions. These conditions are the presence or absence of grammatical or semantic markers, and the reversibility or nonreversibility of constructions. In connection with the presence or absence of grammatical markers, consider the use of inflections in the following sentences: "Mal'chik poshel v les." (The boy went into the forest.); "Pulya popala v serdtse." (The bullet hit the heart.); "Kniga polozhena na stol." (The book is placed on the table.). In all of these instances, inflections which distinguish the nominative case from other cases are missing, making the comprehension of these constructions more difficult than in sentences in which these additional grammatical markers are present. Thus, compare these sentences with "Chelovek uvyaz v bolote." (A man got stuck in a bog.) or Mal'chik nastupil na lyagushku." (A boy stepped on a frog.), where the suffix of the final word indicates that it is the object and not the subject. In English, with only minimal case marking, such an absence of inflections is natural. In Russian, instances in which the nominative and accusative cases are expressed by the same forms are relatively rare. When they do occur, decoding is more difficult.

Another device facilitating comprehension of the construct is the semantic nature of a sentence. This involves the real relationships between things. In some cases, these relationships can be "nonreversible." Thus, we can say "Mal'chik poshel v les." (The boy went into a forest.); "Pulya popala v serdtse." (The bullet hit the heart.); "Flag razvivaetsya na kryshe." (The flag flutters on the roof.); "Oblako plyvet po nebu." (The cloud floats in the sky.). But we cannot say *"Les poshel v mal'chika." (The forest went into the boy.); *"Serdtse popalo v pulyu." (The heart hit the bullet.); etc. We cannot use these latter constructions because they express impossible forms of interaction between real things.

Therefore, reversible constructions give rise to significant difficulties in comprehension. In these cases, even the presence of inflections may not alleviate the difficulties. Consider the following examples of reversible constructions: "krug pod kvadratom" (a circle under a square); "kvadrat pod krugom" (a square under a circle); "krug v kvadrate" (a circle in a square); "kvadrat v kruge" (a square in a cirlce). In these instances, all of the constructions are equally possible. The reversal of word order produces an acceptable, but quite different construction.

The same thing occurs in more complex construction in which temporal relationships are expressed with the help of auxiliary words. For example, "Ya prochel gazetu, pered tem kak pozavtrakal." (I read the paper before I ate breakfast.). This may be reversed to form "Ya pozavtrakal, pered tem kak prochel gazetu." (I ate breakfast before I read the paper.).

Comprehension becomes even more difficult when inversion as well as reversibility are involved. In cases of inversion, the order contradicts the order in which the actual events occur. To decode constructions that involve inversion, an added operation is required to overcome this conflict. The following sentence involves both reversibility and inversion: "Ya pozavtrakal posle togo, kak prochel gazetu." (I ate breakfast after I read the paper.). In this case, the succession of the words is not the same as the succession of events. Thus, "posle togo, kak prochel gazetu" (after I read the paper) means that I read the paper earlier and ate breakfast afterward, requiring the listener to make a mental transformation of the construction.

Similar difficulties arising from inversion may also be seen in the change from the active to the passive voice. In this case, the subject is moved to the end of the construction and the object is placed at the beginning.

Word Order

We have already stated that in the grammatical constructions of Russian (as well as in other Indo-European languages) the subject of the action appears near the beginning of a sentence while the object toward which the action is directed occurs near the end. This correspondence between the order of words and order of things ("ordo et connexio idearum u Ordo et connexiv rerum") helps make the construction comprehensible.

The influence of word order is most clearly seen when a construction is reversible and cannot be decoded with the help of morphological or semantic markers. In such cases, word order is the only possible instrument for deciphering the meaning of the construction. Instances of this in Russian are rare, but they do occur. For example: "Plat'e zadelo veslo." (The dress brushed against the oar.); "Veslo zadelo plat'e." (The oar brushed against the dress.). In English, a language that does not rely heavily on inflections, the role of word order is much more important. Often, one can understand a reversible construction in English solely on this basis. For example, in "The boy hit the girl." and "The girl hit the boy.", the difference in meaning can be understood only on the basis of word order.

In constrast, reversible constructions which include a morphological case marker (in the form of an oblique case inflection) are easier to understand because they do not need any additional transformations. The following may serve as examples of such constructions: "Mal'chik udaril devochku." (The boy hit the girl.); "Devochka udarila mal'chika." (The girl hit the boy.). Similarly, in cases where the interpretation of a construction relies heavily on word order, the process is much easier in the case of nonreversible constructions. Here, a semantic marker plays the role of an auxiliary marker. The following are examples of such constructions: "Oblako zatumanilo solntse." (The cloud obscured the sun.); "Solntse zatumanilo oblako." (The sun obscured the cloud.). The semantic impossibility of the second sentence facilitates comprehension.

However, in cases involving semantic inversion, decoding is more difficult. This is precisely what occurs when a word in an oblique case (which identifies the object toward which the action is directed) appears at the beginning of a sentence, and the word identifying the performer of the action appears near the end. Consider the following example: "Petyu udaril Vanya."[14] (Vanya hit Petya.). In this case, comprehension requires additional operations. These may be guided by devices such as prosodic markers (e.g., special stress on a significant word). Comprehension becomes significantly more complex. It may involve successive operations and may be reflected in speech: "Petyu udaril Vanya . . . aha . . . znachit

---

[14] In Russian, the accusative ending of Petya (Pet*yu*) indicates that Petya is the direct object. This is so even though the noun appears at the beginning.—*J. W. Wertsch*

Vanya udaril . . . a Petya postradal." (Vanya hit Petya . . . aha . . . that means, Vanya hit . . . and Petya was hit.).

Perhaps the most striking example of such cases is provided by a change from the active to the passive voice. In this case, the form disrupts the correlation between the succession of words and the succession of events. It includes a new factor which requires an additional transformation.

We have already noted that in Russian, as in other Indo-European languages, the subject appears at the beginning of the sentence while the object appears near the end. In other, more ancient forms of language, however, the structure S→O→P (subject→object→predicate) may be seen instead of S→P→O (subject→ predicate→object) (cf. Greenberg, 1963).

In passive constructions, however, the subject appears in the instrumental case and near the end of the sentence, while the object appears in the nominative case and at the beginning of the sentence. Naturally, this form of inversion creates considerable difficulties. These difficulties can be overcome by transforming the sentence. Thus, compare "Petya udaril Vanyu." (Petya hit Vanya.) and "Petya udaren Vanei." (Petya is hit by Vanya.). The question is, who was the recipient of the action? Comprehension of the first sentence is a direct process, while understanding the second requires additional operations, including stress on the key word and the further transformation of the entire construction (e.g., "Petya udaren Vanei . . . aha . . . znachit Vanei . . . Znachit Vanya udaril, a Petya postradal."—Petya was hit by Vanya . . . aha . . . that means by Vanya . . . Vanya hit, and Petya was hit.).

The same can be observed in other cases. Thus, the process of understanding the passive construction "Volk ubit tigrom." (The wolf is killed by the tiger.) requires considerably greater effort than is required by the direct active construction "Tigr ubil volka." (The tiger killed the wolf.). In order to understand the passive construction, we often need methods which remove the inversion.

It is only in languages where the passive exists on an equal footing with the active (e.g., Georgian) that passive constructions do not require additional transformations. In these languages, the meaning of such constructions is perceived directly. A psychological analysis of the processes which occur during the transition from the active to the passive (or from the affirmative to the negative) has been carried out by several investigators (e.g., Miller, 1962). Therefore, we shall not discuss these processes in greater detail here.

We know that several conditions can influence the ease with which a construction will be comprehended, including the presence or absence of grammatical or morphological markers, the use of reversible or nonreversible constructions, and the conflict between word order and the order of the events designated by the sentence. While some constructions enable the listener or reader to understand the sense of the given constructions directly, others do not. In these latter cases, comprehension becomes possible only when additional transformations are performed.

Comparative Constructions

The last type of construction used to express the communication of relation-ships is the comparative construction. In contrast to the constructions described earlier, comparative constructions have an entirely different purpose. They do not express the mutual interrelationship of the components of a single event. Rather, they are used to portray the relationship between two objects by com-paring them.

That is why, in addition to utilizing some of the means we described earlier (e.g., inflections, prepositions, and word order), comparative constructions also rely on a special link that expresses the comparison. For example, consider the following constructions: "Petya sil'nee Vani." (Petya is stronger than Vanya.); "Olya temnee Soni." (Olya is darker than Sonya.). In order to understand the construction "Olya svetlee Kati." (Olya is fairer than Katya.), one must presup-pose that Katya is fair. Only by performing the additional transformation ". . . and Olya is even fairer," does the meaning of the sentence become comprehensible.

Further difficulties are encountered if the listener is asked a question which involves inversion. This situation arises if one is told, "Olya is fairer than Katya.", and then is asked "Who is darker?" In this case, additional transformations of the following type are necessary: "Olya is fairer than Katya . . . That means she is fair. And Katya is less fair . . . that means, she is darker." It is only after such auxiliary transformations that the meaning of the construction becomes clear.

Sometimes, comparative constructions become especially complex. As a result, the analysis of how they are comprehended has become an important device in intelligence testing. Classic examples may be found in Burt's tests where items which involve a twofold comparison are included (such as, "Sonya is fairer than Olya but darker than Katya."). These constructions have been studied by psycho-logists and linguists such as Clark (1969, 1970, 1974). Their research has greatly facilitated the analysis of the difficulties involved in comprehending comparative constructions.

The psychological difficulties in the comprehension of these twofold compara-tive constructions stem from the fact that one and the same object (Olya) possesses a positive feature when compared with another (she is fairer than Sonya) and a negative feature when compared to a third object (she is darker than Katya). This means that one and the same thing simultaneously enters into two relationships. Moreover, these relationships are of an opposite nature. In trying to understand this construction, a phenomenon emerges which, as Bever (1970, 1974) so aptly put it, is similar to double vision, "or "mental diplopia." There is good reason to compare the difficulty in understanding constructions of this type with the kind of "impossible" logical figures described by Gregory.

When we isolate one combination, it negates the other; and if we separate the second combination, it negates the first. The difficulty of constructions like

"Olya is fairer than Katya, but darker than Sonya." is precisely in their opposition or the dual relationship in which an object is found.

Therefore, even in relatively simple sentences one may find syntagmas which require complex transformations in order to convert a succession of words into a simultaneously perceivable scheme. This situation provides further support for the fact that syntagmatic structures involve paradigmatic principles of organization and that in certain instances sequentially presented constructions must be converted into complex hierarchically organized constructions.

COMPLEX SYNTACTICAL STRUCTURES

So far, we have been speaking of the paradigmatic components in relatively simple syntactical structures—"brat ottsa" (brother of father); "krug pod kvadratom" (a circle under a square); and "Olya svetlee Kati" (Olya is fairer than Katya.). Let us turn briefly to the problem of the semantic organization of more complex utterances. Complex sentences with subordinate clauses represent a considerably more complex form of a "hypotactic" construction than those discussed above. In these cases, we no longer are dealing with a hierarchy of individual words that are mutually subordinated to one another. Rather, we are concerned with a hierarchy of entire sentences, one of which (the main clause) governs the other (subordinate clause).

New difficulties in connection with auxiliary words ("kotoryi—which, who). When they are used, the listener must understand which member of the main clause is modified by elements of the subordinate clause. The difficulties are apparent where the subordinate clause immediately follows the main clause, becoming even more marked, however, when the subordinate clause is embedded in the main clause, thus creating the additional difficulties associated with a "noncontiguous" construction.

Let us look a bit more closely at the psychological difficulties that arise in these cases. We shall begin with the simpler constructions, which have subordinate clauses and then consider the more complex ones. Take a construction such as "Etot dom prinadlezhit mel'niku, kotoryi zhivet na krayu derevni." (This house belongs to the miller who lives at the edge of the village.). Here we are, in fact, dealing with two sentences: (1) "Dom prinadlezhit mel'niku." (The house belongs to the miller.) and (2) "Mel'nik [kotoryi] zhivet na krayu derevni." (The miller [who] lives at the edge of the village.). The auxiliary word "kotoryi" (who) is coreferential not with the house, but with the miller. The listener or reader must understand this. Naturally, the coreference of "kotoryi" (who) and "mel'nik" (miller) is simplifed by the semantic fact or marker "zhivet" (lives). It takes a person, and not a house, as its subject. However, even in this case the use of "kotoryi" (who) presents difficulties in psychological processing.

Analogous difficulties arise when a semantic marker is absent. For example: "Devochka uvidela ptitsu, kotoraya sela na kryl'tso." (The girl saw the bird which landed on the porch.). This example has two sentences: (1) "Devochka uvidela ptitsu." (The girl saw the bird.) and (2) "Ptitsa sela na kryl'tso." (The bird landed on the porch.). However, the word "kotoraya" (who, which) could be coreferential either with the word "devochka" (girl) or the word "ptitsa" (bird). We understand the construction because of the contiguity of "ptitsu" (bird) and the subordinate clause "kotoraya sela na kryl'tso" (which landed the porch).

However, even under conditions which facilitate the comprehension of these constructions, the process whereby one identifies the referent of "kotoryl" (who, which) presents a complex problem. This is precisely why this coordinating word was either reinforced by the repetition of the name of the object or was altogether avoided in older forms of the language. In the latter situation, it was often replaced by the word "on" (it, he), thereby converting the complex subordinate clause into two simple clauses.

As examples of reinforcement by repetition, we may cite the following constructions which are often seen in ancient documents: "Dom prinadlezhal rybniku, kotoryi rybnik zhil na krayu derevni." (The house belonged to the fishmonger, which fishmonger lived at the edge of the village), or "Ploshchad' razdelyala kanava, kotoraya kanava byla vyryta Prokhorom." (The square was divided by a ditch, which ditch had been dug by Prokhor). Examples of the second type of construction—in which "kotoryi" (who, which) is avoided altogether and replaced by the paratactic conjunction "i" (and)—may be found in archaic English. We come across such instances in the story of Robin Hood. For instance, the sentence "He heard Sir Guy's horn blow, who slew Robin Hood." has been changed to "He heard Sir Guy's horn blow and he slew Robin Hood." In place of the word "who," the word "and" was used. This replaces a hypotactic construction with a paratactic one.

Unfortunately, complex constructions often occur in literary and journalistic writing. The following is a quote from a newspaper: "Pidzhak Kennedi, v kotorogo popali dve puli, imel dva otverstiya, kotorye byli imi sdelany, chto oznachaet ruzh'ya, iz kotorykh strelyet ubiitsa, raspolagalis' s dvukh storon ulitsy, po kotoroi ekhal prezident." (Kenndy's jacket, which was hit by two bullets, had two holes, which were made by them, which means that the guns, which the killer used, were placed on two sides of the street along which the President was driving.). It is natural that such constructions complicate text comprehension. It is important for the psychologist to appreciate these difficulties so that he/she can provide guidance on how to simplify texts.

The above example touches on the issues involved in decoding noncontiguous constructions with multiple hierarchical subordination. These constructions have been studied by several American psychologists, in particular by Miller and his associates (1962, 1965, 1967). The difficulties that arise in comprehending such constructions are evident by examining a series of syntactic structures which are made successively more complex through the use of multiple subordinated propositions connected by "kotoryi" (who, which). The following sequence is an illustration: (a) "Kartina poluchila premiyu na vystavke." (The picture received a prize at the exhibition.); (b) "Kartina, kotoruyu narisoval khudozhnik, poluchila premiyu na vystavke." (The picture, which the artist drew, received a prize at the exhibition.); (c) "Kartina kotoruyu narisoval khudozhnik, kotoryi prodal svoi proizvedeniya v komissionnyi magazin, poluchila premiyu na vystavke." (The picture, which the artist drew, who sold his works to the commission shop received a prize at the exhibition.); (d) "Kartina, kotoruyu narisoval khudozhnik, kotoryi prodal cvoi proizvedeniya v kommisionny i magazin, kotoryi byl organizovan Soyuzom khudozhnikov, poluchila premiyu na vystavke." (The picture which the artist drew, who sold his works to the commission shop which was organized by the Union of Artists received a prize at the exhibition.).

Multiple use of subordinate clauses is illustrated in the diagram below. The items require increasingly complex forms of processing information. In order to comprehend this construction, the listener or speaker must inhibit impulsive, premature decisions and process the information in such a way that widely separated elements can be brought together to form a hierarchy of multiple subordinated clauses. Such cases highlight the psychological difficulties involved in understanding noncontiguous constructions. One must retain widely separated components of the sentence in operational memory and then join together into a single sense.

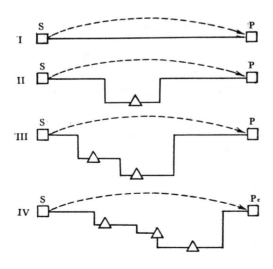

SEMANTIC INVERSION

Yet another type of construction presents significant comprehension difficulties. Until now, we have been examining the problems of understanding sentences that are linked with grammatical devices. However, there is an entire class of difficulties that arise because of the semantic structure of the sentence. A typical example is what we shall term "semantic inversion." Semantic inversion requires particularly complex transformations before the sense of a sentence can be understood.

Perhaps the simplest example of semantic inversion occurs in experiments where a subject is presented with two lines of unequal length and is asked to point to the one which is identified by an utterance. If the subject is asked "Kakaya iz linii bolee dlinnaya?" (Which one of the lines is more long?), he/she will be able to do this without difficulty. This construction includes two positive links: "bolee" (more) and "dlinnaya" (long). Similar results will be obtained in response to the question "Kakaya iz nikh bolee korotkaya?" (Which of them is more short?). In this case, the auxiliary word "bolee" (more) is not taken into account, and the hearer takes the cue from the basic semantic marker "korotkaya" (short).

However, if the same subject is asked "Kakaya iz nikh menee korotkaya?" (Which of them is less short?), greater difficulties will arise. Both "menee" (less) and "korotkaya" (short) are negatively characterized. It is only through an auxiliary transformation ("menee korotkaya znachit bolee dlinnaya"—"less short" means "more long") that the subject will be able to arrive at the correct answer. This may also be seen in the construction "Odin uchenik skazal, 'Ya ne privyk ne podchinyat'sya pravilam.'" (One student said, "I am not used to not following rules."). In this case, the subject is asked to decide whether this individual was a disciplined or an undisciplined person. On the one hand, we see here two negative characterizations. The first is "Ya ne privyk" (I am not used to), and the second is "ne podchinyat'sya pravilam" (not following rules). If we think over what is involved in this sentence, it will become clear that "ne privyk" (am not used to) and "ne podchinyat'sya" (not following) mean "privyk podchinyat'sya" (used to following), and that this means the pupil was a disciplined person. In order to understand this construction involving semantic inversion, we have to convert the double negative to a single affirmative.

As a second example, consider the sentence "On byl poslednii v klasse po skromnosti." (He was the last in the class with regard to modesty.). It is not possible to decode the meaning of this construction directly. On the one hand, "On byl poslednii" (he was the last) is concerned with something that is negative; on the other hand, "On byl skromnil" (he was modest) is concerned with something positive. However, the entire expression "poslednii po skromnosti" (last with regard to modesty) means "pervyi po samouverennosti" (first with regard to self-assuredness). In order to understand this sentence, semantic inversion is required, i.e., one must transform the given construction into its opposite.

Construction involving semantic inversion are not easy to understand directly. Their comprehension presupposes complex processing, and involves replacing a double negative with a single affirmative statement, an operation that entails inhibiting impulsive decisions.

CONCLUSION

From the above, we may arrive at a conclusion which has great significance both for psychology and for linguistics.

In addition to the syntagmatic structures of language which are involved in the production of a sequential chain of speech signals and which usually communicate events, there exist paradigmatic structures. These usually communicate relationships and entail the mastery of complex, hierarchically structured codes of language. Whereas simple syntagmatic structures can be comprehended directly, the decoding of paradigmatic structures often requires additional operations in order to transform a structure into another, more comprehensible one.

Paradigmatic structures can make use of a number of devices for their formation. Among these devices are inflections, auxiliary words, and word order. The decoding of complex paradigmatic structures may involve transformations which remove components of the construction that are difficult to understand. Comprehension can be simplified if the required grammatical and semantic devices are available, and can be made more difficult in the absence of such markers.

Only a careful linguistic and psychological analysis of the structures involved and of the devices and strategies which can be used to decode these structures will enable us to describe how meaning is encoded and decoded in language. This remains one of the main problems in psychology and linguistics.

Chapter 10
Speech Production

In this chapter we shall examine the psychological process involved in the *formation* of an utterance. This process begins with a thought, proceeds through the inner scheme of the utterance and inner speech, and culminates in expanded external speech.

THE MOTIVE OF AN UTTERANCE

The initial motive for any speech utterance is the need to formulate something in speech. The motive of an utterance may be either a demand—termed "-mand" (demand) by Skinner (1957)—or some informational communication— labeled "-tact" (contact) by Skinner. In addition, we can identify a third motivating factor, connected with the desire to formulate one's thought more clearly, which we shall provisionally call "-cept" (concept). These, then, are the three types of motives that may lie behind a speech utterance.

If none of these initial motives is present, speech will not occur. This is precisely the situation in a state of sleep or when there are massive bilateral lesions of the frontal lobes (particularly their deep parts). Another serious disturbance in the motivational sphere can be seen in autism, where the patient is totally cut off from the world. One of the symptoms of autistic patients is the complete absence of active utterances despite the retention of the potential for speech.

It is incorrect to think that speech production always entails the same structure or that motives play the same role in the production of every utterance. Extremely simple utterances, e.g., exclamations or verbal responses to some sudden stimulus, require no special motive and in the proper sense of the term, should not be called speech utterances. Involuntary utterances occur, for instance, in response to pain, fear, or stress and do not require any special complex motive; they have become automatized. Also, belonging to this class are affective exclamations, such as "To the devil with it!", "Gosh!", and sometimes words of abuse that one is accustomed to using.

It is interesting to note that these utterances often are retained even where massive lesions of the brain resulting in extreme damage to speech activity have occurred. We can cite the instance of a patient suffering from severe disturbance of speech functions (aphasia) who could not formulate the simplest request or elementary communication. The patient broke into a storm of abuse when he became angry over attempts to remove him to a mental hospital, abuse clearly indicating expanded speech—absolutely unexpected of such a patient. However, when the state of stress had passed, all speech faculties of the patient remained impaired as before. The ability to speak appeared to be extremely short-lived. It is apparent that the patient's exclamations were not regulated by any complex cognitive motives and therefore could not be considered to be part of complex speech communication.

In addition to simple forms of speech, there are more complex forms. These comprise the class of genuine communications. Foremost among them is *dialogic speech*. An example of dialogic speech is a conversation in which the subject responds to questions. A characteristic feature of this type of speech is that the process is shared by two persons. A question is asked by one of them and an answer is provided by the other. The motive for the utterance is the question asked by one of the interlocutors, the other needs no inner motive for the production of an utterance. As with involuntary speech, a firm, independent motive for the utterance is not required. In this case, speech is more a reactive process than an active one.

Psychologists are quite aware of the different forms of dialogic speech. The simplest form involves reponses to questions where an answer simply repeats or reproduces a part of the question and no special, new, creative activity is required. Examples of this type of dialogue are fragments like "Did you eat today? Yes, I ate." or "Does your head ache? Yes, it aches." In these cases, there is no need to search for the source of the utterance. The source is part of the interlocutor's question, and the utterance itself turns out to be only a reproduction of a fragment already included in that question. All that is needed is an echolalic or imitative reproduction of a part of the question. This form of speech may remain unimpaired even in patients with massive lesions of the brain, when other complex forms of activity are disrupted. Massive lesions of the frontal lobes which almost completely prevent the performance of any activity typically do not affect echolalic responses to questions.

Of course there are more complex forms of dialogic speech. Among them are responses to specific questions. More specifically, we are concerned with cases in which the answer does not reproduce a part of the question. Here, the subject himself/herself must actively find and formulate the answer, introducing something new into the conversation. For example: "What did you eat for dinner today?" followed by the reply "Today I had cutlets for dinner, and after cutlets I had stewed fruit."; or, "What are you doing this evening?" followed by the reply "I shall study for a while in the evening and then perhaps go visit some friends." The motives for the utterance can, to some extent, be found in the question, but they differ from the example cited earlier where it was enough for an answer to give an echolalic reproduction of the question or part of it. Such a technique will not work in this case. The subject must search for the answer himself/herself, selecting one of several possible alternatives and limiting the extraneous associations that arise.

This form of dialogic speech is psychologically more complex than the earlier form. The subject must carefully listen to the question since this creates the basic motive for his/her utterance. Then he/she must select one of several alternatives and formulate a new, active utterance. It is clear that this type of response presents a far more complex form of speech. It is therefore understandable that in cases of massive lesions of the frontal lobe where the echolalic response remains intact, the second type of response becomes very difficult or impossible.

A third form of speech is independent *monologic speech*. It does not occur in response to an interlocutor's question, but is the realization of the speaker's own thought. Both motive and thought must be sufficiently firm, having passed through a sequence of steps in the process of creating a speech program. If this inner motive is lacking, or if the subject is unable to formulate such a motive, the production of expanded monologic speech will be impossible. This happens, for example, in the case of patients with severe damage to the frontal lobes. Problems also arise if the person cannot firmly retain his/her initial thought which would generate the program of his/her utterance. This may also mean that the ability to formulate monologic speech will be lost even if simple forms of dialogic speech are retained.

Disturbance of monologic speech as a result of the absence of a motive clearly distinguishes frontal lobe patients from other patients. In the latter case, the motive for a speech utterance is present and there is no inactivity syndrome, but the patient may suffer from a disruption of the means of speech. Thus, patients with different forms of aphasia (e.g., with word finding difficulties) are characterized by the fact that they actively search for ways to form utterances. It is precisely this active search for possible means of speech communication and expression of thoughts that sharply distinguishes them from frontal lobe patients. Hence, we can distinguish those cases where monologic speech is absent due to inactivity from those cases where it is attributable to the impairment of the means of speech communication. As we shall see, this distinction plays a very important role in the psychological analysis of localized brain lesions.

THE UTTERANCE PLAN

The motive is only the initial factor in speech production. In and of itself, it does not have any specific content. The next stage in the process of speech production is the *utterance plan*, which some linguists term *the initial semantic graph*. The content of the utterance is determined at this level. The overall scheme of the utterance is established at this point. It is the first point at which the *theme* of the utterance (that which the speech will be about) is separated from the *rheme* (the new material to be included in the utterance). Psychologically, this may be described as the stage in which the general subjective sense of the utterance is formed. A characteristic of this stage is that the subject begins to understand what it is that is to be transformed into an utterance. Later, this subjective sense will be converted into a system of expanded speech meanings that are comprehensible to others.

This brings us to one of the central problems of psychology. One would have supposed that the concept of a thought is one of the clearest notions in psychology, but this turns out not to be true. However paradoxical this may sound, thought remains largely uninvestigated in psychology. Several factors contribute to this paradox. First, analyses of the relationship between a thought and an utterance usually are based on the erroneous assumption that a thought is some kind of ready-made formation and that speech serves merely to *embody* it. As Vygotsky pointed out long ago, the process of the transition from thought to speech actually is much more complex than generally assumed. According to him, *speech does not simply embody a thought*. Rather, a thought passes through several stages in the process of becoming *formed*, or, as Vygotsky said, *a thought is completed in speech*. This is a complex process of the formation of a speech utterance that still remains to be investigated. It involves the conversion of an unclear thought into clear and expanded chain of speech.

The second factor that makes the psychological description of thought so complex is a methodological problem—the difficulty of separating the subject matter of thought from the act of observing this thought. It is not easy to reflect on the flow of one's own conscious thought and to continue thinking. Naturally, this interferes with describing the processes involved in thought and its role in speech production. These difficulties account for the fact that attempts to describe thought have made little headway.

As an illustration of these problems, we may cite the research conducted by the so-called Würzburg School, the first school of psychologists to make thinking their special topic of investigation. Among those psychologists was a group of German researchers (such as Kulpe, Ach, Messer, and Bühler) who were active at the end of the 19th and beginning of the 20th century. The methodology for investigating thought used by these psychologists was as follows. A subject was given a problem to solve and was asked to describe the precise nature of thought involved. They were asked to report whether this thought involved sensory images, whether it included elements of speech, etc. In order to investigate this, Würzburg School psychologists typically gave their subjects complex intellectual problems. For example, a complex sentence was read to the subject and he/she was asked whether it was correct and what its main intellectual content was. Or he/she was asked to respond to a question by describing the processes that occurred while at the same time comprehending it. It is from this that the researchers hoped to discover what happens during the process of extracting the main sense of a sentence. Since the subjects in these studies were usually highly educated people, such as professors and senior lecturers in psychology, the investigators thought that their results would be reliable.

The results of these investigations were paradoxical. The subjects agreed overwhelmingly that the thinking process involved neither sensory images nor words. After listening to the sentences, subjects usually did not identify any sensory images. When sensory images were perceived, they tended to distract subjects from the thought that gave rise to them. At the same time, it was shown that the comprehension of sense did not necessarily require any verbal formulation. This finding resulted in a negative description of the act of thinking as an act that involved neither imagery nor verbal formulation.

The members of the Würzburg School thought that they could identify at least two necessary components in a psychological description of the thought process. On the one hand, they identified the *intention or directionality* toward a solution, and, on the other, they identified the act of *"perceiving a relationship."* The latter component involved the emergence of a ready solution, which is sometimes tied to a particular logical feeling. Other experiments of the Würzburg School led to similar conclusions. These studies were conducted in order to analyze subjects' understanding and selection of logical relationships (part-whole, whole-part, genus-species, species-genus). These studies led to the conclusion that sensory (image-bearing) and verbal components play only a minor role in thinking and sometimes are altogether absent. Obviously these conclusions are unsatisfactory, because instead of providing a positive description of thinking, they characterize it in a negative way. Clearly, the relation between thought and expanded speech could not be understood on the basis of these studies.

Vygotsky proposed an important innovation in the scientific investigation of thought. He argued against the notion that a thought is a completely developed formation and that speech serves simply to embody it. Instead, he argued that thought is *completed* in the word, i.e., he argued that the *thought itself is formed with the help of the word or speech.* This argument was based on the fact that the transformation of an unclear thought into clear speech is an extremely complex process that passes through several stages. According to this approach, one of psychology's most fundamental tasks is to investigate the *transition from subjective sense, which is not yet formulated in words and is comprehensible only to the subject, to a system of meanings formulated in words and comprehensible to others.* That is, the conversion of sense to meaning is the central issue in speech production.

What a speaker wishes to convey is already subjectively known to him/her. The question is how this gives rise to an utterance, how the initial, subjective sense is transformed into an expanded system of verbal meanings, comprehensible to others. Clearly, this process of speech production, or the conversion of an initial subjective sense into an expanded objective system of meanings, is comprised of a number of stages.

THE INITIAL SEMANTIC GRAPH

We shall now deal with the distinct stages in the complex process of transforming a thought into expanded speech. Until recently, very little was known about the structure of the basic thought underlying an utterance. An important development in this area has been made in recent years in generative approaches to linguistics. Investigators in this field have taken on the task of examining the stages in the process of speech production. Among the many linguists and psychologists who examined this problem were de Saussure (1922) in France; Hjelmslev (1936, 1954) in Sweden; Rommetveit (1968, 1974) in Norway; Bloomfield (1926, 1933), Chomsky (1957, 1965), Lakoff (1971, 1972), and McCawley (1968, 1972) in the U.S.; Halliday (1970, 1973) in Great Britain; and Apresyan (1974), Zholkovskii (1964, 1967), and others in the USSR.

The notion of a semantic graph represents an attempt to describe the structure of the thought that is later converted into expanded speech. Initially, the semantic graph of an utterance involves two parts. In linguistics those are termed the "theme" and the "rheme." The part that identifies what is already known and serves as the subject of the utterance is usually designated as the theme. The part that identifies something new about this subject and introduces some new data into the utterance is the predicative structure of the utterance and is the rheme. These two parts constitute the initial thought or the system of simultaneous connections that figure in the future utterance. These connections make up the semantic model. This model consists of a group of separate sets or elements of the utterance and a group of vectors or connections among these elements. It is this model that provides the unity or coherence to the utterance as a closed sense system.

Let us consider the example of an utterance that has been analyzed in detail by several Soviet investigators: "Vanya tverdo obeshchal Pete, chto vecherom on primet Mashu samym teplym, serdechnym obrazom." (Vanya firmly promised Petya that in the evening he would receive Masha in the warmest, most cordial manner.). This sentence contains the two basic components of theme and rheme. The theme, or basic subject of the utterance, is Vanya. The rheme of the utterance is the fact that he will receive Masha in the evening and that this meeting with her will occur in the warmest, most cordial manner. Thus the sentence contains the idea that Vanya expects Masha in the evening, that he will receive her cordially, and that he will therefore have warm feelings toward her. The rheme, or predicate, enriches this theme by eliciting several semantic connections.

In order to turn this semantic graph into an expanded speech utterance, one must carry out another extremely significant operation—the operation of *converting this semantic model or graph into a scheme of a sequentially organized speech utterance*. This necessity leads to the next stage in the formation of a speech utterance—*inner speech*. This was a major concern for Vygotsky.

INNER SPEECH

Inner speech is a necessary stage in the production of external speech. In order to convert a nonsequential semantic graph into a sequentially organized utterance, it must pass through a special stage involved with the transition from thought to the speech utterance. By passing through this stage, the inner *sense* is transformed into a system of expanded, syntactically organized speech *meanings*. The nonsequential semantic graph is converted into the form of a successively unfolding "tree." The transformation of the initial thought into a sequentially organized speech utterance is not carried out in a single, instantaneous step. It involves a complex recoding of the initial, semantic graph into a syntagmatic speech schema. This is why Vygotsky argued that thought is not embodied in the word, but is *completed* in the word. It is in this process that inner speech plays a decisive role.

Let us recall some of the points we made earlier about inner speech. It is known that inner speech appears in a child when he/she encounters difficulties in a task setting. This inner speech emerges at a comparatively late stage on the basis of earlier expanded utterances addressed to others. These utterances later begin to be addressed to the speaker himself/herself. The development of inner speech passes through several stages, including external speech, fragmented external speech, whispered speech, and finally abbreviated speech for oneself.

Inner speech does not have the same morphological structure as expanded speech. It is reduced and amorphous and has a predicative function, due to the fact that the subject of the utterance (the theme) is known to the speaker and therefore is absent in inner speech. What is primarily represented in inner speech is the predicative part of the future utterance (the rheme). The predicative character of inner speech is the basis for the conversion of the initial thought into an expanded, syntagmatically structured, speech utterance. Although inner speech consists only of fragmentary words, it retains those functions which characterize these words and their potential bonds. For example, a word such as "to buy" in inner speech retains its valencies (to buy *something*, etc.); when the predicate "odolzhit'" (to lend, to borrow) appears in inner speech, it retains all of its rich valencies (to borrow from *someone*, to borrow *something*, to borrow *for a certain period*). The retention of these potential bonds characterizes inner speech and serves as the foundation for the expanded speech utterance. Thus we see that inner speech, itself arising through the contraction of earlier expanded speech forms, retains the capacity to "re-expand" and to turn into syntagmatically organized external speech.

As we shall see later, if inner speech is disturbed (as it is when certain types of brain lesions occur) and the potential lexical functions connected with its fragments are destroyed, then the clear meaning of the grammatical subject of the utterance may be lost. In such cases, the initial intention cannot be transformed into a syntactically organized utterance, and we may witness the peculiar phenomenon of a patient's being able to repeat words spoken to him/her with ease but not being able to expand them into a complete utterance. The patient will be limited to single word naming, thus turning an integrated utterance into a succession of isolated nominative units or names. We shall return to this syndrome, which is characterized by "telegraphic style," in a later chapter.

THE FORMATION OF AN EXPANDED SPEECH UTTERANCE

Let us now consider the last stage in the process of converting a thought into an expanded speech utterance. In spite of its great importance, this stage has been studied much less by linguists and psychologists than the stages we discussed earlier. There are two crucial factors in analyzing an expanded speech utterance. First, the utterance is part of ongoing social interaction which involves the communication of information from one person to another. Second, it is composed not of a single sentence, but of a chain of mutually connected sentences. These sentences make up a single integrated system and possess the quality of a single integrated structure.

The extreme complexity involved in integrating successive utterances into a coherent text (as opposed to the production of an isolated sentence) has been noted by many writers, beginning with Humboldt (1905, 1907). Humboldt pointed out that the language used in communication is not "Ergon" (i.e., related to individual things and relations), but "Energeia" (i.e., included in the complex process of communication that unfolds across time). This idea was also discussed by several writers of much later period: Austin (1962, 1969); Grice (1957, 1968); Halliday

(1973, 1975); Lakoff (1971, 1972); Rommetveit (1968, 1974); Wertsch (1974, 1975); Wittengenstein (1972). They pointed out that sentences always occur in a practical or a speech *context* and that the context must take into account not only the intention of the speaker, but also the attitude of the listener. These sentences together form a text and cannot be studied outside of their context, or, to use Rommetveit's (1974) term, they cannot be studied "in vacuo." In this connection, writers such as Rommetveit (1968, 1974), Halliday (1973, 1975) and Wertsch (1974, 1975) pointed out that sentences included in a text possess not only referential meaning (which points to a specific object or event), but also social-context meaning (which is concerned with the communicative context).

It is precisely because of this, as these writers pointed out, that a bare linguistic analysis of speech production is insufficient. Such linguistic analysis must be viewed as only one of the factors in a broader *psychological*, and perhaps even sociopsychological, analysis (Rommetveit, 1968, 1974; Halliday, 1973; Wertsch, 1974, 1975). A psychological analysis takes into consideration the communicative situation, the motives of the speaker, the nature of the information being conveyed, the attitude of the hearer, etc.

The speech production processes we have discussed so far do not yet provide a complete account of the expanded speech utterance. In order to develop such an account, we must examine the theme, or what the utterance is about and the rheme, or what the utterance will convey—i.e., we must examine the counterparts of the inner speech theme and rheme in the external utterance. The inner speech entities must be substantially expanded into an entire chain of connections in a complex program. One of the most important requirements of this, of course, is that both the theme and the rheme should remain stable. The set created by the task of conveying certain information should be able to inhibit other influences which might divert attention from it. If this does not happen, then the expanded text loses its coherence. It ceases to be a closed semantic system and becomes a system that is exposed to all kinds of outside influences. We shall have occasion below to deal with this kind of breakdown when we consider early stages in ontogenesis and certain pathological conditions, where the overall text ceases to be subordinated to the initial goal. Instead, we find individual, unconnected fragments rather than a text with a single coherent purpose. These facts support the notion that a speech utterance can profitably be considered as a complex form of speech *activity*, which in principle possesses the same psychological structure as any other form of psychological activity.

The notion of activity has been studied extensively in Soviet psychology (e.g., A. N. Leont'ev, 1959, 1975). As is true with all other forms of mental activity, we must identify in speech activity the motive which gives rise to it, the goal that it serves, and the task that arises as a result of setting this goal in a certain context. That is, our analysis of speech activity must distinguish between the individual stages or *acts* and the *operations* that carry out these acts. Such an analysis must take into account all the units that make up speech production (A. A. Leont'ev, 1969, 1974).

Two very important factors in speech production (a form of speech activity) are the formulation of an utterance's goal and tailoring the goal directed processes to specific concrete conditions confronting the speaker. That is, the goal directed processes can vary, depending on the communicative context, the nature of the information the speaker wishes to convey and the person to whom this information is addressed. Speech production presupposes an adequate operational memory. Without it the speaker cannot carry out his/her tasks. It must rely on a complex system of "strategies" to make it possible for the speaker to isolate the sense of the utterance and inhibit influences which could divert attention from that sense— or, this operational memory must allow the selection of those speech formulations which correspond to the task.

All of this presupposes that speech production involves the creation of an initial schema. This schema gives rise to a succession of connections in an utterance as well as the sense included in its components. At the same time, an utterance necessarily involves constant control of its components. In complex cases, it involves the conscious selection of the necessary speech components from among many alternatives. The selection may take the form of probes which occur in the flow of "intellectual activity." Intellectual activity has been examined in recent years from the theoretical perspective developed by Gal'perin (1959, 1976) and his collaborators. Their research provided the foundation for viewing the basic units of a speech production not in terms of individual words or sentences, but in entire meaningful groups which are distinguished by the speaker. The speaker divides the entire text into a chain of successive meaningful components or "chunks," thus providing an adequate transition from one meaningful group to the next (Miller, 1967). As we shall see, the psychological structure that ensures a smooth expanded speech utterance can be different in different forms of speech (e.g., oral and written speech). It depends both on the complexity of the task and on the degree of automation of the speech processes. All these factors play a role in the preservation of the unity of a text.

THE ONTOGENESIS OF THE SPEECH UTTERANCE

It would be incorrect to assume that expanded speech utterances appear suddenly in ontogenesis. Psychologists are quite aware that speech production undergoes protracted development during childhood. This has been recognized during recent decades as the result of the work of several psychologists—e.g., Braine (1971); Brown (1973); Halliday (1975); Leopold (1939–1949); Slobin (1970).

Facts emerging from this research indicate that children's speech production begins with isolated words and proceeds to isolated sentences. Only in the last stages is speech production characterized by complex expanded texts. Halliday (1975) correctly noted that even the first forms of children's vocal responses are always addressed to adults and serve as the most primitive form of verbal communication. For example, in the English speaking environment that he studied, Halliday found that the sound "eh" (with a steady tone) in a certain context may mean "give me" or "do this." The same sound, when pronounced tensely and with a high tone, may mean "do this immediately," but when pronounced softly and in a falling tone, it may mean "I am sleepy" or "that's nice." This indicates that even during early pre-linguistic stages a child's vocalizations serve as simple forms of communication. At this stage the compositional and intonational components, as well as the practical communicative context, must be taken into account.

The child's speech possesses many of the same features during the following stage, the stage of holophrastic utterances, and also during the subsequent stage of utterances, and also during the subsequent stage of "two-word sentences." These stages have been studied very carefully by Brown (1973). During these stages, one ought to examine the individual lexical components which are at first diffuse and later become more complex grammatically. However, at these stages speech remains context bound, and the meaning of the child's utterances remains incomprehensible if we do not take situational and intonational factors into account.

The development of the communicative function of a child's speech is by no means complete when the child begins to master simple grammatical forms and begins to reply appropriately to questions. Observations show that even at this stage utterances do not represent a firm "closed semantic system," i.e., the child's speech has not yet acquired the firm semantic coherence which is an important feature of a mature speaker's utterances.

The characteristics of a text at this stage are easy to identify if we give a child of 2½ to 3 years of age a semantic problem such as telling us what he/she has just seen at the zoo. A child of this age may begin to carry out the assigned task correctly by enumerating everything that he/she saw in the zoo. However, the circumstances that create a closed semantic system seem to be so unstable that he/she is easily distracted. Irrelevant facts float to the surface of the child's consciousness in a seemingly uncontrolled way. His/her story therefore may take on the following character: "Well, I saw a bear in the zoo, and he is so big, and everyone is frightened of him . . . And you know Kolya has a dog; he barks and guards the house and they feed him meat . . . . "

Only gradually, as the child reaches school age, do both the motive and the schema of the extended text assume a firmly established character. At this point, the execution of this program begins to be based on a closed system of complex narration and is limited to the specific task. It is possible that the transition to this phase of speech production is closely connected with the formation of inner speech in the child. We know that inner speech appears much later in ontogenesis than external speech. That is why a child, who already possesses external speech, as manifested in social dialogue, may still be unable to produce stable, coherent monologic speech. This is largely attributable to the fact that inner speech, with all of its predicative functions, is still not sufficiently well formed. Precisely because of this, the transition to monologic speech is still incomplete, even while dialogic speech is mastered quite well. Only when external speech has become abbreviated and converted into inner speech does it become possible to carry out the opposite process, i.e., the expansion of this inner speech into an external, connected text with its characteristic semantic coherence.

A great deal of research has demonstrated the complexity involved in mastering basic morphological structures and lexical and syntactic forms. We would argue that once a child has mastered these operational components of expanded speech, he/she goes through an equally complex path to develop real speech activity. This activity is guided by a motive, is subject to a specific goal, and constitutes a constantly regulated, closed semantic system. The ontogenesis of the ability to produce complex, expanded texts is a process still insufficiently studied. We can only hope that this gap will be filled by the coming generations of psychologists.

SUMMARY

By way of general summary, we would like to stress that one should not think of speech production as a simple act of converting a ready-made thought into an equally ready-made system of speech formulations and then into an expanded text. There is every reason to agree with Vygotsky that thought is completed, rather than embodied in speech and that the transition from thought into speech involves several stages. First is the motive of the utterance, followed next by the initial thought, a psychological structure that still remains largely a mystery. Afterwards, the thought, which includes meanings that are comprehensible to the speaker but are not yet expanded enough to be understood by others, is converted into a schema through the apparatus of inner speech. These components of speech activity are involved in communication and have the same structure as many other mature human activity. Psychology still lacks sufficiently reliable data to characterize the individual stages of this complex process. This task will constitute an important branch of future research.

Chapter 11

Basic Forms of the Speech Utterance: Oral (Monologic and Dialogic) and Written Speech[15]

This chapter examines the basic forms of the speech utterance including an analysis of the mechanisms and features that distinguish one form of speech utterance from another. We usually deal with two forms of expanded external speech, *oral speech* and *written speech*. Oral speech may, in turn, be divided into two basic forms, *dialogic speech* and *monologic speech*. The main issues in the psychological investigation of these two forms of speech are how linguistic (synsemantic) and extralinguistic (sympractical) elements are related and how grammatical forms and semantic structures are used in each of them. We shall examine the structure of each of these speech forms separately.

[15]In this chapter, the term "speech" often appears where "language" would normally occur in English texts (e.g., "written speech" instead of "written language"). This represents a more literal translation than is sometimes used. The distinction between speech ("rech'") and language ("yazyk") is important, however, since use of the former term indicates an emphasis on an active psychological process or activity, whereas use of the latter reflects an emphasis on the linguistic code. Therefore, the terms have been kept separate.—*J. V. Wertsch*

ORAL SPEECH

Oral speech may occur in three basic forms: exclamations, dialogic speech, and monologic speech. The first form, exclamations, cannot be termed speech in the real sense. It is not the communication of any specific information or relationship with the help of language. Rather, exclamations are affective speech productions, elicited by any type of unexpected stimulus. For that reason, we shall not examine this form of speech in detail.

Oral dialogic speech may occur in the form of answers to questions or in the form of conversation, while oral monologic speech may occur in the form of a narrative. The narrative may be descriptive (i.e., the communication of a certain event), or it may take the form of an analysis of the logical and causal relations involved in an event. The obvious question arises, then, as to whether oral dialogic speech and oral monologic speech have an identical grammatical structure.

ORAL DIALOGIC SPEECH

There is every reason to believe that oral dialogic speech should possess unique grammatical characteristics, both because of its origin and because of its psychological structure. Oral dialogic speech is different from monologic speech in several respects. First, an utterance in oral dialogic speech does not originate with an individual's ready-made internal motive, intention, or thought. The processes involved in an utterance are shared by two persons, one who asks questions and another who replies. Consequently, the speaker may not have his/her own motive for an utterance.

In addition, other important features distinguish dialogic speech from monologic speech. Among them is the crucial fact that the person answering a question is already aware of the subject or the general theme of the conversation. Very often the conversation takes place in a clear-cut situation, and knowledge of the situation may govern the speech utterance of the person replying to the question. This awareness of the situation is the second important feature which determines the grammatical structure of oral dialogic speech.

The third characteristic of oral dialogic speech is that participants can rely on extralinguistic elements, i.e., they do not have to rely solely on the system of grammatical structures. Accordingly, while mimicry, gestures, intonation, and the use of pauses are involved in all forms of oral speech, they play an especially important role in oral dialogic speech.

All of these factors help determine the grammatical structure of oral dialogic speech. One structural characteristic of this kind of speech is that it allows a considerable degree of grammatical incompleteness. Various parts of a fully expanded utterance may be omitted or replaced either through an awareness of the situation or through pheonmena such as gestures, mimicry, and intonation. Precisely this makes possible what is known in linguistics as ellipsis, i.e., the omission of elements of a fully expanded utterance.

Despite this grammatical incompleteness, oral dialogic speech is quite adequate for communication. The fact that a maximum expansion of utterances is not obligatory for oral dialogic speech can be illustrated by several examples. Dialogic speech variants range from extremely contracted and reduced forms where great significance is attached to situational and gestural-intonational components, to the most complete and expanded forms of oral dialogic speech. These latter cases rely on synsemantic or grammatically expanded speech structures rather than sympractical forms.

Let us examine some instances of dialogic speech which vary along this dimension. First, imagine that several people are waiting for a bus and are exchanging short remarks with each other, e.g., "Is it coming?" "Yes." "Which one?" "No. 5." The question "Is it coming?" with the response "Yes.", and the question "Which one?" with the answer "No. 5.", do not possess any stable independent meaning of their own. They become comprehensible only when the speech situation is understood by both participants in the dialogue. In this case, the theme of the conversation remains beyond the bounds of the speech utterance. It is unnecessary for the person asking the question to formulate his/her question in a fully expanded utterance (e.g., "What do you think, is a bus coming or not?"). Similarly, it would be pointless to formulate the second question in an expanded form (e.g., "What in your opinion is the number of the bus that is approaching?"). Since the point of the conversation is understood, the speaker only mentions the rheme (i.e., what can be said about the bus). In actuality, the content of the rheme is also not made completely explicit. Only certain fragments of it appear ("Yes."; "No. 5."). It would be strange if this person had responded with complete grammatical forms—"Yes, it seems the bus is coming." or "Probably it is Bus No. 5.". Grammatical completeness in these cases is superfluous, it is quite enough to be aware of the situation. An intonation expressing regret if the number of the bus is different from the one expected, or satisfaction if it is the same, makes the situation clear.

ORAL MONOLOGIC SPEECH

Oral monologic speech (e.g., narrative) differs from oral dialogic speech in several important respects. At the same time, it retains several features common to all forms of oral speech. In oral monologic speech, the speaker is responsible for both the motive of the utterance and for its general scheme. The motive and the scheme must be sufficiently stable to determine the flow of the entire expanded, monologic utterance. This utterance, in turn, can be divided into meaningful chunks. These form an integrated, "closed" structure. The program which is created by the motive and the general scheme of the utterance must inhibit extraneous associations that could destroy this closed system. Furthermore, this program must restrain the speaker from repeating again and again the elements of the utterance that have already occurred. That is, the program must inhibit those forms of mental processes often termed "perseveration." It is easy to see what would happen to a report or a lecture if the program guiding the utterance were unstable, if the monologue ceased being a closed semantic system, or if the subject were to be constantly diverted to uncontrolled, extraneous associations or inert stereotypes. Precisely these phenomena can be observed during early stages of speech development and in certain forms of speech pathology caused by brain damage.

The organization of expanded (monologic) speech depends on the stability of the motive and the ease with which the initial semantic graph moves through inner speech to deep, and then surface, syntactic structures. In addition, however, important features of monologic oral speech also depend on the speaker's goal and on the concrete conditions in which the expanded oral speech is embedded. If we are dealing with a simple narration of something one has seen or experienced, and if this narration is addressed to an interlocutor who is already familiar with the general situation and shares the speaker's motive, oral monologic speech can flow quite smoothly. In those situations, grammatical incompleteness or ellipsis is sometimes acceptable, and there may be no need to use special devices for identifying the components that comprise the utterance.

If we are dealing with a connected, sequential account of information, such as that found in lectures and reports, the semantic structure of monologic speech must be significantly different. The speaker's task is to present the information in a consistent and logically structured form. This involves highlighting the most significant parts and maintaining a clear logical transition from one point to another. For this reason, considerable time may have to be spent on the preparation of this type of oral monologic speech. The lecturer himself/herself must highlight the semantic chunks, place them in clear logical patterns, and make decisions about the use of devices such as intonation, pauses, and stress during different points in the narration. Such preparation, naturally, requires a great deal of experience. Only the experienced lecturer, narrating familiar information, can shorten this period of preparation significantly.

In situations where a speaker is trying to make the listener conscious of the inner sense and emotional motives behind a text rather than simply conveying information, monologic speech takes on a different structure. A typical example of this kind of speech is the speech of an actor. The psychological analysis of this type of speech as well as the pedagogical preparation required for producing it have been carefully examined in Russian and Soviet literature by such outstanding theoreticians of the theater as Stanislavskii (1951, 1956) and Knebel' (1970; also see Knebel' and Luria, 1971). The experienced director who wishes to develop an actor's oral (and especially monologic) speech, does not give an actor the complete script of his/her role at the beginning of the rehearsal period. Rather, the first task is to master the character, to explore the motives of the role the actor is portraying, so as to understand exactly how the character would act in various settings. Only after a period of "living" the role is the actor given the script and begins trying to master it.

Clearly, this process requires a prolonged period, during which the role becomes an inseparable part of the character. The actor's utterances (including monologic utterances) begin to be interpreted through the character. Hence the actor begins to make use of intonational and gestural devices, and his/her monologic speech aquires the smooth flow that gives the audience the impression of naturalness and sincerity. Again, it is only with a very experienced and talented actor that this process of role preparation may be shortened.

Thus oral monologic speech provides the best demonstration of the fact that thought is not simply embodied in speech. Rather, we see that the production of oral monologic speech represents a complex process of transforming the initial intention into connected speech, in which the sense becomes clear. Vygotsky noted this fact in his notion that "thought is completed in speech."

There are several characteristics unique to oral monologic speech. However, this form of speech also has several things in common with oral dialogic speech. For example, oral monologic speech is addressed to a living interlocutor who hears it and responds. These responses enable the speaker to modify oral monologic speech during communication, i.e., to omit what is already known, to add and elaborate what is not known, etc. In this way, oral monologic speech in certain instances may be transformed into a latent form of dialogic speech and may be modified by external forces, thereby revealing various stages of development.

Like oral dialogic speech, oral monologic speech also has at its disposal expressive devices or markers other than the linguistic code. Among these are prosodic markers like intonation, stress, and pauses, as well as extralinguistic devices like mimicry and expressive gestures. All of these devices can be used to supplement the linguistic code by emphasizing what is new and important or by revealing the significant elements of sense. It is not difficult to see that changes in the use of devices such as intonation and mimicry can impart a different sense to identical syntactic constructions. Like oral dialogic speech, oral monologic speech also allows for ellipsis. Its grammatical structure sometimes approximates the incomplete grammatical structure of dialogic speech. Finally, oral monologic speech may be tied to practical action in different ways. In some cases, it may accompany practical action; in others it may be isolated from practical action and may assume the character of a special, independent speech act. In both circumstances, the grammatical structure of oral monologic speech may vary.

It is customary to distinguish two main forms of oral monologic speech. Some psychologists have used the terms "drama" and "epic" to identify these forms. The dramatic construction of oral monologic speech is a reproduction of the real situation being depicted in the communication. In addition to the grammatical structures of the expanded speech utterance, gestures, intonations, and action may also be used. The grammatical structure of this form of oral monologic speech is characterized by several devices. As a rule, direct forms of speech, which reproduce forms of everyday dialogic speech, are used. Thus intonational and prosodic components play an important role.

Let us turn to an example of dramatic monologic speech. It depicts a woman describing a scene she has witnessed in a bazaar:

> I approach her, and she shouts, "Why are you coming up here? Where do you think you are going, breaking into the line?" And I say to her, "It's none of your business, I know myself where I am going!" And she says, "Haven't you been brought up right?"....

It is easy to see that this form of monologic speech directly reproduces the situation that it describes. That is why sympractical and extralinguistic devices as well as the direct speech forms which occur in the dialogic speech play such an important role. Therefore, in this form of oral monologic speech, ellipsis is allowed.

A quite different form is found in cases of monologic speech that psychologists would identify as epic. A typical example is the epic of the blind poet Homer, who renders his narrative in a monotonous, outwardly unvarying manner. A person who makes use of epic speech uses almost no expressive means. This speech practically never allows direct forms which would reproduce the typical structures of dialogic speech—precisely why this form of speech does not make use of the rich system of extralinguistic markers and does not permit ellipsis. It relies on a grammatically expanded form and uses indirect speech and complex forms of government. Thus, in dramatic oral monologic speech, the form approximates the form used in action and dialogue, whereas in epic oral monologic speech the form approximates written language.

WRITTEN SPEECH

Written, monologic speech may appear in the forms of written communication, written reports, written narration, written expression of ideas or arguments, etc. The structure of written speech differs radically from that of oral dialogic and oral monologic speech, differences based on a number of psychological factors. Written monologic speech is speech without an addressee. This means that the speaker is solely responsible for the motive and the initial plan. If the motive is contact (-tact) or a demand (-mand), the writer must mentally represent to whom the speech is addressed. In this case, the speaker does not witness any immediate responses to his/her communication and has no external stimuli that can serve to modify his/her mistakes. The writer is solely responsible for controlling the activity involved in the production of written speech. If the motive of this speech is to make a concept more precise (-cept), written speech again has no external addressee, so the person writes only in order to clarify, verbalize, and expand an idea.

Written speech has almost no extralinguistic expressive devices. It does not presuppose that the addressee has knowledge of the situation. Consequently, it cannot make use of gestures, mimicry, intonation and pauses. These devices, which can play a role in monologic oral speech, can be utilized only minimally in written monologic speech through italics, paragraph divisions, etc. Thus, the information conveyed by written speech must depend primarily on the appropriate use of linguistic devices which allow the writer to produce grammatically expanded utterances. It follows that written speech is maximally synsemantic and that the grammatical means it uses must be adequate for the expression of information. The writer must structure communication in a style that will enable the reader to be able to move from the expanded, external speech to the inner sense of the text without relying on anything except the grammatical forms of the written communication.

It is also important to note that the process of understanding written speech differs radically from the process of understanding oral speech. What is written can always be reread. One can return at will to all the links in the communication, something that is impossible in the understanding of oral speech.

There is yet another basic difference in the psychological structure of written and oral speech. The difference is due to the fact that these two types of speech have different origins. Oral speech evolves naturally in the process of social interaction between children and adults. This speech is sympractical in the earlier stages and later becomes a special independent form of oral speech communication. As we have already seen, elements of the practical situation, such as gestures and mimicry, continue to play a role in oral speech even at later stages.

Written speech is quite different in its origins and psychological structure. Written speech emerges as the result of special learning. It begins with the conscious process of mastering all the devices of the written expression of thought. In the earlier stages of its formation, the object involved is not so much the thought which is to be expressed as it is the technical devices of designating the sounds, letters, and words. These devices are not the focus of consciousness in comprehending oral dialogic or monologic speech. This is exactly why a child who is learning to write is concerned not so much with thoughts as with the means of their external expression. The modes of expression of the sounds, letters, and words are the object upon which the child's conscious action focuses. It is only later that these become the object of subsidiary operations.

As opposed to oral speech, which is formed in the process of actual social interaction, written speech is from the very beginning a conscious voluntary act in which the means of expression are the main object and focus of attention. The problems raised by the need to distinguish phonemes, represent these phonemes with letters, combine letters into words, and move from one word to another remain, for a long time, the object of conscious action in written speech. It is only when written speech is automatized that these conscious actions are transformed into unconscious operations.

Thus written speech differs from oral speech both in its origin and in its psychological structure. The main reason for these differences lies in the fact that written speech requires a conscious analysis of the means of expression. For this reason, written speech involves several levels which are not distinguished in oral speech. Written speech involves several processes at the phonemic level, such as the search for individual sounds and their contrasts, the coding of individual sounds into letters, and the combination of individual sounds and letters into complete words. To a much greater extent than in oral speech, written speech also involves decisions at the lexical level. These might involve choosing appropriate words and searching for suitable expressions. Finally, written speech also involves conscious operations at the syntactic level. Again, these occur automatically or unconsciously in oral speech. As a rule, the writer constructs sentences consciously. The decisions involved are based not only on existing speech habits but also on rules of grammar and syntax.

Thus, written speech differs radically from oral speech in that it must be produced on the basis of the rules of expanded (explicit) grammar. This is what makes the substance of written speech comprehensible in the absence of accompanying gestures and intonation. That is also why the structure of monologic, written speech does not approximate that of oral dialogic speech. In written speech, sentence length is usually greater than in oral speech. Also, written speech rarely uses direct quotation, and relies heavily on complex forms of control, e.g., relative clauses, which are rarely encountered in oral speech.

Written speech is an important device in thought processes. Written speech becomes a useful means for clarifying thinking because it involves conscious operations with linguistic categories. These can be carried out at a far slower rate of processing than is possible in oral speech, and one can go over the product several times.

It is therefore obvious why we often utilize written speech not only to convey prepared information, but also to process and clarify our thinking. The idea that it is often best to put things down in writing in order to make oneself clear is completely sound. This is precisely why written speech is of enormous significance for processing thought. It represents work performed on the mode and form of an utterance. It emerges with particular clarity when one is working on a report or a scientific paper or when we look at the work of a translator or an editor. For example, translation is by no means confined to the technical operations of translating from one system of codes into another. On the contrary, it is a complex form of analytical activity, in which the logical structure of thought itself is the basic object.

THE RELATIONSHIP BETWEEN ORAL AND WRITTEN SPEECH:
TYPES OF WRITTEN SPEECH.

Several relationships exist between written and oral speech. Oral speech is accompanied by gestures, intonation, and pauses, and it allows one to use abbreviations, ellipses, and agrammatisms. In certain examples of dialogic or dramatized monologic speech, these peculiar characteristics are especially prevalent. Written speech, on the other hand, always remains speech in the absence of an interlocutor. The devices for encoding thought into utterances which are used unconsciously in oral speech become the subject of conscious action in written speech. Written speech does not rely on extralinguistic means. It must therefore possess adequate grammatical completeness in order to permit complete understanding.

The relationship between oral and written speech can be quite interesting in the case of a person who is just beginning to learn to write and is therefore not able to use written speech with sufficient automaticity. Let us turn to an examination of the written speech of a mature person who has not yet mastered all aspects of writing. The written speech of such a person still reveals many characteristics of oral speech, but also reflects the activity of consciously learning the techniques of language needed for writing. For example, if we examine a letter written by such a person it usually looks something like the following: "Hello, dear Mommy, Daddy, sister Nina and brother Kolya. I am your sister Katya writing to you. I want to convey . . . and . . . to you, and to tell you . . . and . . . " The written speech simultaneously reflects some forms used in oral speech and some forms associated with the conscious act of writing itself. Here we see that the writer tells the addressee who is writing what he/she wishes to convey. The writer formulates not only the substance of what he/she wishes to convey, but also the acts that he/she performs while writing. That is, a person who is at this stage of mastering written speech writes in the same way that he/she speaks and acts.

In such cases, written speech is quite different from the written speech of a person accustomed to using it as a special instrument of communication. In cases of the latter type, the opposite process may occur. The rules of written speech, having become sufficiently automatized, begin to be transferred to oral speech. Such a person begins to speak in the same manner that he/she writes. We have in mind here cases of formal styles in oral speech which do not involve ellipsis or errors. For such a person, live oral speech may be deprived of elements of intonation and gestures. His/her speech may become hypergrammatical and converted into dead, formal, and grammatically overelaborated speech. It has the properties that characterize written speech but seldom seen in live oral speech.

To deal with the different relationships between written and oral speech at different stages of learning written speech, we shall have to rely on to another branch of science—stylistics. This discipline is quite developed in linguistics and deserves the special attention of psychologists in the future.

Chapter 12
Comprehension of the Components of a Speech Utterance: the Word and the Sentence

We have examined the process of producing an expanded speech utterance and found that it begins with an intention and ends with the expanded speech communication. We demonstrated that this process may be considered one which proceeds from the internal sense of an utterance to a system of expanded speech meanings that enable the speaker to convey information to the listener.

Let us now turn to a psychological analysis of the process of *comprehension* or, as it is sometimes called, decoding. In many respects, this process is the reverse of speech production. It begins with external speech, moves to an understanding of the meaning of the utterance, and then moves to the subtext or sense.

Analysis of speech comprehension is one of the most difficult and, strange as it may seem, one of the least discussed problems in psychology.

THE PROBLEM

The problem of speech decoding or comprehension has been approached by psychologists in several different ways. Some investigators argued that in order to understand the sense of an utterance it is enough to understand the meaning of each word and to understand the precise grammatical rules governing word combinations. In that view, comprehension of a message is determined by the presence of concepts on the one hand and an understanding of the grammatical rules of the language on the other.

Obviously, these factors are necessary for understanding speech. However, those two factors alone do not explain the process whereby we decipher the sense of an oral or written utterance. Other psychologists therefore argued for a quite different account of comprehension. They proposed that it begins with a search for the general idea of the utterance. This constitutes the primary focus of the process that only later shifts to the lexical-phonemic level (the specification of the meaning of individual words) and to the syntactical level (the deciphering of sentence meaning).

This analytic approach supports the notion that the process of understanding an expanded speech communication does not correspond to the order in which the information is communicated. It does not first involve individual words that reach the listener (the lexical phonological level) and then the sentence (the syntactic level). Such an approach has been adopted by some authors—Fillmore (1972), Lakoff (1972), McCawley (1972) and, very recently, Wertsch (1974, 1975). Accordingly, the process of comprehending a communication is very complex. Some of the component subprocesses involve the perception of word meaning, and others involve the decoding of the syntactical rules for their combination. However, this is still not the entire picture. The complexities involved indicate that even in the earliest stages of comprehension certain hypotheses or presuppositions emerge and that the main property of this process is exploration, which leads to a selection from a number of alternatives.

The listener or reader never is confronted with the problem of understanding isolated words or sentences. Neither words nor sentences occur "in vacuo." Rather, the processes involved in comprehending words or sentences are subordinated to another action. They are auxiliary *operations*, and it is only in certain cases, such as decoding texts in a foreign language, that they are converted into *actions*. The basic process involved in comprehension consists of deciphering the meaning of the whole message. The meaning forms its inner sense, or what Wertsch (1974) labeled, its "external coherence." This, in turn, imparts a greater depth to the communication. It is its "subtext" or "internal coherence."

Comprehension is always aimed at searching for the context of an utterance. Sometimes this involves the linguistic or synsemantic context, and sometimes the extralinguistic or situational context. Without this, it is impossible to understand the entire text or to evaluate the elements in it correctly. That is why the authors mentioned above argue that there are no "context-free" elements of an utterance and that we must examine the process of forming relevant hypotheses or presuppositions which determine the concrete meaning of words or phrases in a speech utterance.

According to authors such as Fillmore (1972), Halliday (1970), Lakoff (1972),

McCawley (1972), Rommetveit (1968), and Wertsch (1974, 1975), speakers' "strategies" are based on presuppositions. These presuppositions provide the initial mechanism for deciphering incoming communication. All of this makes the decoding of speech an active and complex process.

The second, equally essential factor involved in speech comprehension concerns knowledge of basic semantic or deep syntactic structures. These are at the foundation of each component of the utterance and express emotional or logical systems of relationships. As already noted, this aspect of the system is especially important when the deep syntactic structure differs from the external surface structure. In this connection, investigators such as Miller (1967) have been correct in pointing out that complete comprehension of each part of each sentence in a communication can be attained only by transforming the surface grammatical structures into the underlying semantic or deep structures. These may differ from surface structures to varying degrees. According to these authors, there can be no real comprehension of speech without this process. The linguists and psychologists who have argued for the existence of a deep structure along with a surface structure of language made a significant contribution to the study of communication.

Finally, there is a third group of psychologists and linguists who have correctly pointed out that hypotheses regarding basic semantic structures and deep syntactical structures are not sufficient for a complete account of comprehension. This group of investigators, especially Vygotsky (1934), argue that there is yet another important step in the comprehension of speech, a step consisting of transforming the external structure of a text to the "subtext" or "sense" involved in speech. It is not enough to understand the direct meaning of a communication. In addition, it is also essential to identify the inner sense which lies behind these meanings. In other words, one must take into account the extremely complex transition from the system of meanings to the system of sense. By specifying the inner sense of the communication, one can make the transition to an analysis of the motives that lie behind the acts of the persons or events described in the text.

The following example will illustrate this phenomenon. In Griboedov's *Wit Works Woe* ("Gore ot uma"), Chatskii's last exclamation, "Karetu mne, karetu!" (The coach, give me the coach!), has a relatively straightforward meaning. It reflects Chatskii's request for the coach so that he can leave an evening party. However, the sense of this request is far deeper. It involves an expression of Chatskii's attitude toward the society he is leaving. It is precisely this fact that belongs to the sphere of phenomena that linguists and psychologists understand as presupposition.

Thus, the sense of an utterance may differ from its external meaning. The problem of complete comprehension is one of not confining oneself to reproducing the external meaning. One must pass from the surface text to the subtext or from meaning to sense, and then one must move on to the motive behind the communication. This is what accounts for the fact that a text can be understood or "read" at various levels. There is little doubt that individuals differ much more in their understanding of sense than in their understanding of meaning.

The importance of the transition from the meaning of a text to its sense is well-known to writers, actors, and directors, and analysis of this process ought to occupy an important place in psychology. The transition from the comprehension of external meaning to the understanding of inner sense is perhaps one of the most important, though least studied, aspects of cognitive psychology.

Let us now move on to an analysis of the sequence of steps involved in comprehension. We know that the process of comprehending a spoken or written text begins with the perception of individual words, followed by the perception of individual sentences, which leads to the perception of an entire text. Finally, the general sense is identified. This sequence should be understood only as a logical sequence. As already noted, we are not suggesting that the comprehension of a text actually proceeds in this manner and consists of a successive transition from the word to the sentence and from the sentence to the text.

In reality, the processes of decoding meaning and understanding sense are far more complex. In most cases, even the process of understanding individual words takes place simultaneously with the perception of sense fragments. Sometimes the comprehension of an individual word may even follow the perception of sense fragments. In such cases, a word's context reveals its meaning and later on its sense. This shows that the logical sequence of "word—sentence—text—subtext" should not be understood as a chain of real psychological processes which unfold across time. However, it is important to understand the processes involved in the perception of each component, and that is why we shall examine them one at a time.

WORD COMPREHENSION

It would appear that comprehension of the individual words in a communication is the initial and simplest step in the process of decoding speech. However, as noted in the very first chapters of this volume, comprehension of a word's meaning, and to an even greater degree comprehension of the distinct sense in which a word is used in any given instance, involve complex psychological processes. Let us consider separately the factors that combine to form these complex processes.

It is well known that every word is homonymous, i.e., it has numerous meanings, and also, numerous senses. Therefore, in order to determine its object reference and to concretize its meaning, a process of selection is necessary every time it is used. There must be a selection from several alternative possible meanings of the word. These alternatives are determined, first of all, by the context in which the word is used.

Homonymy of words is not limited to obvious homonymy. The following are examples of obvious homonymy. The Russian word "kosa" may mean either an agricultural tool (sickle), a sandbank (shallow) in the sea, or a girl's plait. The word "klyuch" may mean a device for opening a lock (key) or a water spring, etc. The meaning can be determined from the context. Thus: "Devochka zaplela dlinnuyu kosu." (The girl made herself a long plait.); "Nuzhna ostraya kosa, chtoby skosit' etot lug." (A sharp sickle is needed to cut this meadow.); "Dlinnaya peschanaya kosa daleko vykhodila v more." (A long sandy bank ran far out into the sea.); "Klyuch ot moei kvartiry podkhodit k dversi soseda." (The key to my apartment fits my neighbor's door.); "Voda vzyataya iz klyucha, b'yushchego iz-pod gory, byla kholodnoi i svezhei." (The water taken from the spring that came from the mountain was cold and fresh.).

There are also cases of latent homonymy when the meaning of a word is broader and more complex psychologically than it is normally thought to be. This can easily be seen if we analyze names that designate objects. The Russian word "ruchka" has numerous meanings. It can mean a pen for writing, a door handle, the arm of a chair, or a child's little hand. The Russian word "boi" may mean a battle during a war, or the breaking of crockery, or the striking of a clock. The same thing can be said of adjectives. The word "prokhladnyi" (cool) may refer to the weather or an emotional response; the word "ostryi" (sharp) may refer to a needle or to a discussion (i.e., a sharp exchange). Homonymy may also be found in verbs. The Russian verb "podnimat' " (to raise, to lift) may mean to lift something from the floor, to raise one's hand, to raise a question, etc. The verb "razdelit' " (separate) may express the separation of one part of something from another, as in "razdelit' na dve chasti" (to divide into two parts), or it can be concerned with unity or agreement, as in "Ya razdelyayu mnenie etogo cheloveka." (I share that person's views.). Similarly homonymy can be observed in auxiliary words. The preposition "v" (in, into) has quite different meanings in such contexts as "v lesu" (in the forest), "v mysli" (in thought), "v isstuplenii" (in a frenzy), etc.

It is quite obvious that to understand any utterance one must select the meaning of a word from several alternatives. Furthermore, the process of understanding a word does not simply consist of selecting the relevant meaning from the possible uses of a word which are usually noted in a dictionary. A word may also differ in its sense in a particular context. The word "pyatno" (stain, spot) has quite a different sense in such contexts as "pyatno na solntse" (a spot on the sun), "maslyanoe pyatno na kostyume" (an oily stain on a suit), "pyatno na reputatsii" (a blot on one's reputation), etc. The word "starost' " (old age) is used in quite a different sense in such contexts as "pochetnaya starost' " (venerable old age), "boleznennaya starost' " (sick old age), and "degradatsiya ot starosti" (degradation due to old age). In order to comprehend a word in a text, it is not enough to know its normal object reference and meaning. In each instance of use one must select the appropriate meaning and sense from a large number of alternatives. This choice is determined by the situational as well as the linguistic context.

What we have said so far still does not provide a complete psychological analysis of word comprehension. In order to carry out an adequate psychological analysis of this process, one must also take into account the fact that there are different semantic levels of word meaning and that the reader or listener must select the proper level (which itself may shift). The choice of an appropriate level of word meaning is entirely determined by the context in which a word occurs. Thus, in the context of cooking, the Russian word "ugol'" (coal, charcoal) means a type of fuel, whereas in the context of a chemical treatise the same word designates a complex chemical concept—the element C (carbon). The Russian word "set'" (net) has one meaning when used in the context of fishing, but the same word in a scientific context may mean a "system of connections" or a "network" (e.g., a network of neurons).

If one does not perceive the meaning of words at different levels, or if one perceives the meaning of words at an inappropriate level, comprehension of the text will be disrupted. It is not difficult to see that it will never occur to an uneducated person, for whom the word "ugol'" means a type of fuel, that the word can also be used to refer to a diamond. On the other hand, for a person who is used to formulating scientific concepts, the word "ugol'" can be used to refer both to a kind of fuel as well as to a diamond.

We should also point out that in certain forms of mental illness (e.g., schizophrenia) one can see an inability to select the appropriate sense of a word. This is both the chief symptom of the disease and a major factor that prevents patients from arriving at an appropriate interpretation of information.

From what we have said, it is obvious that it would be a mistake to think that a word has stable meanings which remain identical across conditions. Words are homonymous or polysemantic. In order to comprehend a word, it is necessary to select both its object reference and its meaning and sense from among numerous alternatives. This selection is possible only by taking into account the context in which the word is used. This selection of the appropriate meaning of a word is a complex psychological process, a process that should be carefully studied in order to develop a description of the mechanisms involved in speech comprehension.

CONDITIONS FOR COMPREHENDING WORD MEANING

The process of selecting the required meaning of a word from a number of possible alternatives is influenced by several factors. The first of these is how frequently the word is used in a language. It is quite natural that if the word "podnyat'" (to raise, to lift) is frequently used in the sense of lifting something from the ground and is practically never used in the sense of raising a question, the former meaning of the word will be perceived more readily than the latter.

Conversely, when understanding the second meaning of this word it will be necessary first to reject the more frequently encountered meaning.

This difference can create comprehension difficulties for subjects from different professional backgrounds. If the word "selezenka" (spleen) is quite familiar and has a definite meaning for a physician, it is natural that the word "selezen'" (drake, male duck) will turn out to be more difficult for him/her to understand due to the possibility of confusing words which have a similar sound structure. On the other hand, for a poultry farmer, the word "selezen'" occurs with far greater frequency in the concrete meaning of a bird. That is why when a poultry farmer hears the strange word "selezenka" he needs to inhibit the more habitual meaning of the word "selezen'." This difference naturally produces some difficulty in analyzing the word.

These problems are of particular importance for students of a foreign language. In their case, words frequently occurring in practical experience are comprehended more easily than less familiar words. Furthermore, this experience with frequently occurring words can even lead to errors in evaluating the meanings of less familiar words. As an example, we can quote the instance of a Russian who had only recently settled in the U.S. For a long time, he understood "molted coffee" to be "molotyi kofe" (ground coffee). It was only later that he discovered the word "molted" had nothing to do with the familiar word "molotyi," but was the name of the firm which produced the coffee.

The inclusion of various words in a variety of practical settings and the varying frequency with which certain word meanings appear are factors that can result in certain types of comprehension problems. These difficulties arise when a person who is attempting to comprehend words with unusual meanings "semanticizes" them, i.e., establishes their sense on the basis of familiar words. As an example, we can cite the case of a patient who had difficulties in word perception because of damage to the speech zones of his cerebral cortex. He understood the unfamiliar, low-frequency word "mokritsa" (woodhouse)[16] as "wet weather" on the basis of an analogy with "rasputitsa" (the time in winter and spring of bad roads). For further details on this and other cases, see Luria (1947, 1962, 1975a). On the other hand, one may find instances where the word "rasputitsa" (the time in winter and spring of bad roads) is incorrectly semanticized as "dissolute woman" on the basis of an analogy with the masculine gender noun "rasputnik" (a profligate). This kind of semanticization of little known words, when sense is established by analogy with a word that occurs more frequently and is more familiar, appears in the process of comprehending a text which includes unfamiliar words.

The second, and perhaps main factor determining the choice of the meaning of a word is the *context*. The importance of this factor is especially evident in the comprehension of obvious homonyms. Thus, the word "truba" (trumpet,

---

[16]The Russian word "mokryi" means "wet."–*J. V. Wertsch*

chimney) in the context of an orchestra obviously calls to mind the meaning of a musical instrument, whereas the same word in a description of a house is always understood as referring to a chimney.

A related problem arises in the comprehension of latent homonyms. Whether the word "ruchka" will be understood to mean a pen, a child's hand, or the arm of a chair will depend on the context in which the word is used. This also applies in the case of the word "podnyat'" which, depending on the context, may mean to lift from the ground, to raise one's hand, to raise a question, etc. The Russian word "ekipazh" (carriage, crew) may in one context be perceived as a means of transport, and in another as the crew of a ship or an airplane. These examples show clearly that word comprehension is by no means a direct, immediate act. They show that the process of selecting the meaning from among many possible alternatives depends both on the frequency with which a particular meaning occurs and, most importantly, on the context in which it occurs.

It is interesting to note that for some people word meaning does not evolve on the basis of contextualized speech (i.e., in live communication), but consists of acquiring the dictionary meanings of individual words. In those instances, there may be considerable difficulty in comprehending the meanings of words in actual communication. Perhaps the most striking instance of this phenomenon is word comprehension by deaf-mute individuals for whom word meaning does not evolve as a result of participating in live communication. A deaf-mute child learns word meaning by acquiring individual words. If the word "podnyat'" is presented as meaning "to bend down and lift an object from the floor," then it turns out to be quite difficult for him/her to comprehend the meaning of this same word in a context where the speaker has in mind "raising one's hand." The second meaning remains incomprehensible unless it is explained to him/her that in this context the word has quite a different meaning. The comprehension problems of deaf-mute people has been studied in detail by several Soviet researchers (e.g., Boskis, 1963; Korovin, 1950; Morozova, 1947).

Similar phenomena occur in the learning of a foreign language, a process that begins not with contextual speech, but with the dictionary meaning of individual words. This method of learning a language inevitably leads to difficulties, similar to those mentioned above, which can be considerably alleviated if the learner begins with the context and uses the dictionary meaning of individual words only secondarily. The psychology of foreign language learning is a special, well-developed branch of psychology. Therefore, we shall not dwell on it in greater detail here.

The process of word comprehension is always a process of selecting one meaning from numerous possible alternatives. This process involves analyzing the general context in which a word is used and inhibiting inappropriate associations that may arise in connection with the word's sound structure or alternate meanings.

The difficulties we have mentioned can become particularly pronounced in certain types of pathology. For example, the meaning of a word may be reduced to a single item, it may become alienated and confused with the meanings of similarly sounding words or, finally, it may emerge in inappropriate contexts. We shall describe these difficulties at a later point in this volume. The psychology of text comprehension must take these difficulties into account because when a listener or reader fails to recognize the polysemantic nature of words and the decisive role of the context, this may lead to difficulties in comprehension.

THE COMPREHENSION OF SENTENCES

The next logical stage in the decoding of communication is sentence comprehension. It is not difficult to comprehend simple sentences, such as "Dom gorit." (The house burns.)[17] or "Sobaka laet." (The dog barks.). These sentences are of the form $(S \rightarrow P)$. It is also not difficult to comprehend more complex sentences, such as "Mal'chik udaril sobaku." (The boy hit the dog.) or "Devochka p'et chai." (The girl drinks tea.), i.e., sentences of the form $(S \rightarrow P \rightarrow O)$. Even somewhat more complex sentences, such as "Malen'kii mal'chik udaril dvorovuyu sobaku." (The little boy hit the watch dog.) or "Bol'naya devochka p'et gor'koe lekarstvo." (The sick girl drinks the bitter medicine.), i.e., sentences of the form $(Adj \rightarrow S \rightarrow P \rightarrow Adj \rightarrow O)$, do not present any real difficulties in understanding. This is explained by the fact that the surface syntactic structures of these sentences do not differ from their deep syntactic structures, and that the sequence of the events expressed in the sentences corresponds to the order of words.

One can expect to observe greater difficulties in the comprehension of sentences in which the surface (syntactic) structure differs from the deep structure. In such instances, a transformation is required for the comprehension of the sentence. This transformation is involved in the transition from the surface (syntactic) structure to the deep logical syntactic structure.

Thus, even though the sentences "Petya dal slivu." (Petya gave a plum.) and "Petya poprosil slivu." (Petya requested a plum.) have identical surface (syntactic) structures, they differ in their deep logical syntactic structures. In the first instance (Petya gave a plum.), the sequence of events corresponds to the order of words $(S \rightarrow P \rightarrow O)$. In the second instance (Petya requested a plum.), matters are more complicated. The sentence signifies that Petya requested of someone, who is not explicitly mentioned in the phrase, to give to him (Petya) a plum. The transfer of the plum involves a reverse interpretation. A transformation is involved because an interpretation of the sentence requires that the listener or reader understand that another party (the logical subject) who is not explicitly identified is

---

[17]Luria's Russian examples here are in the present imperfective. They could be translated into English either as "The house burns." or "The house is burning." We have chosen the former because it provides a better parallel to the examples in Luria's argument.—*J. V. Wertsch*

going to give the plum to Petya. The subject is taken for granted. This is what makes it possible for young children to understand the first sentence (Petya gave a plum.) without difficulty, while the action expressed in the second sentence (Petya requested a plum.) can be correctly understood only at an older age.

Even greater difficulties arise in the comprehension of polysemantic sentences. Thus, "Petya prishel k Ole s Sonei." can be understood in two ways: "Petya and Sonya arrived at Olya's." or "Petya arrived at Olya's, who lives with Sonya."[18] That is why the comprehension of polysemantic sentences requires additional markers. In the example we are considering here, these markers may consist of emphasis and pauses that enable the speaker to group the sentence elements in various ways.

Much greater comprehension difficulties arise in sentences that express relations and make use of complex grammatical devices for expressing these relations. Even simple constructions which express relationships, such as "Sokrat—chelovek." (Socrates is a human being.) or "brat ottsa," (brother of father), may create difficulties in comprehension. These difficulties emerge if the listener perceives the words as simply indicating two images (i.e., Socrates + human being, or brother + father). Such direct interpretations of the parts of the construction prevent the understanding of the relations involved.

This kind of difficulty may be observed in mentally retarded children and in certain forms of speech disorders resulting from brain injuries (so-called "semantic aphasia"). Even greater comprehension difficulties emerge when speech includes more complex grammatical structures (such as subordination) and when complex surface structures conflict with the deep syntactic structures. In those cases, additional devices are involved in comprehension.

Some of these devices concern the transformation of grammatical structures. Such transformations bring the surface grammatical structure into line with the deep syntactical structure and facilitate the direct comprehension of sentence meaning. Other means, e.g., expanded semantic devices in the form of external speech supports, are also available to aid comprehension. It is only at later developmental stages that these external auxiliary supports are removed and the comprehension of grammatically complex sentences can occur as a series of abbreviated mental acts. At these later stages (e.g., the case of an experienced listener or reader), this transformation occurs so fast and effortlessly that the comprehension of complex grammatical constructions may mistakenly be assumed to be direct of immediate.

Let us consider some examples demonstrating these comprehension difficulties. We shall outline the type of grammatical constructions which cause the greatest difficulties and the methods which can assist in overcoming them.

[18]The ambiguity arises here in Russian because of the morphological inflections.—*J. V. Wertsch*

The first type of construction that causes difficulties in comprehension is the inflection. Perhaps the most straightforward example of this is the attributive genitive in Russian. Several of its properties make comprehension difficult. As noted earlier, an example of this is the reversible construction "brat ottsa" (brother of father) and "otets brata" (father of brother). Several factors are involved in its comprehension. First, one must understand that the construction involves one person who is identified through the relationship between two nouns. One must also understand that putting the noun in the genitive case gives it the meaning of an adjective. Moreover, as previously noted, the adjective in Russian usually precedes the noun. In this case, however, a noun is in the genitive case, and this means that the item that functions as an adjective is placed in second position. Therefore, in order to understand this construction we have to transform it by placing the second noun, which is in the genitive case, in the first position.

In some cases even this is inadequate and it becomes necessary to use external markers, such as demonstrative pronouns, to comprehend the construction. These allow the speaker to identify the main subject of the utterance and to show that the second word has only a relative, attributive meaning. External markers are often encountered in everyday speech. In the present example, the expression "brat ottsa" (brother of father) may be replaced by the expression "brat moego ottsa" or "brat etogo ottsa" (brother of my father or brother of this father). This facilitates the comprehension of the construction.[19]

Analogous difficulties arise in the comprehension of constructions in which one cannot determine the relationship among elements on the basis of inflections alone. In these cases, the meaning of the construction depends on word order. Among such constructions are sentences like "Plat'e zadelo veslo." (The dress got entangled in the oar.) and "Veslo zadelo plat'e." (The oar got entangled in the dress.),[20] where the listener cannot rely on inflections to identify the relationships among elements of the communication. The sole criterion for determining syntactic role is the place a word occupies in the entire construction and the context in which the given construction occurs. Additional external markers—additional pronouns, stress, and pauses—cannot facilitate comprehension as they did in the constructions we considered earlier. That is why it is necessary to construct an inner auxiliary

---

[19]In certain languages, for instance in Turkish, this additional marker typically takes the form of "etogo ottsa ego brat" (of this father's his brother). A similar construction may be seen in the "Saxon genitive" (Des Vaters sein Bruder), which is used frequently in everyday speech.

[20]One cannot rely on inflection here to determine the syntactic role of the items "plat'e" (dress) and "veslo" (oar), because (a) both words are in the neuter gender and (b) there is no inflectional distinction between nominative and accusative cases in the neuter gender. Thus, when "plat'e" serves as the subject (in the first sentence) and hence is in the nominative case, it has the same inflection as when it serves as the direct object (in the second sentence) and hence is in the accusative case. The same can be said of "veslo."—*J. V. Wertsch*

image—e.g., "Devushka vykhodila iz lodki i ee plat'e zadelo veslo." (The girl was getting out of the boat and her dress got entangled in the oar.) or "Mal'chik greb i ego veslo zadelo plat'e devushki." (The boy is rowing and his oar got entangled in the dress of the girl.). This expanded image removes the difficulties inherent in the construction. It is only after a certain amount of practice that the expanded process becomes automatized and acquires a contracted form.

The greatest difficulties of this type occur in connection with complex reversible constructions using prepositions. Examples of this kind of construction are phrases like "krug pod kvadratom" (a circle under a square) and "kvadrat pod krugom" (a square under a circle). It is very difficult to comprehend the meaning of these constructions directly. In order to make these constructions comprehensible, one must use several auxiliary transformations. The transformations may expand the original form to various levels of detail. For instance, a transformation may serve to split up the expression "krest pod krugom" (a cross under a circle) into the form "krug, a pod etim krugom—krest" (a circle, and under this circle—a cross). Sometimes a more expanded program of transformation may be used. We have been able to examine transformations while analyzing how patients with semantic aphasia try to comprehend complex constructions. We should also note that these transformations play a role in restoring the learning ability of patients suffering from such disturbances.

As a rule, patients who are unable to understand logical relations directly (cf. Luria, 1962, 1971, 1975a) are able to grasp the sense of the aforementioned constructions only by using subsequent transformations to help them arrive at the sense of the construction in an indirect way. For instance, these transformations may involve identifying the main element of an utterance. Thus, a patient may use the following line of reasoning: "The word 'krest' is in the nominative case which means it is the subject, 'pod' means underneath (the substitution of the relative meaning of 'pod' for the absolute meaning). 'Pod krugom' means that the circle is placed at the top and the cross at the bottom. 'Krest pod krugom' means that the cross is placed below and the circle is placed above."

We see, in this case, a construction involving two nouns, one in the nominative and the other in the instrumental case, and one preposition. It can be understood only if each of the elements can be converted from relative to an absolute element. In that way the simultaneous relationship is converted into consecutive links in a chain. Only by using such transformations can one get round the difficulties caused by the complex communication of relationships. In the example we used, we see something of a "magnifying glass of time." It enables one to explicate the program of successive operations used to decode the complex communication of relationships which relies on prepositions.

Perhaps the most interesting group of grammatical constructions that cause comprehension difficulties are relative clause constructions which make use of the auxiliary word "kotoryi" (which, who). The simplest forms of these constructions—e.g., "gazeta, kotoruyu ya chital utrom" (the newspaper which I was reading in the morning) or "devushka, kotoraya smotrela v zerkalo" (the girl who was looking in the mirror)—do not create any noticeable difficulties. This is because the surface syntactic form corresponds to the deep structure, and because the expressions depict a nonreversible action. We can say "devushka, kotoraya smotrela v zerkalo" (the girl who was looking in the mirror), but we cannot say "zerkalo, kotoroe smotrelo v devushku" (the mirror which was looking into the girl).

The comprehension of such constructions when partial reversibility is possible is somewhat more difficult. An example is "devushka, kotoraya krasila bugy" (the girl who was painting her lips [i.e., applying lipstick]). The reverse construction, "guby, kotorye krasili devushku" (the lips which were painting the girl), is impossible.

The greatest difficulties arise when a construction involving the relativizer has multiple meanings and when additional operations are needed to specify which element of the sentence is being referred to by "kotoryi." For example, difficulties like these arise when we consider the problems involved in comprehending noncontiguous constructions, especially if these noncontiguous constructions involve multiple relations. Consider the following example: "V shkolu, v kotoroi uchilas' Dunya, s fabriki prishla rabotnitsa, chtoby sdelat' doklad." (Literal translation: To the school in which Dunya was studying, from the factory came a woman worker, in order to give a lecture.). In order to understand this construction, one must bring together elements that are widely separated in the sentence. Thus, one must combine "V shkolu" and "prishla rabotnitsa" (To the school, came a woman worker) on the one hand, and "V shkolu" and "sdelat' doklad" (To the school, to give a lecture) on the other. Furthermore, one must inhibit the link that naturally arises between the elements "Dunya" and "s fabriki" (Dunya, from the factory). One can comprehend this sentence only by conducting an analysis that inhibits the seemingly natural hypotheses and combines noncontiguous elements of the construction.

The greatest difficulties occur in the case of a multiple hierarchy of relations. Consider the classic illustration proposed by Miller: "Kartina, kotoruyu narisoval khudozhnik, kotoryi prodal ee kollektsioneru, kotoryi sobiral proizvedeniya iskusstva, kotoryi nedavno umer, poluchila premiyu na vystavke." (Literal translation: The painting, which the artist drew, who sold it to a collector, who collected works of art, who died recently, received a prize at the exhibition.) Or consider "Ivan uekhal v otpusk, kotoryi byl predostavlen emu nachal'nikom kotoryi byl naznachen direktorom instituta kotoryi byl tol'ko chto organizovan po spetsial'-nomu resheniyu kotoroe bylo prinyato ministerstvom, i nichevo ne znal ob etom vosprinyal eto poruchenie kak ser'eznoe zadanie." (Literal translation: Ivan went on a vacation which was granted to him by his boss who was appointed by the director of the institute, which had just been organized in accordance with a special decision, which was adopted by the ministry, and knew nothing about this.)

It is evident that in both of these constructions multiple, hierarchically organized subordination is combined with noncontiguous placement of elements
which are related in sense. In such cases, comprehension requires that one establish
a complex hierarchy of relations, thereby combining noncontiguous components.
This involves an entire chain of transformations which divide the construction
into a chain of isolated sentences and thus allow one to specify the elements
identified by the relativizer "kotoryi" (which, who).

Analyzed quite thoroughly in psychology and of special interest is the comprehension of comparative constructions. Comparative constructions are typical
examples of the "communication of relationships." Rather than being aimed at
providing information about an object or person, they concern relationships between them. Therefore, it is natural that the comprehension of such constructions
should give rise to special difficulties. No great difficulty may arise in the case
of simple comparative constructions, such as "Petya sil'nee Vani." (Petya is
stronger than Vanya.) or "Olya svetlee Soni." (Olya is fairer than Sonya.) Investigators have discovered that the comprehension of these constructions includes:
(a) the isolation of the initial (entailed) meaning of one of the elements (Vanya
is strong); (b) the coordination of this initial meaning with the second link (But
Petya is even stronger); and (c) a synthesis (e.g., Petya is stronger than Vanya.).
Thus, in order to understand comparative constructions one must transform the
sentence by breaking up the construction into two elements, each of which changes
a relative form into an absolute one.

Greater problems are encountered in decoding difficult constructions. These
involve a threefold comparison, including comparison of opposing characterizations. It turns out that the comprehension of these constructions is so complicated
that they are now used as a special part of intelligence tests. An illustration of
these constructions is the well-known statement "Olya svetlee Soni, no temnee
Kati." (Olya ia fairer than Sonya, but darker than Katya.), where the construction
is very difficult to comprehend. The difficulty arises because of the need to
establish a simultaneous relationship among three objects (Olya, Sonya, and Katya)
which involves opposing characterizations ("fairer" and "darker"). To understand
such constructions, one must break them up into a chain of components and
determine how the components are characterized. Then one must transform the
comparison of two contrasting values into a comparison of one.

We can describe the process of understanding this construction in terms of
the following transformations: (a) identification of an absolute characteristic
(Olya is fair); (b) replacement of the abbreviated comparative construction (Olya
is fairer than Sonya) by another, expanded construction (Sonya is also fair, but
Olya is fairer. Olya is fairer than Sonya.); (c) transformation of the second inverse
characteristic (darker) into the positive characteristic used earlier (Olya is darker
than Katya = Katya is fairer than Olya); (d) the reconstruction of all three elements of the construction (Olya, Sonya, Katya) into a single, consecutively joined

series (Olya is fairer than Sonya and Katya is fairer than Olya). This results in a series with the single characteristic of darkness Katya–Olya–Sonya. It is evident that the above complex program of actions is not open to direct evaluation. Very few people are able to decode such a construction directly. Even an intelligent, well-educated person can usually do so only by expanding the construction into a series of successive actions which include transformations. Only in this way can subjects avoid what psychologists such as Bever (1970, 1974) termed "mental diplopia." This results from the fact that one link is related to the second one positively, but inversely to a third.

When discussing difficult grammatical constructions, we touched on semantic inversion. Typical examples of this are constructions that include two negatives, such as "Ya ne privyk ne podchinyat'sya pravilam." (I am not used to not obeying rules). These two negatives can be understood here if we transform them into a single positive, such as "Ya privyk podchinyat'sya." (I am used to obeying.). Therefore, "I am not used to not obeying rule." means "I am used to obeying rules." Similarly, in constructions of the type "On byl poslednii po skromnosti" (He was the last person with regard to modesty.), "poslednii po skromnosti" (the last person with regard to modesty) may mean "pervyi po samouvrennosti" (the first person with regard to self-assuredness). Here again, comprehension of such constructions requires substituting a positive meaning for two negative ones.

It is evident that the difficulty in understanding these constructions is connected with the fact that one must inhibit an impulsive interpretation and mentally reverse it, i.e., one must convert two negative ideas with a single positive one. It is only when the mental processes have become automatized that this process of comprehension begins to occur with ease. However, when certain slight changes occur (e.g., fatigue) accurate comprehension is possible only by resorting to expansion.

The psychological analysis of sentence comprehension and the construction of a hierarchy of successively more complex increments is a subject for further research. It is self-evident that an important task awaits the psychology of comprehension, a task connected not only with analyzing the comprehension of individual words, but also sentences. This task depends both on semantic-syntactic complexity as well as subject's mental state.

What we have said illustrates the types of difficulties that may arise in the comprehension of what appears to be quite simple sentences. We have also seen how these difficulties increase with an increase in the complexity of the construction, and we have outlined some approaches for dealing with comprehension difficulties encountered in grammatical constructions. It is obvious that a continued psychological analysis of comprehension difficulties that arise with complex grammatical forms can be very useful both for avoiding unnecessary difficulties while compiling texts and for identifying the methods which can help overcome these difficulties.

Chapter 13
Comprehension of the Sense of a Complex Message: Text and Subtext

In this chapter we shall analyze the psychological process involved in understanding a complete message. The analysis of this process is a crucial problem for psychologists who are concerned with the processes of speech comprehension. We shall investigate all of the processes involved in the transition from an expanded utterance to the sense of the utterance. When dealing with this problem, we are moving from an analysis of the system of external meanings in a speech utterance to an analysis of its inner sense. This is sometimes expressed in terms of a transition from understanding words, sentences, and even entire texts, to the comprehension of the subtext or sense, and finally the motive that lies behind the text.

In the case of literature, understanding the sense and the motive is perhaps the main point. For example, the sentence "The light is burning.", apart from its external meaning, may convey any one of several different senses: The sense may be found in the thought, "How wonderful that the electricity has been restored!"; or, the sense may be something quite different, such as "How careless you are, you have forgotten to turn off the light again!" The depth of "reading into" a text or finding its subtext or inner sense may vary greatly. As we have already said, this variation may distinguish one person from another to a far greater degree than the depth and fullness of the comprehension of the external meaning.

How does this entire process of identifying the sense occur? In other words, how do we move from expanded speech to inner sense and finally to the motive of an individual described in the text or even to the motive of the author of a literary text? In our discussion of these issues, we shall begin with the relatively elementary process involved in comprehending the meaning of a coherent text and end with the more difficult problems involved in the transition from the meaning of the text to its inner sense.

THE INTERTWINING OF SENSES OF SENTENCES

It would be a mistake to think that texts consist simply of a chain of isolated sentences and that in order to understand texts it is enough to understand the meaning of each sentence. It is essential to realize that sentences are not isolated links. Each sentence "intertwines with" or "takes in" the meaning of the preceding one. It is because of this process (what Vygotsky termed the "intertwining" or "infusion" of sense)[21] that the essential content of a text can be understood.

The following short text illustrates this process: "I took off my jacket. There was a tear in it (i.e., in the jacket). It (i.e., the tear) occurred when I was walking past a fence. There was a nail in it (i.e., the fence) which (i.e., the nail) was left there by workers when they (i.e., the workers) were painting the fence." One can easily see that the comprehension relies heavily on the intertwining of the sense of each sentence with the others. However, the difficulty in interpreting this text is due to the fact that this intertwining does not remain stable. The object under discussion constantly changes so that every sentence involves a referent different from the one mentioned in the preceding sentence.

Sometimes this process of the intertwining of senses is particularly complex. For example, as we have seen, this occurs when the comprehension of a complex utterance requires bringing together noncontiguous elements. The following examples provide an illustration. First, consider the sentences: "Birds catch beetles and caterpillars. They protect our fields and forests." Here the pronoun "they" does not refer to the same objects identifies by the immediately preceding noun, i.e., "beetles and caterpillars." Rather, it is coreferential with the noncontiguous words "birds." Second, consider the following example: "Life was difficult for the young boy Muk, and when a serious illness struck his father, matters became much worse for him." Obviously, to understand this sentence one must not use the proximity between "father" and "him"[22] to determine coreferentiality.

---

[21]Vygotsky discussed these notions in the last chapter of *Thought and Language* (1934).—*J. V. Wertsch*

[22]The Russian version of this is: "Tyazhelaya zhizn' byla u mal'chik Muka, a kogda zabolel otets, emu stalo sovsem plokho." In this text, the word "father" (otets) appears immediately before "him" (emu). Therefore, in Luria's example the two items are contiguous.—*J. V. Wertsch*

Rather, one must see the connection between the words "Muk" and "him," words that stand far apart in the text. If a communication were simply a chain of isolated phrases and sentences and if there were no intertwining of senses, proper understanding of the entire text would be impossible. The process of intertwining of senses is the fundamental condition for ensuring the comprehension of an entire text. It is therefore regrettable that this process and the various structures involved have been very inadequately studied up to now.

THE IDENTIFICATION OF "SENSE NUCLEI": ANALYSIS THROUGH SYNTHESIS

The examples cited above show that the processes involved in the intertwining of senses or the unification of noncontiguous elements of an utterance are often quite complex. Sometimes the contributing items in a text are not grouped together, but require a complex search activity. This orienting activity, which is aimed at the identification of "sense nuclei" and bringing them together, is perhaps most obvious in reading. It is here that it has been studied more thoroughtly than anywhere else. Eye movement studies have been conducted to examine the processes involved in identifying sense nuclei and unifying widely separated components of a complex message. These studies have made it possible to examine the process of comprehension in its mature form.

It was found that the movement of eyes during reading is not of a linear nature. The reader's gaze does not move smoothly from one word to another and from one sentence to another, stopping only at the most important informative elements. Rather, eye movements are quite complex. The gaze often returns to what had been read earlier, comparing noncontiguous portions of the text. These observations indicate that the process of understanding a text is an active search process which not only identifies individual sense nuclei, but also compares them by returning to text segments that have already been read. In other words, this process involves both the identification and unification of sense nuclei. This process of active analysis, of clarifying the content of a text through comparison, has frequently been labeled the process of analysis through synthesis.

During early stages of development, this process of identifying and comparing the major sense nuclei in a text (i.e., analysis through synthesis) is expanded. To the degree that reading is mastered, the process can be accelerated and contracted. As a result of this development, reading begins to be transformed into a skill of rapidly identifying what is important. It no longer requires a separate external process of comparing noncontiguous elements in a text. In this regard, I cannot help remembering how Vygotsky read books. It was enough for him to take a book in hand and to run rapidly through the text "diagonally." This process allowed him to extract the essential sense of a text without needing to return repeatedly to sections that had already been read. The ability to identify important sense nuclei quickly, and then to establish the sense of the text, is the secret to rapid reading. Rapid reading does not simply involve quick eye movement. It derives from the ability to identify what is significant and to penetrate the sense of the text, to arrive at its general idea.

Before the automatization of the reading process can take place, readers often must utilize several auxiliary means to help them identify what is important in a text, make comparisons, and arrive at the general idea of the text. Several devices for identifying what is important are used in any written text. Among them are the practices of separating a text into paragraphs, emphasizing individual elements by using italics, using conclusions to summarize paragraphs or parts of the text, and highlighting sections of a text through subheadings.

Auxiliary devices in oral speech help to identify the important sense nuclei and arrive at the general sense of the text. Among these devices are stress, intonation, pauses, and "oral spacing" in the form of varying the tempo of speech. An experienced reader begins reading a text by relying on devices like italicized words and paragraph indentation. These help accelerate the process. It is only then that he/she begins to locate the internal components and paragraphs of the text. The italicized words now stop playing a decisive role for the experienced reader. Similar factors make it possible for an experienced lecturer to make use of intonation and pauses to facilitate text comprehension by the audience. A careful analysis of these auxiliary devices which facilitate the process of assimilating the general sense of the text ought to become an important topic in psychology.

Now that we have outlined the external devices for highlighting the important sense units or sense nuclei of a text, we can turn to a much more important problem. This problem is concerned with the indicators that enable us to identify the crucial units of the text, i.e., those units which are necessary for understanding the meaning of the entire text. Obviously, all the individual elements are not equally important in conveying the general sense of the text. Along with the central elements in the text there are secondary elements. If the central elements of the text are changed, the general sense of the text changes; but if the secondary elements of the text are changed, its general sense may remain virtually the same.

The analysis of which elements in a text carry the sense nuclei that can help the reader understand the entire sense of the text is a comparatively new field of research which has previously been explored very little. Hence, it is the subject matter of a comparatively new branch of linguistics—the semantics of text.

We have already noted that any text can be divided into two, often unequal, parts. The first is the "theme" of the text, i.e., the part that points to the subject of discourse. This part deals with what is already old and known. The second part, the "rheme," is comprised of all that is to be said about this subject. It adds something new to it and is actually the basic substance of an expanded communication. It is evident that the theme and the rheme do not necessarily coincide with individual grammatical elements such as nouns and verbs, and that the logical subject may not coincide with the grammatical subject, just as the logical predicate may not coincide with the grammatical predicate.

In oral speech, the part of a sentence carrying the central sense may be highlighted by accent. The sentence "Ya poshel v kino." (I went to the movie.) acquires quite different senses when stress is put on "I" (resulting in "I," and no one else, went to the movies) rather than on the verb "poshel" (in which case the sense would be "I *walked* to the movies and did not go there by means of any *transport*," in other words, "I didn't mind walking to the movies."). Finally, the stress can be placed on the object (in which case the sense would be "I went to the *movie* and not to the theater."). The same thing may be observed in an entire text.

The semantics of text is the subject matter of a special areas of research. Particular significance is attached to the problem of identifying the parts of a text, without which its meaning is incomprehensible. Put another way, this is the problem of identifying the elements of a text which, if changed, would result in a different general sense. Recent investigations have begun to show how much the sense of an entire text may change if one of its elements is removed or altered. These investigators have also begun to identify precisely which key elements form the basis of the sense nucleus that determines the meaning of the whole text.

As an example of the aforementioned studies, we may cite the work of Khomskaya's early research. She used a method in which an experiment began with the development of an orienting response in a reader to an isolated sentence. When this conditioned reflex toward the sentence had been sufficiently formed, subjects were presented with altered sentences or texts in which some link had been excluded, new links had been introduced, or, all the lexical items had been changed while the general sense had been retained. Khomskaya examined how an altered sentence or text elicited or failed to elicit the response developed earlier. For instance, an orienting response was developed to the sentence "A body submerged in water loses as much of its weight as the weight of the volume of water displaced by it." After an orienting reflex had been created to this sentence, the reader was given individual words—such as "body," "submerged," "in water," "loses," "weight," "displaced," "volume," and "of water"—and the intensity of the response to each of these words has assessed. This analysis showed that different words in the text triggered orienting responses of varying intensities. The investigator was therefore able to identify the significance of individual words or components as sense nuclei in a sentence.

The objective investigation of the semantics of texts is still at a very rudimentary stage. One can only hope that it will continue to develop.

THE PROBABILISTIC APPROACH TO MESSAGE COMPREHENSION

Prior to this point, we have proceeded on the assumption that the comprehension of a text depends on its *formal structural* properties. By this we mean we have assumed that the comprehension of a text becomes more difficult whenever the intrasentential or intersentential structure becomes more complex. Within the sentence we have seen that a chain of words involved in simple coordination (parataxis) requires less analysis than complex subordination (hypothaxis). We have seen that simple contiguous structures are understood with greater ease than complex noncontiguous structures, that direct structures are understood more easily than inverted structures, etc. As we have seen, similar phenomena occur at the level of texts. A simple text that utilizes apposition or contiguity is understood with greater ease than a complex text that involves subordination and noncontiguous constructions.

This is evident from the following comparison. First, consider a simple text: "Otets i mat' ushli v teatr, a" (Father and mother went to the theater, and) "doma ostalis' staraya nyanya i deti," (at home were left the old nanny and the children)— (Father and mother went to the theater, and the old nanny and the children were left at home.). Then consider a more complicated text involving subordination and noncontiguous constructions: "V shkolu, gde uchilas' Dunya," (To the school, where was studying Dunya,) "s fabriki prishla rabotnitsa," (from the factory came a worker woman,) "chtoby sdelat' doklad," (to give a report.)—(A worker woman came from the factory to the school where Dunya was studying to give a report.).

Several questions can be answered on the basis of the second sentence. For example, one can provide answers to the following questions: Who came? Where was the report given? Where did she come from? In order to do this, one must separate the individual sense nuclei and their intertwinings. Only after such an analysis can the content of the text be understood. It is not difficult to see that in the second example this analysis requires an active, complex process.

In addition to analyzing the formal structure of texts, another important form of analysis is required. The level of difficulty in comprehending a text and the need for varying degrees of active analysis depend on the *content* of the text as well as on its formal structure. In particular, the level of difficulty and the need for active analysis depend on the probability with which elements in a text can be predicted. The expected probability of occurrence of sense components in a text can vary greatly. In some cases, the ending of a sentence is highly predictable given its beginning and thus the probability of predicting the end approaches unity. In other cases, the beginning of a sentence does not determine its ending and thus leaves open the possibility of a number of alternatives.

Obviously, sentences of the first type can be comprehended more easily than those of the second type. In the first case, comprehension may be based on a single guess which does not require any special analysis. Where the probability of predicting subsequent sense components in a sentence is quite low because there are many possible alternatives, a simple guess will be inadequate for understanding the sentence. In those instances, sentence comprehension requires a prolonged and active analysis.

In each example given below, the reader is asked to complete the sentence whose beginning has been provided. It will be evident that the probability with which a single, obvious ending can be provided can vary greatly. The sentence beginnings are presented in order of increasing indefiniteness.

(1) "Nastupila zima i na ulitsakh vypal glubokii . . . (sneg)" (Literally: Set in winter and on the streets fell deep . . . snow). In this case, the missing word "sneg" (snow) will occur to all readers. Its probability in this sentence is close to one.

(2) "U menya zaboleli zuby i ya poshel . . . (k doktoru v apteku, v polikliniku, etc.)" (I had a toothache and I went . . . to the doctor, to the drugstore, to the poly-clinic, etc.). At least two or three alternatives are available which can be used to complete the sentence correctly. The probability of occurrence of any one of these endings is from .3 to .5.

(3) "Ya poshel v zoopark i uvidel tam . . . (I'va, tigra, zhirafa, ili znakomogo, ili novyi prud, etc.)" (I went to the zoo and saw there . . . a lion, a tiger, a giraffe, or an acquaintance, or a new pond, etc.). In this example, there are even more alternatives to choose from, and the probability of occurrence of any one of these is still smaller.

(4) "Ya poshel na ulitsu, chtoby kupit'sebe . . . (gazetu, botinki, bulku, etc.)" (I went out to the street in order to buy myself . . . a newspaper, some shoes, a roll, etc.). Here the probability that a particular sentence ending will occur is even lower because the preceding context does not point to any one specific choice.

From the above examples, it is clear that as the probability increases that a specific sentence ending will occur, the listener can rely more heavily on guessing or prediction rather than an active analysis of the text. Some sentence beginnings can be completed in only one way. In those, the sentence ending is completely determined. In contrast, there are sentence beginnings for which the probability of any particular ending is not very high. Obviously, then, one cannot rely solely on prediction to understand the sentence.

The same principle applies to entire texts. In some texts, a general set toward a single narrow sense is created. In those instances, every part of the text does not play a key role in understanding its general sense. The set produces a predic-tion or presupposition, and active analysis turns out to be unnecessary. On the other hand, there are texts in which the occurrence of a specific sense cannot be predicted with great certainty, and thus prediction or guessing will not suffice. What is required is an active, complete analysis. This involves comparing the ele-ments of the text with one another, creating an hypothesis about its general sense, and choosing from the alternatives which emerge during the sense analysis of the text. Therefore, the smaller the probability that a specific item can be predicted from the context, the greater the need for an active analysis of the text and the greater the difficulties in comprehending it.

An extremely important branch of the psychology of text comprehension involves the issue of how the process of decoding text depends on the arrangement of its context and on the certainty with which certain semantic components can be predicted. Information theory, a special field of study, has attempted to introduce a quantitative approach to the study of this problem. It has contributed many new ideas to the study of text comprehension by suggesting that the complexity of the processes involved depends not on the structure and formal organization of a text, but on its content. This approach not only enables us to examine text comprehension from a new perspective, but also allows us to compare the amount of new and old information and thereby measure the complexity of a text through specific numerical units.

We shall not expand on this aspect of comprehension because a detailed analysis would take us too far away from the main theme of the present chapter.

THE COMPREHENSION OF INNER SENSE (SUBTEXT)

The comprehension of a text is not limited to understanding its surface meaning. The meaning of a sentence, the communication of an event or of relationships, or even the general expression of thought in a text is not the final stage of its comprehension. Comparatively simple speech utterances likewise contain an inner sense in addition to the external, obvious meaning of the text. This is true of all utterances, ranging from the simplest to the most complex.

Earlier we mentioned that truly simple utterances encountered in plays may contain a deeper, hidden sense. For instance, the exclamation "It's ten already!" may signify an awareness of the time, but it may also conceal the sense "Oh, how late it is! It's time for me to be leaving." or "How time flies.". An inner subtext or hidden sense, along with the external meaning, exists in almost every utterance in a play. Accordingly, the actor's main task is to convey to the audience not only the external meaning of the text, but also its subtext, i.e., the actor must help the audience "read" the text more profoundly.

Let us turn to examples of how the subtext can be related to the external meaning of the text. In some cases, ordinary narrative text may not involve a double-tier system (i.e., inner subtext in addition to external meaning). In utterances such as "The carpenters used wooden shingles to cover the house." or "The sun lit up the dale brightly.", there may not be any special subtext. The comprehension of these utterances may just be limited to an understanding of their external meaning. Yet even in comparatively simple utterances one may come across a double meaning. For example, the sentence "All the trees in the garden are in bloom." may involve the inner sense "How beautiful the spring is!" or "How fine it is to be young!" as well as the external meaning. Or the sentence "The horses are ready." may involve the subtext "How difficult parting is!"

In addition, there are special utterances in which an inner sense is always present. These utterances cannot be understood without understanding this sense. For example, expressions with a figurative meaning belong in this category. The expression "iron hand" does not refer to a hand made of iron; it is used to refer to an inflexible, strong-willed approach to dealing with something. "He's an ass." does not mean we are talking about an animal; it means we are talking about a foolish, dull-witted person.

An analogous semantic structure is seen in similes (e.g., "He had a character like steel."; "Her eyes were like fathomless lakes."). In all these examples we have a figurative sense, which has to be understood by rejecting the immediate, external meaning of the sentence. It is easy to see that the sense includes an affective evaluation of the fact or event under discussion.

Finally, we have a special form of utterance whose essence is to be found in the figurative sense rather than in the external meaning. There are proverbs. The Russian proverb "Ne krasna izba uglami, a krasna pirogami." (Literal translation: The beauty of a hut is not in its corners, but in the pies that are baked in it.) concerns neither a hut nor pies. Rather, it is concerned with the relationship between the external shape of things and their inner essence. That is why the sense of this proverb is quite different from the sense of another in which similar words are used. This second proverb is "Esh' pirog s gribami i derzhi yazyk za zubami." (Eat your mushroom pie and keep your tongue away from your teeth— i.e., Save your breath to cool your porridge.). In order to understand these proverbs, it is necessary to move away from the direct meanings of the words and substitute the inner sense of the proverb for the concrete meaning. Therefore, the method of analyzing figurative sense (especially in the case of proverbs) has become one of the most important methods of illustrating the depth of a reader's understanding.

In one widely used task, subjects are given a proverb and then asked to choose an item having the same sense from a list of other proverbs. Some of these choices make use of the same words and expressions found in the original proverb while others make use of different words but express the same sense. If the subject understands the proverb, this is manifested by the fact that he/she rejects items that include the same words but involve a different sense and selects those items which make use of quite different words but have the same sense. For instance, the proverb "Ne krasna izba uglami, a krasna pirogami." (The beauty of a hut is not in its corners, but in the pies that are baked in it.) can be paired with the proverb "Ne vse to zoloto chto blestit." (All that glitters is not gold.), even though the same sense is expressed in quite different words.

This distinction between outer meaning and inner sense is especially evident in fables—a literary form that Vygotsky studied a great deal in his early psychological research. For example, the fable "The Lion and the Mouse"[23] involves the sense of being grateful for help given. In contrast, the fable "The Lion and the Fox,"[24] in which we find a number of similar elements, involves the quite different sense that one must beware of perfidy. In sentences with a figurative sense as well as in proverbs and fables, there is a clear conflict between the external text or system of meanings expressed by the text and the inner sense. In order to understand such constructions, one must get away from the direct system of meanings and move to an analysis of the inner sense. This sense is expressed allegorically in the system of expanded, outer meanings.

What we have seen in these examples can be found in any narrative, especially literary text. It is precisely in the case of a literary text (e.g., plays, short stories, novels) that a superficial "reading" does not produce the necessary depth of understanding. The transition from the outer meaning to the inner sense, or from the text to the subtext, is of decisive importance.

Of course this transition is more complex in literary texts than in other types of texts. It is not as obvious as in a proverb or a fable. Rather, a literary work allows for varying degrees of depth in its reading. It is possible to read a literary work superficially, identifying only the words, sentences, or narration of events. On the other hand, it is possible to read a literary work by comprehending the inner sense that is concealed in the description of events. Finally, it is possible to read a literary work with even deeper analysis by going beyond the text, not only into the sense but by analyzing the motives of the characters and/or by understanding the motives of the author. The depth with which one reads a text may be surprisingly varied. Readers may differ in this far more than in the breadth of their grasp of different components of logical relationships expressed in a text.

We should note that depth of reading does not correlate with a person's general knowledge or degree of education; nor does it correlate with the logical analysis of the surface system of meanings. It depends far more on the reader's emotional sensitivity. For some readers, the understanding of a text will remain within the limits of an analysis of external logical meanings even though they might possess great qualities of subtle intellect.

This ability to pass from meaning to sense, and then to motive, is a special aspect of mental activity which may not correlate with the ability to think logically.

---

[23] "A lion was asleep and a mouse ran over his body. The lion awoke and caught the mouse. The mouse begged the lion to let her go. The lion laughed and released her. The next day a hunter caught the lion and tied him to a tree with a rope. The mouse approached stealthily, gnawed through the rope, and set the lion free."–*J. V. Wertsch*
[24] "A lion grew old and could no longer hunt animals. So the lion had to consider how he could live by cunning. He lay in his den and pretended to be ill. The animals came up to him, and he ate them. One day a fox came but would not go into his den. The lion asked the fox, 'Why don't you come in?' The fox replied, 'I can see tracks going into your den but none coming out.' "–*J. V. Wertsch*

These two systems—the system of logical operations in cognitive activity, and the system that ensures the transition to the emotional significance or sense of a text—are quite different psychologically. Unfortunately, the differences have not been adequately investigated in psychology. We should point out that until recently we have not had access to objective methods with which to investigate these phenomena to any great degree. We have lacked methods for analyzing the external structure of perceptual processes as well as the transition to inner sense. These limitations have restricted the exploration of this important aspect of psychology.

Some concrete examples are given below to illustrate this transition from external text to inner sense. They allow us to examine the ways which help us to master different readings of a text while leaving the outer content of the message unchanged. Consider the following excerpt from Gaidar's popular story "Chuk and Gek":

> There lived a man in the forest near the blue mountains. He began to feel melancholy and decided to write to his wife and children to come and join him.

One may understand this as a simple communication of events if one grasps only the outer meaning of the sentences. But one may read aloud these sentences in such a way (e.g., with particular pauses) that encourages the transition from outer meaning to inner sense. There lived a man [in the forest] , near the blue mountains, etc. In this case, the first part, "There lived a man," tells us about someone who lived for a long time cut off from other fellow creatures. "In the forest" indicates his loneliness. "Near the blue mountains" suggests that he lives far away, etc. The process of comprehension is quite different in these two cases: In the first, comprehension is limited to a description of the external situation, in the second, it becomes a communication about a system of inner experience. The pauses and intonation are the devices for making the transition from the level of external, expanded meanings to the level of internal sense. The use of these devices very often turns out to be a decisive factor in realizing this transition from the plane of meaning to the plane of inner sense (cf. Morozova, 1947).

The art of great reciters (e.g., Zakushnyak, Kocharyan, Andronikov, and Zhuravlev) lies precisely in the fact that they are able to use appropriate devices to convey to their audience not only the external meaning of the communication, but also its inner sense and sometimes the motives of characters or the author as well.

So far we have been discussing devices in oral speech that can facilitate the transition from external meaning to inner sense. The same problems arise in understanding written speech, although different devices are used. In written speech, intonation, gestures, and pauses do not play a role; rather, devices like paragraphing and punctuation are used. However, these devices do not fully ensure the transition from meaning to sense. Therefore, the process of understanding the subtext that is concealed by a written text is more complex. It requires a type of independent, inner work which may not be necessary in the comprehension of oral speech.

Let us consider two examples illustrating the complexity of the transition from understanding the external text to the comprehension of the subtext. The following is an excerpt from Shvarts' short story "Strange Girl":

> Marusya, who had quarreled with the boys, sat in a boat all by herself and floated down the river. The boys remembered that there was a dam downstream. They set out in search of her; suddenly Serezha caught sight of some red object, floating on the river. His heart began to thump. It was Marusya's red cap.

This text can be read superficially and perceived as a simple narration of events—the boys' quarrel with the girl, the girl gets into a boat and goes away, down the river there is a dam, the boys look for the girl and find a red cap floating on the river. This type of reading of the text limits itself to surface meanings.

On the other hand, this text can be "read" at a deeper level. The boys' quarrel with the girl leads to her leaving them, and the fact that the boys who ran to look for the girl see her red cap on the water has as its subtext the fact that the girl had perished at the dam. In this instance, the simple detail of a red cap floating on the water signifies a tragedy, the sense of which is precisely what constitutes the subtext of this story. Finally, this same story can be read in an even deeper way, and when it is we may discover a network of motives such as conflicts, quarrels, hurt feelings, and tragedy concealed in the system of events related in the story.

The same possibilities for reading a text at different depths can be seen even more vividly in another short story for which Morozova (1947) has provided a semantic analysis. This story, entitled "The Little Girl from the City," has the following content:

> During the war a woman gave shelter to someone else's little girl. The girl could not get used to this woman. She was shy and shunned her. Suddenly toward spring, the girl brought the woman who had given her shelter a bunch of snowdrops (the first spring flowers which grow even before the snow has melted) from the forest and said, "I've brought you these . . . Mama."

A surface reading of the text reveals just a chain of events—the war, a woman adopts someone else's child, the girl was shy and shunned her and, finally, toward spring the girl brought her flowers from the forest. However, if this same message is read at a greater depth, the sentence "This is for you, . . . Mama" is seen to conceal a subtext which tells the reader that the girl at last acknowledged the woman who had adopted her as her mother. From this single sentence, a deep, emotional content emerges that is the essence of the story. It reveals the emotional content that does not figure in the surface meaning.

In all of the above examples, the central problem is not one of understanding the surface meaning which issues directly from words and grammatical constructions. The central problem is the transition from the external, surface meanings to the inner system of subtexts or senses. It is precisely this which presents the most complex and important issues for psychology.

Although the transition from meaning to sense is a crucial issue in psychology, it is still very inadequately studied. One is more likely to find an examination of this process in literary analysis or in the practical work of directors of plays than in psychology. Stanislavskii (1951, 1956) and his pupils (e.g., Knebel', 1970; also see Knebel' and Luria, 1971) developed an entire system of methods for conveying to the audience the inner subtext or inner sense of an utterance. They tried to analyze how one can change the direction of communication and shift the attention of the audience from the surface meaning to deep structures.

There are two general types of methods that can be used to convey to an audience the inner sense of a message. First, there are external methods. Among these methods are intonation and pauses. As we have already said, the use of these devices may immediately change the sense of a text without changing a single word in it. Consider a sentence like the following: "Tremble, animals, the lion has come out on the road." If we were to read it without expression, it might remain limited to a simple communication of an event. But if we were to read it with appropriate intonation (e.g., "*Tremble*, animals, the *LION* has come out on the road!"), then it would begin to convey the state of fear, humility, or grandeur (it is the *LION* himself that has come out). The sentence "That was quite a walk." pronounced without any intonation does not express anything except a communication of an event. But if a certain intonation is introduced here (e.g., "That was *quite* a walk!" or "That was quite a *walk!*"), then the sentence acquires different senses.

Pauses play a similar role. The sentence "Today, the man, sitting alone in his empty cottage, recalled his past." may be interpreted quite differently if pronounced with pauses. Consider the following version: "Today [the man] sitting alone [in his empty cottage] recalled the past." In the second version, the inner sense is much more accessible.

In addition to external methods for aiding the transition from meaning to sense, there are other methods. Perhaps the best example of these can be found in Stanislavskii's extensive analyses of texts. In Stanislavskii's school, the director who is preparing an actor to convey not only the external events but also the inner sense in a play, never begins by studying the text of the role. Rather, preparation of the director and actor begins with something quite different. The actor is first asked to get accustomed to the image and motives of the character he/she is to portray and to decide what the character would do in various concrete situations. The actor is given the task of improvising, of uttering whatever would express the character's motives. Hence, the actor carries out what Stanislavskii and his colleagues term "material acts." These are external acts which are also interpretations of the character. In this way, preparation for a role begins with a study of the character's motives, followed by portraying several possible acts the character might have performed in various situations. Long before given a text, the actor is getting accustomed to the image of the character. Only on the basis of this preliminary work is the actor, who later will get the text, able to interpret the verbal expression of this text. He/she does this through the system of motives and through the character of the person which he/she has already mastered.

It is in this manner that actors master a role. It involves the transition from mastering motives to creating the character of the person who is to be portrayed. The text of the play is interpreted through these motives and this image. The text thus acquires an expressive significance because it portrays not the meaning, but the sense the text; it enables actors to make the audience conscious of the sense of the message.

If an actor is given the text as a first step and if the stages of mastering the character's motives are excluded, the reading of the text will be limited to conveying the meanings. It will not reach an effective communication of the sense, which is the essential task of an actor.

The analysis of the process of understanding the sense of an utterance, and the transition from meaning to sense and motive, remain a major issue for cognitive psychology. One can only hope that in the future the processes that make this transition possible will become the subject matter of careful, detailed, and objective psychological experiments. There is no doubt whatsoever that such research would represent a new and important stage in scientific psychology.

Chapter 14
Language and Discursive Thinking: The Process of Deriving a Conclusion

In previous chapters, we emphasized that language plays an extremely important role in the formation of human cognitive processes and human consciousness. We touched on a series of problems concerned with the production and comprehension of speech, the relationship between oral and written speech, the relationship between speech and thought, and the development and breakdown of the processes involved in speech. All these areas are studied by a new discipline that stands on the borderline between psychology and linguistics. This discipline, which has made rapid strides during recent years, is psycholinguistics.

However, there is another important question we have not touched on so far. The word and the sentence, as basic forms of language, are not the only means that make possible higher forms of the reflection of reality and the expression of thought in speech. As we pointed out at the very beginning of our analysis, the acquisition of speech makes possible that transition from sensory to rational analysis. This is perhaps the most important event in the evolution of mental life. It is because of language that humans can delve into the essence of things, transcend the limits of direct impression, organize their purposeful behavior, unravel complex connections and relationships which are not accessible to direct perception, and transmit information accumulated over generations to other persons.

Moreover, language plays another essential role which goes beyond the limits of organizing perception and ensuring communication. The existence of language and its complex logical-grammatical structures enables humans to *derive conclusions* on the basis of logical arguments. This can be done without having to rely on direct sensory experience. It is easy to see that this property of language makes possible the most complex forms of discursive (inductive and deductive) thinking. These forms of thinking are the main forms of human productive intellectual activity.

The aforementioned characteristic clearly distinguished human conscious activity from the mental processes of animals. As was suggested earlier, an animal can accumulate experience only through direct perception or, at best, on the basis of "extrapolation" from material derived through direct perception. Those are the processes that we see in Krushinskii's well-known experiments. In his studies, a dog could see a piece of meat through a hole in a pipe. The meat was moving slowly through the pipe. The dog ran to the end of the pipe and waited for the meat to emerge. The "conclusion," based on impressions, enabled the dog to extrapolate the movement of the bait and respond by going to the place where it should have appeared. However, this example of "reasoning" can be explained by the presence of a direct perceptual situation.

We now know that mental development in the animal world is limited to complex inherited programs of behavior and new connections formed as conditioned reflexes. These conditioned reflexes can range from elementary to complex forms, the latter accounting for the extrapolation of direct impressions. In contrast, because humans can use language, their potential is much different. The basic fact here is that humans can derive conclusions not only from their direct impressions but also from the general experience of humankind. They have access to the experience of generations, and therefore can often arrive at conclusions without having to return to direct, sensory experience. This fact, which results from being able to use language, characterizes human production thinking.

Let us now turn to a detailed examination of this process. We have already pointed out that the word provides the mechanism for abstracting and generalizing, a mechanism created in the process of human social history. We have also noted that the combination of words in a sentence enables humans not only to indicate an object and include it in a system of relationships, but also to formulate and express thoughts. Finally, we have pointed out that because they possess "valencies," many words require the appearance of other words which complement them. This fact causes the "feeling of incompleteness" which disappears only with the emergence of another word which completes the lexical structure at issue. All of these mechanisms have been created in the course of thousands of years and are the basic instruments of the formation of consciousness.

However, there also exist larger and more complex linguistic units. These enable humans not only to name and generalize objects and formulate word combinations, but also to ensure a new process which is absent in animals, namely, the process of deriving a productive logical conclusion. It takes place on a purely verbal-logical plane, thus enabling humans to draw conclusions without turning to direct external impressions. This device, which has evolved over the course of several thousand years of social history, involves the logical combination of several utterances. When taken together, several utterances form the device that makes logical thinking possible. One such device is the syllogism. It can serve as a model for those techniques of language that make logical thinking possible, and allows the operation of deriving conclusions from general hypotheses.

Syllogisms have been the focus of attention since ancient times and were especially important to thinkers during the Middle Ages. In a typical syllogism, there are two initial premises, i.e., two separate ideas connected with each other not only by their sequential presentation, but also by logical relationships (this latter connection being more important). In the simplest form of a syllogism, the first, or "major," premise includes a certain general or universal idea. The second, or "minor," premise reveals how some object belongs to the category formulated in the major premise. The combination of the major and the minor premises induces a feeling of logical incompleteness. This leads to the formation of a conclusion based on the general rule that the regularities which characterize all objects in a set must also characterize individual objects in the set.

Let us consider the following very simple syllogism: "Precious metals do not rust. Platinum is a precious metal. Consequently, platinum does not rust." What is it that explains the psychological structure of this syllogism? What do we need in order to accept this syllogism? To begin with, in order to use this syllogism, one must accept the first premise as a universal statement. This premise, in our example, states that all metals, without exception, which belongs to the class of precious metals, possess the quality of not rusting. This universal statement is what serves as the basis for all of the subsequent steps. The second, minor premise states that a certain concrete object, platinum, belongs to this class of metals. Consequently, it has all the qualities mentioned in the first premise about precious metals. The third part of the syllogism, the conclusion, is the result of including the concrete object in the general system formulated in the first premise. It enables one to transfer the quality of the enitre group mentioned in the first premise to the given object.

A syllogism is a device of logical thinking that has evolved over the course of social history. It completes the system of necessary logical connections, thereby enabling us to derive a conclusion solely on the basis of a verbal-logical system. No additional data from experience is required. The logical necessity is psychologically expressed in what we may term "a feeling of logical coherence." An intellectually advanced person who hears the major and minor premises will inevitably experience a feeling of incompleteness, which can be removed only by deriving the final conclusion, thereby completing the logical system.

We shall not discuss here the large number of different types of syllogisms that have been identified in modern logic. The important point for us is that any of these syllogisms represents a complex, historically evolved, verbal-logical mechanism. They make it possible to derive conclusions solely by coordinating two verbal premises. The productivity of the logical matrices used to arrive at logical conclusions allows humans to acquire new information both from individual observations, which can then be included in a system of generalizations, and from general premises, which formulate universal human experience through language.

The possibility of arriving at conclusions on the basis of the logical mechanism that we have just described naturally undergoes certain changes during evolution and during ontogenesis. During the initial stages, the process of deriving a conclusion from a syllogism is not adequately developed. It requires additional supports. During later stages of development, syllogistic reasoning becomes so habitual that at one time psychologists believed that the experience or feeling of logical necessity was a fundamental property of spiritual life and not a product of prolonged socio-historical development. Psychologists of the Würburg School interpreted the presence of these feelings as a primary and universal property of mental life which depends neither on concrete images nor on speech. The experience of logical coherence for part-whole, and species-genus relationships, as well as for cause-effect relationships, belong to such logical feelings. Also included among feelings of logical coherence are experiences that arise when one brings two premises into a relationship.

Gestalt psychologists proposed some similar ideas. They regarded the feeling of logical incompleteness as a consequence of those formal laws devised by them in their study of the process for completing incomplete schemes. These psychologists developed a phenomenology of logical thinking. The need for this phenomenology is what led to the creation of an entire science of logical thinking. We shall not undertake a complete analysis of that thinking here. Rather, we shall address two other issues: (1) describe the psychological conditions that form the basis for deriving a logical conclusion and evoke the logical experiences mentioned earlier; (2) trace how these operations of verbal-logical conclusions have evolved historically. This will involve a comparison of conclusions which are derived through the basis of strictly formal foundations with conclusions which are derived on the basis of individual practical experience. We shall see that these two types of derivations involve different stages in the historical evolution of consciousness.

As we have already said, there are three conditions making possible the process of deriving a logical conclusion, a conclusion based solely on the premises and therefore not involving additional data from practical experience. The first condition is that the position expressed in the major premise should, in fact, have a universal character, i.e., it should state a universal fact which does not admit any exception. If this is not true, then the major premise will not express an obligatory meaning and will not be able to serve as the starting point for any further argument. The second condition is that there should be complete belief in this major premise. The subject must accept the major premise without comparing it with his/her own individual experience and without doubting that it provides a law from which one can arrive at a conclusion. The third condition is that the two premises must not be considered as two isolated statements. Rather, they must be enclosed in a single logical system, the first part of which is the major premise (statement of the universal fact) and the second part is the minor premise (statement relating a particular object to the category mentioned in the major premise). If the two prmises are perceived by the subject as separate, isolated statements, the feeling of logical incompleteness will not occur and there can be no derivation of a conclusion.

It would be a mistake to think that this system has been in existence during all the stages of human social history or that it appeared suddenly. Several facts indicate that the syllogistic formula is a product of gradual socio-historical development. There is good reason to believe that all three characteristics of the syllogism mentioned above first appeared rather late in social history. In particular, there is good reason to believe that the appearance of syllogistic thinking can emerge only during those stages of cultural development when activity realized through the help of language becomes an independent process. That is, this process does not depend on direct practice and constitutes a special form of theoretical activity. Research has shown that this form of theoretical activity does not exist during the early stages of ontogenesis or during the comparatively early stages of socio-historical development. Let us consider these cases separately.

The ontogenesis of intellectual processes, in particular, the processes involved in deriving logical conclusions, has been the subject of a great deal of research. The work of Piaget (1955) and his followers occupies a special place in this research. These investigators collected a great deal of data concerned with genetic epistemology. Their research is quite well known. Given our present interests, we shall provide only a brief review of this work.

The first and the most widely known fact of interest for us here concerns the "law of conservation," or the "law of reversibility" described by Piaget and Inhelder (1969). A manifestation of this law is the child's ability to break away from direct sensory impressions and move to the stage of "concrete operations" which includes verbal-logical operations in their simplest form.

This transition is manifested as follows. If we pour liquid into a wide glass vessel and then transfer it into a tall narrow vessel in front of the child's eyes, the directly perceived level of the liquid will rise. Now, if we ask the child, under these conditions, if the quantity of the liquid in the narrow vessel remains the same as it was before in the wide vessel, the child, whose reasoning is governed by direct impressions, will say that the quantity of liquid has changed. He/she may state that the quantity has increased (by focusing on the changed level) or that it has decreased (by focusing on the diameter of the vessel).

It is only later that the child can break away from direct impressions and work with abstract reasoning. When this occurs, the types of answers seen earlier disappear, and the law of conservation begins to govern reasoning about quantity. The dependence of the preoperational child on direct impressions and the inability to include the link of verbal-logical generalizations in reasoning are reflected in the fact that he/she cannot derive a universal conclusion from his/her observations. For a child of 3 or 4 years of age, the category of universality does not exist. We have every reason to believe that at this age the operation of deriving a conclusion from a single, universal statement is not yet possible. Observations indicate that children in this age group base their conclusions not so much on universal categories (the point of departure for deriving a logical conclusion) as on their individual practical experience. That is why one is fully justified in saying that a child of 3 or 4 years of age possesses neither the power of induction (i.e., going from individual facts to a universal law) nor the power of deduction (i.e., deducing individual facts from a general premise). Instead of using these operations, the child arrives at a direct conclusion on the basis of external impression, a process that Piaget, with complete justification, termed "transduction."

Piaget's observations of the reasoning processes of a very large number of children from 3 to 5 years of age failed to yield evidence of even a single case of universal reasoning. When a young child observes that certain things sink in the water while others float, he/she does not carry out further analyses of these facts, analyses that would lead to replacing his/her direct impressions with a general reason for why some things sink and others float. For example, a child might say, "This thing sinks because it is red.", "This one sinks because it is big.", "This one sinks because it is made of iron.", "Boats sail because they are light.", and "Ships sail because they are big." Such answers reveal that the child's answers are based on direct impressions rather than on an abstract general property. This constitutes the basis for what Piaget and other authors have termed "syncretic thinking."

Many of the same properties have been observed in developmental research concerned with deriving conclusions from syllogisms. Observations have shown that young children interpret the two premises of a syllogism not as a system in which the second part is included in the first, but as two isolated statements. Therefore, they are unable to take the major premise as a universal fact, to include the second premise in this universal fact, and to derive a logical conclusion. Instead, the child bases his/her conclusions on direct experience, and does not turn his/her attention to the theoretical operation based on the relationship of the two figures of the syllogism.

Studies conducted by Piaget illustrate this. Children were given a syllogism, such as: "Some of the inhabitants of the town N are Bretons. All Bretons of the town N perished during the war. Were there any inhabitants left in the town N?" The conclusion from this syllogism, which can be easily derived by a developed consciousness, remains inaccessible for the child. The usual reply to the question in this study was, "I don't know. No one told me anything about it." These observations enabled Piaget to identify several stages of verbal-logical development during childhood.

He argues that between 2 and 7 years of age the child passes through the stage of "pre-operational" thinking, that there is no hint of the ability to use independent logical relationships or derive conclusions in syllogisms. During this stage, the child derives conclusions on the basis of direct experience, bypassing any hierarchically constructed, logical operations. The second stage, recurring between the ages of 7 and 10 years, is what Piaget calls the stage of "concrete operations." Logical operations make their appearance during this stage, although they function only in connection with the concrete visual plane of experience. In Piaget's opinion, it is only when the child reaches the age of 11 to 14 years that he/she makes the transition to the stage of "formal operations." At this stage, the child masters verbal-logical codes which enable him/her to pass from one argument to another on the formal logical plane.

There is no doubt that Piaget's data are based on sound empirical research. However, there is some evidence that raises doubt in our minds about whether the sequence in which these stages occur is necessarily fixed. We also question whether it is not possible, given properly structured teaching, to achieve a significant leap that would enable children of a much younger age to master the elements of theoretical thinking and therefore to use instruments of theoretical thinking, such as syllogisms. Experiments carried out by Gal'perin (1959, 1976) and his colleagues have shown that it is possible for children as young as 5 to 6 years of age to develop the ability to derive a conclusion from a syllogism. They have shown that this is possible if the reasoning process is expanded and the child is given the chance to learn certain forms of theoretical thinking by first relying on concrete means and then switching to external verbal reasoning.

Thus, according to Piaget, a child of 3 to 4 years of age is still totally unable to reason on the basis of general statements. During the second stage (children of 4 to 5 years of age), one may observe the beginning of this kind of reasoning. During the third stage (children of 5 to 6 years of age), these features begin to appear more regularly and permanently. This provides grounds for using significant characteristics of objects to form a universal rule. Finally, during the fourth stage (children of 6 to 7 years of age), this condition of universality begins to become stable. A child of this age can derive conclusions in a syllogism.

The data from research conducted by Zaporozhets and his colleagues are relevant to this claim. The results of their research are presented in Table 1. These data indicate that it is possible to teach a child syllogistic reasoning. Thus, the operations involved in the transition from concrete thinking to theoretical,

TABLE 1

PERCENTAGE OF CORRECT SOLUTIONS OF A SYLLOGISM

	3-4 years	4-5 years	5-6 years	6-7 years
Before learning	0	4%	20%	98%
After learning	0	52%	96%	100%

verbal-logical thinking can be traced to their initial stages in early childhood.

Ontogenetic investigations of thinking provide valuable material for analyzing the gradual process of mastering theoretical, verbal-logical thinking. However, one cannot rely completely on such material. In early ontogenesis, it is difficult to separate maturation from learning. These two processes are related in a very complex way. Furthermore, in the early stages of ontogenesis children have not yet developed full-fledged practical activity. Accordingly, we cannot observe the degree to which verbal-logical thinking is independent of fully developed, concrete-practical thinking.

For these reasons, it becomes evident that unique and valuable data about the interrelationship between practical and theoretical thinking can be obtained by examining changes in intellectual activity during socio-historical development. Attempts have repeatedly been made to analyze the socio-historical development of thinking. However, since most of these attempts have been based on theoretically unacceptable positions, the resulting data suffered from serious shortcomings. One group of investigators argued that the whole development of thinking, beginning with the level of direct practice and ending with the level of complex theoretical activity, can be explained in terms of the number of concepts involved. This hypothesis, naturally, oversimplifed the analysis of the formation of intellectual processes. An attempt to account for differences in thinking on purely quantitative grounds can hardly be satisfactory.

A second group of investigators, among whom is the well-known French psychologist Levy-Bruhl, argued that during the early stages of development, thinking is of a prelogical, magical character. This point of view, once widely shared by various investigators, is clearly unacceptable. It ignores real forms of thinking which are part of the concrete historical development of the forms of mental activity connected with the changes in the modes of economy and forms of social life. That is, this approach ignores forms of thinking that are connected with socioeconomic life.

It is clear that scientific analysis of the development of thinking is impossible unless one begins with a careful investigation of the forms of social life that characterize a particular stage of historical development, and unless one links progress in the area of intellectual processes with changes in the forms of practical life—because these forms of practical life provide the basis for the formation of new kinds of thinking.

During 1930–1931, we had an opportunity to study people in our country who had undergone a rapid and radical change in the socio-historical conditions of their life. These people lived in what was almost a natural economy. They had remained nonliterate, and their primary form of activity was purely practical activity. As a result of societal changes and the cultural revolution, they were integrated into a culture in a very short time. Nonliteracy was stamped out, and elementary forms of individual economic life were replaced by a collective economy. These changes could hardly help but lead to the appearance of new forms of thinking.

The subjects we studied were quite bright. They were fully capable of managing their agricultural economy, sometimes requiring them to solve extremely complex practical problems connected with the use of irrigation canals. However, their mental processes were closely connected with their practical activity. Their theoretical thinking had not evolved into a special form of activity and their life was characterized by the predominance of concrete practical forms of activity. After the introduction of collectivized agriculture and the eradication of nonliteracy, they began to develop theoretical activity at a rapid rate. This development began with the mastery of elementary forms of classroom skills and proceeded to complex forms of discussing problems connected with the planning of their economic life. These radical changes in the community under observation led to distinct progress in their intellectual activity. This progress could easily be observed when we studied the attitude of these people toward syllogisms.

We found that when subjects who had not been exposed to theoretical activity were asked to repeat a major and a minor premise and a question, and then to derive the conclusion, their behavior differed greatly from what is characteristic of a normal, mature adult who has been educated in school and who has had experience with theoretical thinking. As a rule, these subjects found it difficult even to repeat an elementary syllogism consisting of a major and minor premise. Thus, when confronted with the following syllogism: "Precious metals do not rust. Gold is a precious metal. Does it rust or not?", they usually repeated it as two isolated sentences. For example, they might say "Do precious metals rust or not?"; "Does gold rust or not?" It was clear that the premises were perceived as isolated questions and that the logical connection between the major and the minor premises had not been mastered.

It is characteristic that even subjects who correctly repeated this syllogism and drew the correct conclusion immediately added irrelevant remarks: "Yes, I know this. I have a gold ring. I've had it for a long time. It does not rust." If they were given the syllogism "All men are mortal, Muhammed is a man, therefore . . . ", they would answer, "Of course, he will die, I know that all men die." This small addition—"I know this myself"—is of great psychological significance. It indicates that what is really taking place here is not so much the process of deriving a conclusion as the mobilization of available information. In these cases, the syllogism provides an impulse for applying concrete knowledge, rather than for extracting a genuinely logical conclusion from the premises.

In order to test this hypothesis, we conducted the following experiment. Subjects were given two groups of syllogisms. Syllogisms in one of these groups were drawn from their direct practical experience, syllogisms in the other were purely abstract. They were taken from a field in which the subjects did not have any practical knowledge. The following is an example of the first type of syllogism: "Cotton grows in all places which are humid and warm. In the place called N it is not humid and warm. Does cotton grow in N or not?" An example of the second type of syllogism is: "In the Far North, where there is snow all year round, all bears are white. The place N is situated in the Far North. Are the bears in N white or not?" The cases were quite different. This difference confirmed our hypothesis that the intellectual activity of our subjects differs greatly from what we normally see. Their reasoning proceeded by mobilizing their practical experience rather than by deriving conclusions solely on the basis of theoretical premises. When confronted with the first type of syllogism, our subjects usually answered, "Yes, of course, cotton probably would not grow there. I know that cotton grows only places where it is warm and humid." When confronted with the second type of syllogism, they usually refused to answer, saying that they did not possess knowledge on the subject. Thus they might answer, "I've never been there and don't know. I don't want to tell a lie, I won't say anything. Ask someone who has been there. He'll tell you!"

It becomes quite clear that these subjects did not take the theoretical premises as something possessing universal significance. They did not derive appropriate conclusions from it. They preferred to derive conclusions by mobilizing their practical experience. Thus, they were unable to master the system of syllogistic relationships when these syllogistic relationships did not rest on their practical activity.

However, thinking that is limited in this way was not found in members from another section of the population of this same region. These people had completed short-term courses, had actively participated in the newly created collective economy, and had therefore been involved, to some extent, in theoretical activity. Such subjects could derive a conclusion from syllogisms. Instead of simply relying on the process of recalling data from their own experience, they used a theoretical mode of operation. They used the syllogism as a method of deriving conclusions from a premise which went beyond the bounds of their direct experience. It was only in a few instances that they resorted to concretizing the available data. In these cases, the conclusions they derived from the syllogism bore a mixed character. They were connected partly with the system of logical relationships and partly with concrete experience.

TABLE 2

THE OPERATION OF DERIVING A CONCLUSION FROM A SYLLOGISM

Subjects	Type of response		
	Refusal to answer	Conclusion with additional concretization	Formal logical conclusion
Subjects from backward regions, nonliterate	54%	39%	7%
Collective farm, active members	5%	30%	65%
Pupils of elementary schools or those attending courses	0	10%	90%

We also studied the performance of a third group of subjects who were culturally more advanced than the members of the first two groups. For members of this third group, deriving a conclusion from a syllogism was quite easy. The results of our study are presented in Table 2.

These figures reveal that the ability to derive logical conclusions is in fact the product of historical development. During the early stages of social development, when active, concrete forms of practice predominate, formal logical conclusions are not yet easily formulated, and subjects are limited to concrete practice. The radical restructuring of socioeconomic structure, which is accompanied by the introduction of literacy and culture, results not only in a broader range of concepts and the mastery of more complex forms of language. It also enables people to master techniques of logical thinking that allow them to go beyond the bounds of direct experience. An example of this is the syllogism, a device for theoretical thinking.

We see that among other things, language enables humans to go beyond the limits of immediate experience and derive conclusions on the basis of abstract, verbal-logical hypotheses. Among the constructions provided by language in this regard are the logical structures which may be modeled in a syllogism.

It is precisely because of this that the transition to complex forms of social activity enables one to master those linguistic devices which make possible the transition to a new level of consciousness, the level of theoretical thinking. This marks the transition from sensory to rational processes. It is a fundamental property of human conscious activity. Thus we see that humans are not only an active agent, but are also the product of socio-historical development.

Chapter 15
The Cerebral Organization and Pathological Disruption of Speech Production

In our final chapters, we shall examine a problem only touched upon earlier, i.e., the problem of the cerebral organization of speech activity. This will involve both the production and the comprehension of speech. By examining the cerebral organization of speech, we enter into what is perhaps the most interesting and important—for a materialistic psychology—sphere. Despite the fact that this issue has been studied for a hundred years, we still know all too little about the processes involved.

METHODS

Two main methods are usually used to study the relationship between cerebral organization and mental activity. One is the comparative evolutionary method, and the other is the analysis of changes in activity which result from focal brain lesions. The first method has been used widely throughout the history of science. By examining the relationship between brain structure and associated behavioral characteristics at various stages in evolution (usually in animals), we can derive conclusions about the cerebral mechanisms of complex forms of mental activity.

Unfortunately, the comparative anatomical method is of little use for studying many of the problems that interest us. The main difficulty arises because of the complex and unique organization of speech activity. The evolution of the brain of animals has taken tens of millions of years. It is only as a result of this prolonged process that we see the formation of the highly organized brain characteristic of vertebrates, mammals, primates, and finally humans. The yardsticks that apply to the evolution of language, however, are quite different. The evolution of language involves a relatively short period. Language was created over the course of 40,000, 50,000, or perhaps 100,000 years; it can hardly be compared with the extremely slow evolutionary process involved in the evolution of the brain. That is why an analysis of the development of language can scarcely help us arrive at any significant conclusions about the cerebral organization of different forms of speech activity.

Concrete data confirm this conclusion since the brain of humans who are at a low level of historical development but who still belong to the species homo sapiens differs hardly at all from the brain of modern, highly developed humans. But the organization of speech activity in these two types of humans is quite different. Thus, an analysis of the transformations which occur in the evolution of the human brain can tell us almost nothing about the properties of human language and about the processes of speech communication.

Nor can we expect anything more from an ontogenetic analysis of the brain. The development of a child's brain occurs relatively fast, but even this pace of development is not comparable with the extraordinarily fast pace at which a child learns language. In a very short time, sometimes within 6 or 10 months, children master the basic deep grammatical structures, learn the basic rules of language structure, and pass on to complex forms of speech utterance. Hence, an ontogenetic comparison of the brain provides us with very little material for understanding language development.

Given these problems, we can see why a study of the cerebral organization of speech processes must rely largely on the second method of analyzing how speech activity undergoes a change as a result of focal lesions of the brain. This method is in complete accordance with Pavlov's well-known position that "Through the process of separating and simplifying, pathology reveals what is otherwise whole and hidden from us in the physiological norm."

The study of changes in speech activity resulting from focal brain lesions was begun over 100 years ago. As early as 1861, French anatomist Broca (1861) made an observation that proved to be extremely important for the study of this problem. He showed that a lesion of the posterior third of the inferior frontal gyrus of the left cerebral hemisphere leads to a distinctive pathology. Patients with this type of lesion may not be affected by paralysis (including paralysis of the speech apparatus), but they may lose the ability to speak. This occurs even though it appears that patients of this type fully retain the ability to understand speech addressed to them. Thirteen years later, German psychiatrist Wernicke (1874) described another phenomenon which was of no less significance. He showed that patients who have a lesion of the posterior third of the left superior temporal gyrus retain the ability to produce smoothly articulated speech. However, their ability to understand speech is disrupted. In Wernicke's terms, the "sensory images of the word" are affected in those patients.

Broca's and Wernicke's findings marked the beginning of serious study of the cerebral organization of human speech activity. These two investigators demonstrated that focal brain lesions lead to specific disruptions of speech activity rather than a general deterioration. Their observations led to the conclusion that the *speech process is dependent on a number of simultaneously functioning areas of the cerebral cortex, each of which has its own specific significance for the organization of speech activity*.

Although their observations at first appeared to have opened to the way for the precise analysis of the cerebral organization of speech processes, investigators soon came face to face with difficulties that took several decades to overcome. The main factors underlying these difficulties were, on the one hand, the absence of a theory of language structure, and, on the other, an incorrect understanding of the relationship between language and the brain.

Neurologists and psychologists who analyzed the cerebral organization of speech and observed the effect of localized brain pathology on speech processes had access to a very imperfect theory of language and speech activity. Their approach was based on the associationism which prevailed in the 19th century. As a result, these investigators thought of speech as the association between sounds or articulatory movements and ideas. Investigators who observed symptoms resulting from damage to the posterior third of the inferior frontal gyrus of the left hemisphere (Broca's area) hypothesized that this area is the "center of the motor images of the word" and that damage to its leads to damage to the motor images of the word, while leaving speech movements intact.

The data described by Wernicke were interpreted in an analogous way by associationists. For them, the posterior third of the left superior temporal gyrus represented "the center for the sensory images of the word" or, as Wernicke said, the center for the "concepts of the word" ("Wortbegriff"). Therefore, damage to this center led to the impairment of sensory images of the word while leaving the motor images unaffected.

Following these discoveries, other attempts were made to describe more complex forms of speech disturbances, such as "conduction aphasia" and "transcortical aphasia." However, like earlier approaches, these analyses—by investigators such as Lichtheim (1883)—were based on the same simplified, associative scheme. Obviously, such an oversimplified understanding of the psychological structure of speech activity proved inadequate. Clinical observations of speech disturbances in patients with focal brain lesions were unable to account for this cerebral organization of complex forms of speech activity.

Not surprisingly, there was soon a reaction against these elementary, oversimpli-schemes. Typical among them was that of the so-called noetic school. Several leading neurologists, e.g., Monakow (1914) and Goldstein (1948), belonged to this school. These investigators approached speech as a complex symbolic activity which emerges out of an abstract attitude and plays an important role in carrying out complex forms of categorical thinking.

For these authors, speech was considered to be a complex, unified activity occurring on a conscious plane. They assumed that cerebral lesions inevitably led to the disintegration of the complex symbolic processes involved in the ab-stract attitude or categorical behavior. Phenomena that earlier were considered to reflect the disintegration of speech activity alone, now began to be considered as phenomena indicating a general deterioration of categorical behavior. The emphasis shifted from focal lesions to the overall brain.

It is clear that these views were even less capable of answering questions about the cerebral organization of speech processes. They were no more capable of producing an adequate account of the cerebral mechanisms of speech than the attempts inspired by the mechanistic notions of associationism.

What was required was an overall analysis of the psychological structure of speech activity in order to ensure that an analysis of its cerebral foundations would be possible and productive. This meant dividing real speech processes into component parts in order to uncover their individual stages. It was only with this kind of approach, an approach that took several decades of effort, that researchers were able to provide the necessary environment for develop-ing an adequate account of speech processes and the changes in speech pro-cesses that occur as a result of focal brain lesions. Not until the 1940s and 1950s did the efforts of linguists, psycholinguists, and psychologists result in a theory of speech activity that could be used in the analysis of the cerebral organization of speech processes.

In addition, however, there was a second difficulty in this research. Most re-searchers tried to make a direct comparison between complex forms of speech and focal brain lesions. These psychomorphological conceptions provided the founda-tions for research hypotheses. Most of these hypotheses assumed that very limited areas of the brain govern the complex processes involved in the formation of sounds and the lexical, morphological, and syntactic system of language. Such were the views expressed, for instance, by the German psychiatrist Kleist (1934). He con-structed a map of the brain in which individual regions correspond to individual aspects of human speech activity. A similar position was taken by the British neuro-logist Head (1926). Proceeding from quite different theoretical conceptions, he tried to show that focal brain lesions can lead to nominative, syntactic, and semantic aphasia. However, even these attempts to correlate different aspects of linguistic activity with limited regions of the brain did not meet with success. It remained, there-fore, to overcome this second difficulty as well during the following decades. The idea had to be accepted that cerebral lesions are connected with speech disturbances in a complex *indirect* way.

The general problem confronting investigators in this area of study had two basic parts: On the one hand, they had to be concerned with the psychophysiological factors involved in speech production; on the other hand, they had to be concerned with comprehension, or how the expanded speech utterance is transformed into thought. It was only by investigating the extralinguistic conditions that lie at the foundation of complex forms of speech activity and by identifying the conditions for carrying out the stages involved in speech processing that researchers would be able to correlate these extralinguistic factors with specific areas of the brain. Only then could they provide an analysis of how disturbance of these factors caused by lesions of some part of the cerebral cortex can lead to changes in speech activity as a whole.

By utilizing such a method, we shall identify the types of speech defects that result from lesions of different parts of the brain. We shall analyze how speech activity can be disrupted by a lesion in deep brain structures which are involved in cortical regulation. Then we shall consider lesions of the frontal lobes which govern complex forms of programmed movements and actions. Finally, we shall turn to an analysis of lesions of specific areas of the so-called *speech cortex*. We shall see that these lesions result in disturbances of processes that play a more direct role in the organization of speech. Our account will constitute a brief summary of observations that have been described in detail elsewhere (e.g., Luria, 1947, 1962, 1970, 1974a, 1975a).

As mentioned earlier, speech production involves a complex course of events. It begins with a general motive such as conveying something to another person, or asking for something, or explaining something. Then it passes through the stage of inner speech, which converts the initial intention into a scheme of the expanded speech utterance. The process ends with the expanded speech utterance, with its lexical, syntactic, and semantic properties. We shall consider the stages of this complex process one at a time and try to identify the cerebral systems involved in each.

THE CEREBRAL ORGANIZATION OF THE MOTIVATIONAL BASIS AND PROGRAMMING OF SPEECH PRODUCTION

Speech production must begin with a motive. This motive may be to convey something to another person, to request something, to explain some idea, etc. Clearly, in the absence of such a motive, no speech utterance will occur.

The motivational basis of the utterance is doubly characterized. First, the speaker must be active enough to be able to formulate a speech utterance plan. Without this activation or the necessary cortical tone, no utterance is possible.

Second, the motivational basis of the utterance must be transformed into an expanded speech utterance through predicative inner speech.

These two characteristics are connected with the functioning of different parts of the brain. We know that cortical tone depends on the functioning of the brain stem. More specifically, paths ascending from the reticular formation ensure this. Clinical studies have shown that lesions of the brain stem result in the well-known primary inactivity syndrome. This is manifested in the general behavior of patients as well as in their speech activity. We have frequently observed patients of this type. They lie passively in their beds, make no effort to engage in activity, and their gaze remains fixed on a single point (they find it extremely difficult to shift to another). Their behavior is generally characterized by extreme inactivity.

It is natural that with this type of disruption of activity, speech is impossible. These patients generally do not attempt to speak to anyone or ask for anything. Speech activity is simply absent. This is just one aspect of their general inactive state. This syndrome may appear when a person has recently suffered from some serious brain injury accompanied by small hemorrhages in the brain stem. For example, we once observed a great scientist who had remained unconscious for several weeks after an injury and then manifested symptoms of extreme inactivity. During this period, his behavior was characterized by the fact that his gaze was fixed on a single point in space. He made no attempt to say anything to anyone. Some neuropathologists tentatively made the diagnosis of motor aphasia, but it could not be confirmed because of the patient's general inactivity. Unlike other patients suffering from aphasia, this patient did not even try to produce speech. There was good reason for arguing that the impairment of speech in this case was not so much a special disturbance of symbolic activity, but a type of mutism—that it was a general cessation of speech caused by the patient's overall inactivity. That is why we were not surprised to find that after this period of general inactivity had passed and the normal function of the ascending reticular formation was restored, the patient's speech manifested all of the properties which characterized it before his illness.

This form of primary speech inactivity is characteristic only of very serious cases of injury to the deep structures of the brain. Much more frequently we come across cases where the lowered tone of the cerebral cortex is manifested in a confused, oneiroid state. Those patients cannot orient themselves in time and space, and this is reflected in their speech activity.

Such patients often express ideas that do not correspond with reality, although they are quite capable of naming objects shown to them and repeating words, groups of words, or short sentences. If a short pause is inserted between the presentation of a sentence and its reproduction, or if one diverts the patient's attention by some irrelevant stimulus, the task of reproducing the sentence becomes impossible for them. The recall of words is "contaminated" by words that had been presented earlier. Thus we see that the selective character of speech activity is disrupted.

The disturbances described above can be observed especially clearly in *complex texts*. The semantic elements of these texts become unstable quite easily. They become disorderly and are replaced by the uncontrolled appearance of irrelevant associations. We have recently described these phenomena in more detail elsewhere (e.g., Luria, 1974b, 1975a).

The impairment of speech activity which arises from an injury to the frontal lobes of the brain is of a quite different character. We have already mentioned that the frontal lobes, occupying about one-third of the cerebral hemisphere in humans, have a special function. They make it possible for humans to have motivations and needs, and to plan and carry out purposeful activity. Several studies (e.g., Luria, 1962, 1970, 1974b, 1975a; Luria and Khomskaya, 1966) have demonstrated that the frontal lobes actively participate in the control of ongoing activity by managing "reverse afferentation" signals to the brain. These signals are used in evaluating the success or failure of an ongoing activity and in making corrections. Thus the frontal lobes represent the highest cortical apparatus responsible for programming complex forms of activity, on the one hand, and controlling the flow of this activity, on the other.

Patients who have suffered serious bilateral lesions of the frontal lobes characteristically manifest very serious disturbances in their active conduct. As a rule, the disturbances are reflected in two main symptoms. Since these patients are not able to create the required motivation and programs for behavior, and are unable to control the flow of purposeful activity, they tend to replace active behavior either with echoic repetition of others' actions or with stereotypic repetition of one and the same action. This transition from complex programmed behavior to imitative or stereotypic behavior usually does not evoke any clear emotional reaction or any attempts to correct the behavioral defects.

Similar disturbances can be observed in the speech activity of such patients. As a rule, they lie silently in their beds. They do not make any attempt to engage in active speech communication. They do not make any request of those near them and do not try to formulate any ideas. In general, they do not try to convey anything verbally to those who are present.

Unlike the patients we mentioned earlier with deep brain injuries, frontal lobe patients can answer questions quite easily and do not display any grammatical defects in their speech. However, their answers usually are in the form of echoic repetitions of the question or inert reproductions of an earlier answer. For example, a patient may respond to the question "How are you feeling?" by saying, "How are you feeling?" "How am I feeling?" and then become silent. Sometimes the patient may produce a one-syllable reply after repeating part of the question. Thus, he/she may say, "I am feeling fine."[25]

---

[25]This is more echoic in Russian than in English. Thus, in Luria's examples, the first reply, "How am I feeling?" (Kak ya sebya chuvstvuyu?), is very similar to the second, "I am feeling fine." (Khorosho ya sebya chuvstvuyu.).—*J. V. Wertsch*

These patients will experience greater difficulties when confronted with a question that requires an answer going beyond the bounds of simple repetition. Thus, when asked "What did you have for dinner today?", he/she might reply, helplessly, "What did you have for dinner today?". Frequently, if the dialogue goes on, these patients begin to show signs of speech stereotypes or preservations. They will inertly repeat an earlier answer and will be unable to produce new speech connections that would allow them to answer the question.

Naturally, more complex forms of speech activity are quite beyond the capacity of such a patient. Frequently, he/she may be able to repeat individual words or short lists of two or three words and name objects presented to him/her, but as soon as one moves on to the task of repeating an entire series of words or naming a series of objects, the patient begins to display serious impairments. Being unable to switch from one set of words to another, he/she begins to repeat the same words or repeat the names of the objects already named. This tendency toward echolalia and stereotypic behavior interferes with speech activity in a fundamental way. It makes it impossible to form complex motives and programs of speech utterances (see Luria, 1974b and 1975a, for further details).

This defect is manifested to an even greater degree in more complex forms of speech activity. Patients belonging to this group cannot formulate the theme of a painting or the plot of a story read to them. For example, if they are shown a painting of a man who has fallen through ice next to a sign which says "Caution," they are able to read the sign but are unable to give any interpretation of the picture. At best, they are able to repeat mechanically, "Watch out! bombardment!" or "Watch out! The place is mined!". Very much the same thing occurs when such patients are asked to repeat a story. They may be able to repeat the first sentence or the first part of the story, but are quite unable to proceed beyond that point. The general passivity of speech activity in these patients is the chief obstacle to speech production. This is manifested both in simple and in the more complex types of speech activity.

A somewhat different picture is presented by patients with serious frontal lobe lesions whose main symptom is not so much general inactivity as disinhibition or a general increase in excitability. Patients of this kind manifest a heightened orienting reflex. They are easily distracted and respond in an excited manner to any irrelevant stimulus. Although their disturbance differs from that of the patients described above, their behavior is equally disrupted. When they begin to carry out some task, they lose track of the task quite easily. They are diverted either by echopractical acts or by inert stereotypes. Their behavior is also characterized by a loss of plans or programs of action. Hence, their action ceases to be purposeful and becomes fragmentary. It is easily replaced by irrelevant activities that are not a part of the program of actions. As a result, such patients lose all control over the purposeful execution of their actions.

They may begin to repeat the contents of a story that has been read to them, but very soon their attention is distracted to something else. Consequently, the closed system required to convey the plot of the story is replaced either by uncontrolled irrelevant associations or inert repetition of speech stereotypes that they have just heard. It is clear that the lexical and syntactic mechanisms of speech activity remain quite intact in such patients. However, since the ability to organize information in an organized program is disrupted, they are unable to form any kind of purposeful, intelligent speech utterance.

For example, when patients of this kind are asked to repeat a simple story (e.g., "The Hen and the Golden Eggs")[26] they may repeat the first sentence of the story ("A man had a hen which laid golden eggs."), but then begin to slip into secondary associations. For instance, they might say: "Perhaps this was a man who had his own petty interests. He sold these eggs because he wanted to earn as much money as he could." When the patient reaches the part of the story relating how the man killed the hen and did not find what he had expected, the patient may say: "He opened up the hen's stomach, then closed it, then opened it up, then closed it . . . the door opens the door closes . . . I enter the dining hall, sit down at a table . . . . " The patient easily slips into uncontrolled thoughts about parallel associations which completely dislocate the organized program required to reproduce the plot of the story.

Sometimes the organized transmission of a story plot may be disrupted by inert fragments that arise in the patient's mind. For example, one of our patients who had suffered serious injury to the frontal lobes was quite capable of repeating the first few sentences of a story, but instead of then proceeding to the next stage of the account, he began to perseverate. In the case of "The Jackdaw and the Pigeons,"[27] he said: "The jackdaw landed in its nest, then flew away, then again landed and again flew away, then again landed and again flew away . . . . " In this instance, a connected text was replaced by inert speech stereotypes.

In other cases, a patient's speech may be disrupted and replaced by direct impressions from the immediate speech situation. To illustrate, a patient with serious bilateral injury of the frontal lobes was asked to reproduce the tale of "The Jackdaw and the Pigeons" that had just been read to him. The story begins with the sentence, "The jackdaw heard that some pigeons had plenty of food, so it painted itself white and flew into a pigeon house." The patient "reproduced"

---

[26] A story by Tolstoy: "A man had a hen which laid golden eggs. He wanted to get more of the eggs at once, and so he killed the hen. But inside he found nothing; it was just a hen like any other."—*J. V. Wertsch*

[27] Another story by Tolstoy: "A jackdaw heard that some pigeons had plenty of food, so it painted itself white and flew into the pigeon house. The pigeons thought it was a pigeon, and took it in. However, it forgot itself and cried out like a jackdaw. The pigeons then realized that it was a jackdaw and sent it away. It went back to its family, but they did not recognize it and would not have it either."—*J. V. Wertsch*

this story by saying: "Galka[28] (looking at the laboratory assistant), the girl Galka ... dyed her hair white ..., got her hair set in a permanent wave ... and got admitted into the Neurosurgical Institute ... The neurosurgeon fell in love with her and proposed to her." It is obvious that the plot of the story has been replaced by several direct impressions. Thus, "Galka" (jackdaw) turns into "the girl Galka," and the phrase "painted itself white" turns into "dyed her hair white and got her hair set in a permanent wave." These intrusions were derived from the speech situation in which the patient found himself.

It is not difficult to detect the common feature among the cases outlined above. In all three of those instances, speech production remained intact. The patients' speech was not disrupted from a phonological, lexical, morphological, or syntactic point of view. However, their speech was greatly disturbed. The closed semantic system necessary for reproducing the plot of a story or for providing an organized account of a picture was disrupted. In its place was a system which was open to distractions. Such distractions could be manifested by echolalia, inert reproduction of stereotypes, uncontrolled associations, or interweaving of direct impressions from the speech setting and facts from the text.

Clearly, speech production in those cases was disturbed both by factors that are not specific to verbal activity (e.g., the instability of motives lying at the basis of the utterance), as well as factors directly tied to speech activity itself (e.g., disintegration of the utterance program, uncontrolled interweaving of irrelevant facts from the speech setting, etc.). It is also easy to see that these intrusions are not under the patient's control. He/she does not correct errors. The patient's speech becomes a cycle of uncontrolled association or inert speech stereotypes which substitute for organized speech. This is the general picture of speech disorders occurring in patients of severe injury to the frontal lobe regions of the cerebral cortex.

THE CEREBRAL ORGANIZATION OF SYNTAGMATIC STRUCTURE IN SPEECH PRODUCTION

The observations described above demonstrate how speech can be disrupted due to disturbance of factors such as the motive of an utterance and the general organization of utterance programs. In addition, there are situations that allow us to analyze the cerebral organization of the speech activity itself.

We know that a speech motive—e.g., the need to formulate something, convey something, ask for something, or explain something—requires the creation of a scheme as the next stage of speech production. The initial intention must be

---

[28]The word "galka" in Russian means "jackdaw." "Galka" is also a girl's name.—*J. V. Wertsch*

reconstructed by being transformed into a scheme of a sequential syntagmatic structure. As noted earlier, this stage is connected with *inner speech*. During early stages of ontogenesis, inner speech is expanded. Later, its structure becomes abbreviated and predicative in function. These changes make possible the recoding of initial intention into a connected, sequential speech utterance. It therefore follows that when inner speech is absent, speech production as a whole will also be impaired. In these cases, both the motive and its initial intention may, within certain limits, remain intact. The patient's difficulty is that he/she is unable to transform the initial intention into a scheme of a linear, predicatively constructed sentence and then into a scheme of an expanded text. Unlike those cases described earlier, the impairment here is concerned specifically with speech. It involves the crucial mechanism of recoding the initial motive and intention into speech.

The cerebral mechanisms of such a transformation of the initial semantic graph into an expanded speech utterance are of special interest to us. These processes are, above all, connected with the function of the speech areas of the left frontal lobe. Although we still know very little about the functional organization of the frontal lobes in general, the nature of disorders that occur in cases of injury to the inferior parts of these areas in the left hemisphere can be delineated fairly clearly.

Patients who have injuries to the speech areas of the frontal lobes do not manifest the same type of disorders as patients with bilateral prefrontal lesions. That is, they do not have great difficulties in organizing and controlling complex behavioral programs. Furthermore, they do not suffer from the paresis or paralysis which characterizes patients with lesions of the motor areas of the cerebral cortex. And finally, they do not display the disorders of the complex motor skills which are caused by lesions in the premotor regions of the brain (and which we shall consider later).

Patients with lesions of the speech areas of the frontal lobes are characterized by the fact that they can carry out motor programs that *are assigned to them*, but they experience difficulties when required to *plan* or *independently formulate* behavioral programs. As a rule, these patients are passive. They can easily carry out ready-made tasks, but lack initiative in carrying out their own activity. Their behavior is characterized by the monotonous features typical of patients with frontal lobe lesions.

The speech disorders we shall consider here occur most clearly with lesions of the lower left posterofrontal region and are sometimes connected with an injury to the pole of the left temporal lobe. It is a syndrome well known to clinicians and often described in terms of "failure of speech initiative" or "dynamic aphasia" (Luria, 1975a; Akhutina, 1975). Patients suffering from this form of speech impairment do not manifest any difficulty in articulation and can easily repeat individual words and sentences. They can name objects and even groups of objects without difficulty and do not display those symptoms of preseveration or uncontrolled occurrence of parallel associations typical in patients with lesions of the prefrontal region. A preliminary investigation may not reveal any speech disorders in these patients. However, a thorough investigation will reveal these disorders quite clearly. Obvious difficulties emerge when they move from simple repetition of words or sentences or the naming of objects to the active production of speech.

These defects are manifested even more clearly when those patients are asked to devise an oral account about an assigned topic. In such situations they are quite helpless. They state that they see flashes of individual details in their mind. However, these details do not fall into a pattern. They say that they feel a kind of emptiness before them which prevents them from formulating an expanded speech utterance. One such patient declared that he could characterize his speech impairment very well. He said, "With other people Friday follows Thursday, but with me after Thursday, there isn't anything."

One patient who suffered from this form of speech disorder was particularly memorable. When asked to produce speech on the theme "The North," he said, after a very long pause: "In the North there are bears (again a long pause), . . . this is what I wanted to bring to your attention." When given a similar task, another similar patient said, after a long pause: "In the wild North there stands alone, on a mountain peak, a pine tree."[29] This is a substitution of a ready-made stereotype for an active, creative speech utterance. As a result of this disturbance in the dynamic scheme of an utterance, these patients are unable to use narrative speech. They become silent, almost speechless people, although the entire lexical and syntactic structure of their speech remains intact.

This syndrome is consistently seen in patients with lesions of the postfrontal or frontotemporal regions of the left hemisphere. Its characteristics have led us to conclude that the basic disorder involves the recoding of the initial semantic graph into the predicative scheme which provides the foundation for expanded, narrative speech. One may assume that the basic disorder involves impairment of inner speech. The impairment prevents patients with this syndrome from creating the scheme of an expanded speech utterance. This is what constitutes the essence of damage to the deep syntactic structure, a structure essential for transforming the initial semantic graph into the next schematic stage in the production of expanded speech.

In addition to disturbances of active speech which arise as a result of a lesion in the speech area of the frontal lobes, there are other types of disturbances in speech production. Lesions of the inferior parts of the premotor areas of the left hemisphere affect the syntactic structure of speech to a much greater extent. An analysis of this phenomenon is presented below.

[29]Lines reproduced from a poem by the Russian poet Lermontov.—*J. V. Wertsch*

It is known that the premotor area of the cerebral cortex is involved in integrating individual movements into sequentially organized programs. It is also known that a lesion in this area leaves individual movements intact but disturbs complex motor skills and deprives the patient of the capacity to make the transition from one element of a movement to another. It obstructs the realization of a complex chain of movements which otherwise would form a single kinetic melody.

With regard to speech production, similar disturbances can be seen with lesions in the inferior regions of the premotor areas of the left cerebral hemisphere. These disturbances differ from those described earlier in that they affect the grammatical structure of connected, syntagmatically constructed speech. Typical of these types of speech disorders is the fact that the articulation as well as repetition of individual words or a series of isolated words remain quite unaffected. Similarly, the nominative function of speech remains intact. Such patients can name objects without difficulty. They begin to experience difficulty only when asked to name a series of objects one after another. This involves inhibiting the preceding name of an object and going on to the next one. In such a situation, the patients either have difficulty in remembering the new names, or they inertly repeat the earlier words.

These patients manifest particularly severe speech disruptions when they try to move from naming individual items or repeating isolated words to constructing complete sentences. An astonishing fact about them is that the complex, paradigmatic organization of their speech has remained relatively unaffected. However, they have considerable difficulty in managing its syntagmatic organization because its predicative aspects have been disturbed. Thus, while these patients are quite capable of identifying individual objects, acts, or properties, they find it very difficult to combine individual speech elements into a single, connected sentence. Verbs and auxiliary words are not used, and isolated nominative elements substitute for complex sentences. This results in the phenomenon of "telegraphic style" that is so well known to clinical neurology.

Thus, the patient who is asked to repeat the sentence "Mal'chik udaril sobaku." (The boy hit the dog.) may use only its isolated nominative elements by saying, "mal'chik . . . sobaka . . . " (boy . . . dog . . .). At best, the patient will repeat the substantive words and words which designate action but they will usually appear in their dictionary (citation) forms. In this case, he/she might say, "mal'chik . . . sobaka . . . undarit'" (boy . . . dog . . . to hit . . .).[30] Naturally, this type of disturbance in syntagmatic structure seriously impairs the spontaneous speech of

---

[30] In these examples of patients' speech, the verb occurs in its infinitive form and the nouns appear in the nominative case. In order to be syntagmatically correct in this repetition exercise, the verb would have to be inflected for third person singular, past tense ("udaril") rather than the infinitive ("udarit'"), and the direct object would have to be inflected for the accusative case ("sobaku") rather than being in the nominative ("sobaka").—*J. V. Wertsch*

the patient as well. The following example of the speech of such a patient while trying to relate the history of his injury and the story of his experience at the battlefront is concerned with how the bullet which struck him in the head deprived him of speech and how the surgery gave him back his life. "Well . . . well . . . front . . . well . . . advance . . . well . . . bullet . . . well . . . nothing much . . . hospital . . . operation . . . well . . . speech . . . speech . . . speech . . . ."

It is obvious that this speech impairment is very specific in its nature. It involves the disintegration of the system of syntagmatically constructed grammatical operations. Our research has led us to conclude that this type of speech disorder is based on a disturbance of the grammatical stereotypes that provide the foundation for the syntactically organized utterance (cf. Akhutina, 1975; Luria, 1975a).

We still do not have detailed knowledge of the specific mechanisms that explain this form of aphasia. However, there can be little doubt that lesions in the above-mentioned areas of the cerebral cortex disrupt the predicative function of inner speech. This is the speech mechanism needed for syntagmatically constructed, fluent speech. It is also noteworthy that in such cases one often finds disturbances of other components of the syntagmatic structure of speech. The speech of these patients is noted for its monotony and isolated articulation of individual words. Furthermore, the prosodic structure, one of the distinguishing features of syntagmatically constructed speech, completely disappears. As a rule, their speech is not characterized by a melodically structured system of intonation, but by a system of stress. The fact that smooth speech is replaced by a chain of isolated nominative chunks is the central feature of this form of speech disorder.

So-called "motor aphasia" provides another example of speech disorders in this class. This disorder results from a lesion in Broca's area. Whereas patients suffering from the types of speech disorders outlined earlier could repeat words or name objects quite easily, these abilities disappear either partially or completely in patients suffering from motor aphasia.

Patients with lesions in Broca's area can articulate individual sounds quite easily. They do not manifest the articulatory difficulties that are characteristic of apraxia. However, articulation of a series of sounds is severely impaired. Patients with motor aphasia are unable to make the smooth transition from one sound to a second, and from the second to a third. For example, after having pronounced the sound "b," they cannot switch to the sound "k." When they are asked to repeat the combination "ba-ka," they repeat it as "ba-ba," and the sound cluster "bi-ba-bo" is repeated as "bo-bo-bo." It is obvious that the pronounciation of complete words requires this very type of smooth transition with the accompanying inhibition of the preceding articulation. When asked to pronounce the seemingly simple word "mukha" (a fly) they are likely to produce something like, "mu . . . ma." Their entire motor speech is found to be quite severely impaired.

This observation, which is the primary symptom of Broca's aphasia or motor aphasia, has not been understood by many investigators. As a result, the mechanisms that were the root cause of motor aphasia remained unexplained. We now have little reason to doubt that what lies at the root of Broca's aphasia is the pathological inertness of articulations once they have arisen. This inertness is accompanied by impairment of the elementary kinetic melodies that are required for the articulation of the word. It is caused by the disintegration of kinetic melodies or the kinetic organization of the motor act in the speech sphere. In this type of aphasia, it is not the syntagmatic construction of an entire sentence that is disturbed. Rather, the smooth production of the components of individual words is disrupted. It is evident that this type of speech disorder is limited to the sphere of speech and involves the controlling part of the speech act in its most elementary forms.

Consequently, the remediation of this type of speech disorder usually passes through the stage of telegraphic style. Patients who can pronounce individual words still may find it difficult to combine words in complete sentences. They may continue to pronounce the words in their dictionary (citation) form. The predicative structure of their speech will continue to be impaired and will require special corrective instruction.

There is another kind of motor aphasia that is clearly distinct from Broca's aphasia. We have proposed the term "kinesthetic" or "afferent" motor aphasia, as opposed to kinetic or efferent motor aphasia, for this type of speech disorder. The disorder results from a lesion of the postcentral region of the speech region (Operculum Rolandi). It may outwardly resemble the motor speech disorder described above. However, a closer examination shows that the cause of this speech disorder is not so much the disintegration of kinetic melody or transition from one articulation to another within a word as the inability to find the articulation necessary for pronouncing a specific sound. Therefore, this type of motor aphasia may be considered as a special type of apraxia of the speech organs.

Unlike patients suffering from Broca's aphasia, patients with afferent motor aphasia cannot articulate isolated sounds accurately. They easily confuse the pronounciation of sounds that are close to one another in terms of articulation. Whereas patients with Broca's aphasia can pronounce any sound, these patients begin to mix up similar, contrasting articulemes. For example, they may substitute the alveolars "n" or "d" for the alveolar "l," or they may substitute the bilabials "p" or "b" for the bilabial "m," etc. As a result, they are likely to mispronounce words because they replace some of the articulemes with similar sounds. They may pronounce "baba" as "mama," "khalat" as "khanat," "slon" as "ston" or "stol," etc. It is quite understandable that this confusion of articulemes in apraxia of the speech organs makes these patients' speech unintelligible.

The fact that this disorder is connected with the breakdown of articulation distinguishes it quite sharply from the types of dynamic disorders described above. The differences involved may be observed both in the character of mistakes the patient makes and in the process of remediation or reverse development of the defect. The main task faced by the psychologist in the case of afferent motor aphasia is to restore the correct articulemes. If this difficulty is overcome, the patient may be able to recover without passing through the stage of telegraphic style. The fact that the prosodic aspects of speech and its syntagmatic structure remain intact supports our claim that afferent motor aphasia is quite different from the types of aphasia we described above.

THE CEREBRAL ORGANIZATION OF PARADIGMATIC STRUCTURE IN SPEECH PRODUCTION

Up to this point, we have been describing speech disorders resulting from the disruption of various stages of transition from thought to the expanded utterance. We have seen how speech is impaired as a disruption of the motivational basis of the speech act and how it is affected in disorders affecting subsequent stages in speech production. These may concern the recoding of the initial intention or semantic graph into a scheme of the smooth speech utterance or the breakdown of the predicative function of inner speech. These facts lie at the basis of our categorization of the speech disorders described above (except afferent aphasia) as speech disorders involving a disturbance of the syntagmatic organization of the utterance.

The disorders examined so far, however, constitute only one group of speech production disorders arising as a result of focal brain lesions. A second group involves cases where the transition from thought, through inner speech, to the expanded utterance remains relatively unaffected and the syntagmatic construction of the speech utterance does not manifest any serious defects. These disorders are characterized by the inverse pattern of disturbance. Rather than being a disturbance of the processes involved in the transition from thought to speech, they involve a disturbance of the process of mastering the paradigmatically (hierarchically) constructed linguistic system.

As we have seen, all languages possess an extremely complex paradigmatic structure. In the phonological organization of oral speech, this paradigmatic structure is manifested in the system of oppositions and in the distinctive features which play a useful role in distinguishing among different words. The preservation of a stable phonological structure of a language is an absolute prerequisite for mastering the phonological system of speech.

The lexical, semantic and logical-grammatical organizational levels of language are also characterized by paradigmatic organization. The lexicon of a language consists of the system of words which form a hierarchically constructed semantic system. The word "dog" not only designates a certain animal and calls to mind a certain situation in which one may come across this animal; it also is part of a hierarchically organized system of meanings. Together with "cat," it is related to domestic animals which are contrasted with wild animals. Together with wild animals, domestic animals enter the hierarchy of animals in general, as opposed to plants, etc. Thus, each lexical unit of a language enters into a system of hierarchically constructed semantic relationships which analyze the external world and enable us to categorize it in terms of a network of familiar concepts.

The logical-grammatical structure of language is also organized paradigmatically. The combination of words that make up an utterance may communicate relationships rather than events. Examples of constructions that communicate relationships are: "Sokrat—chelovek." (Socrates is a human being.); "Sobaka—zhivotnoe." (A dog is an animal.); "brat ottsa" (brother of father); and "khozyain sobaki" (the master of the dog). Speech production involves more than the transition from an initial intention through inner speech to the expanded syntagmatically constructed sentence and then to a series of sentences. Speech activity requires the mastery of an entire system of language codes, beginning with the phonological code, passing through the lexical code, and ending with the logical-grammatical code.

The fundamental hypothesis to emerge out of the neuropsychological investigation of the cerebral organization of speech activity is that the process of mastering the paradigmatically constructed system of language codes is based on a quite different set of cerebral systems than the processes involved in the syntagmatic organization of the utterance. Research has shown that this process of mastering the complex, paradigmatically constructed language codes is realised primarily by the posterior gnostic regions of the cerebral cortex, especially in the left hemisphere.

In order to examine the individual aspects of cerebral organization which enable humans to master these paradigmatic codes of language, we shall first consider the cerebral organization of the phonological codes and then move on to the cerebral mechanisms involved in the lexical and logical-grammatical structure of language.

Several components or basic conditions are essential for mastering the codes of languages. Speech production begins with the mastery of the phonological system of a language, a process involving the secondary regions of the left temporal lobe. This is the cortical apparatus responsible for auditory or, more precisely, auditory-speech analysis. The left temporal cortex is joined by numerous connections to the postcentral and premotor areas of the speech cortex and represents the central mechanism for auditory-speech analysis. This is the region that makes it possible to identify distinctive phonological features.

Quite naturally, therefore, a lesion in the speech areas of the left temporal lobe disrupts the mastery of the phonological code of a language. It hampers the process of speech production. However, such a lesion does not affect the process of converting an initial intention into a smoothly flowing speech utterance.

Patients with a lesion of the speech areas in the temporal lobe retain the motivation leading to a speech utterance. They actively strive to express their thought in speech. Since the syntagmatic organization of speech is not severely affected, the prosodic structure of the utterance remains intact. The difficulties that arise in these cases occur when patients try to find the phonological structure required to transform the initial intention into sound. Very often they confuse similar phonemes and sometimes even confuse phonemes that are quite distant from one another. They severely distort the phonological structure of the words they want to express their thought. In clinical psychology, these disturbances are called "literal paraphasias" or distortions in pronouncing the required word.

This process is also complicated by other difficulties. Frequently the meaning of an intended word becomes blurred and leads patients to replace the real word by another word which is close to it in sound or belongs to the same class. Thus, a patient with a lesion of the left temporal lobe may replace the word "vorobei" (sparrow) with a similar sounding word—"muravei" (ant). Or the patient may make mistakes based on other paradigmatic criteria, e.g., replacing "vorobei" (sparrow) with the word "ptichka" (diminutive of bird), "galka" (jackdaw) or even more distant words like "belochka" (squirrel) or "zaichik" (diminutive of rabbit).

These observations support the notion that the system of words designating objects is severely affected. As a result, the nominative function of speech suffers. It is noteworthy that nouns designating objects are affected more than verbs and even more than conjunctions and auxiliary words. The number of items in these latter two classes is relatively small. As a rule, these items are used in the predicative function of the utterance, a function that remains intact in such patients. It is also noteowrthy that the general syntagmatic and intonational-melodic structure of their speech sometimes remains better preserved than the nominative function of speech. These facts sharply distinguish the speech of such patients from that of patients with dynamic aphasia. A patient with a massive lesion of the left temporal lobe, when trying to describe the history of his injury, may produce fragments of the following type: "Well . . . we are going, going . . . and, well . . . then . . . after this . . . suddenly . . . well . . . well . . . I felt extremely unwell . . . and well . . . I don't know anything and it is very painful . . . and, well . . . I don't know . . . I don't know how this happened . . . and then . . . better . . . better . . . better . . . and then I felt quite all right . . . . " It is not difficult to see that the (intonationally intact) speech of this patient possesses some full-fledged syntagmatic fragments but is quite impaired in its nominative composition. It differs sharply from those speech forms in which predication is affected while the nominative organization remains intact.

Thus, the speech of patients with lesions in the speech areas of the temporal lobes is characterized by the preservation of syntagmatic organization with a disruption of paradigmatic organization, the use of literal or verbal paraphasias, and intact intonational-melodic organization.

In addition to the phonological codes of a language, there are lexical and semantic codes. Speech production also requires the mastery of these codes. One cannot but be constantly amazed by the subtlety and variety involved in the lexical and semantic codes and by the processes of selection with which they are manipulated by a mature speaker.

As we have seen, when producing an utterance we select a single item from all the possible lexical and semantic connections. Conversely, we inhibit superfluous lexical and semantic connections. Research has shown that this process of selection can be realized only under conditions in which the extremely complex gnostic regions of the cerebral cortex are functioning normally. This primarily involves tertiary zones of the left parieto-occipital region.

If these regions of the cortex are impaired and the neurodynamics of these affected areas begin to mainfest pathological symptoms, complex processes of selecting appropriate lexical and semantic connections and inhibiting inappropriate ones are disturbed. That is, there is a disintegration of the organized network of semantic systems on which the speech production depends.

Clinical investigations have shown that lesions in these areas of the cerebral cortex inevitably leads to the phenomenon of word forgetting. This is a well-known symptom in clinical medicine and is the main symptom of "amnesic aphasia." It may also result in "semantic aphasia," which is characterized by difficulties in the selection of appropriate meaning.

The mechanisms responsible for these two main symptoms of this disorder were poorly understood until quite recently. It was often argued that the cause is the deterioration or instability of auditory and speech memory and that the main defect involves forgetting concepts or the disruption of connections between them and the sound structure of words. However, this hypothesis turned out to be incorrect. The data presented above in earlier chapters clearly show that the difficulties in word finding and word forgetting result not from the weakening of the memory traces, but from a deterioration in selectivity.

Lesions in the parieto-occipital regions of the cerebral cortex lead to a phasic condition called an "equalizing" state by Pavlov. Unlike the normal functioning of the cortex, in this condition both strong and weak stimuli and their traces are equalized and begin to occur with equal probability. That is why a patient with lesions of these regions of the cerebral cortex faces insurmountable difficulties when trying to find a specific word. Lexical items that are close in sound, in morphological structure, or in sense begin to surface in the patient's mind with equal probability, and the selection of the appropriate meaning accompanied by inhibition of inappropriate associations is made extremely difficult. These factors obviously lead to disturbances in speech production.

In these cases, the motive which gives rise to an utterance and the intention which is to be turned into the speech utterance remain intact. However, the search for verbal meanings that would be appropriate for these motives is severely disrupted. The speech of patients who suffer from semantic aphasia continues to be active, and the entire utterance retains its expressive and intonational-melodic character, but it is characterized by a frantic search for the required words.

Lesions of the parieto-occipital areas of the left cerebral cortex also result in another difficulty in speech production—a difficulty connected with the system of logical-grammatical relations. We dealt with this issue earlier, and we shall return to it in our analysis of comprehension disorders.

CONCLUSIONS

The observations presented in the foregoing pages clearly show that focal lesions of the cerebral cortex do not result in the total failure of speech activity. Lesions of individual regions of the left hemisphere as a rule result in selective impariment of speech production. This fact enables us to use clinical observations to analyze the cerebral organization of human speech activity.

We have seen that lesions of the deeper regions of the brain may cause severe inactivity, as a result of which the motivation for any speech utterance is lost. We have also seen that lesions in the frontal lobes result in the disintegration of complex motivational and behavioral programs and in the control over speech activity. In both instances, speech production suffers greatly. However, the process suffers not because of the disintegration of a language system, but because of a disturbance in a nonlanguage system that influences the control and flow of speech. The substitution of organized speech by echolalia, perseverations, or fusions of secondary associations characterizes this kind of speech disturbance. The closed system of the speech utterance, which normally is subordinated to a definite program, is replaced by a system open to all kinds of secondary influences.

The disturbances in speech production arising from lesions in the speech areas of the cerebral cortex are of a quite different nature. Lesions in the anterior regions of the speech area lead to a disturbance of the process that links the general intention or primary semantic graph with inner speech, and through it the semantically integrated speech utterance.

In some such cases, the entire speech production program is impaired. As a result, the patient who is quite capable of repeating individual words or sentences and naming individual objects, cannot produce a scheme for speech production. This limits such patients to reproducing speech stereotypes.

When the lesion is located in the anterior regions of the speech area, inner speech is affected. The disruption of its predicative function and its established syntactic structures results in a speech disorder in which the nominative function is seriously affected. In those cases, the patient suffers either from dynamic aphasia or from the disintegration of connected, syntagmatically constructed speech.

Speech disorders that are associated with lesions of the posterior, gnostic areas of the cerebral cortex (particularly, of the left temporal and parieto-occipital regions) are, again, quite different. Here, both the motivation and the initial semantic graph of speech remain intact. So too does the transition from this semantic graph to the scheme of predicatively constructed (i.e., syntagmatically organized) speech. In the examples we studied, the impairment affected the process of mastering phonological, lexical-semantic, and logical-grammatical codes. Speech disorders that arise in these cases are characterized by the disintegration of the complex paradigmatic organization of speech. Depending on the location of the lesion, these disturbances are manifested either as an inability to master the phonological system and the associated articulations of a language, as an inability to select appropriate lexical aspects of the utterance, or as an inability to manipulate complex logical-grammatical relationships. In all of these instances, however, the syntagmatic construction of the utterance remains intact.

Chapter 16

The Cerebral Organization of Pathological Disruption of Speech Comprehension

Having completed our outline of speech production and its disturbances, we shall now examine the processes and cerebral organization of speech comprehension. Since the comprehension or decoding of an utterance has not been analyzed in as much detail as speech production, we shall encounter greater difficulty in providing an account of this process.

The process of speech comprehension is the reverse of the process of speech production. Comprehension begins with the perception of a speech signal characterized by phonological, lexical-morphological, and logical-grammatical structure. It goes through the stage of decoding this signal on the basis of the language codes involved, the stage of isolating the general thought of the utterance, and finally, the stage of identifying the sense which underlies the communication.

This clearly leads us to assume that, like speech production, speech comprehension falls into two main phases. The first phase is concerned with decoding the language codes, and the second is concerned with the transition from these language codes to the deeper sense of the communication. We shall try to throw some light on each of these stages and to identify the cerebral systems that underlie them.

233

THE LOSS OF COMPREHENSION AT THE PHONOLOGICAL AND
LEXICAL LEVELS OF LANGUAGE

The comprehension of a verbal communication (regardless of whether it is spoken or written) begins with the decoding of sounds. We have already said that this phonological code of a language is comprised of a system of phonemic contrasts, each involving one or more distinctive phonemic features. A change in features changes the sense of the perceived word.

We have also mentioned that the temporal region of the left hemisphere plays a major role in the process of phonemic decoding. Injury to this region does not result in a loss of hearing acuity, but it does deprive a person of the ability to make crucial discriminations in hearing. Patients with this kind of injury continue to be able to distinguish among nonspeech sounds, such as the clinking of dishware and musical notes, but they are no longer able to distinguish among meaningful phonemic features and identify how a speech sound fits into the phonemic system of a language. This is a serious deficit, since the latter operation is what makes these sounds bearers of linguistic sense. This kind of injury leads to the confusion of similar, and sometimes even quite dissimilar, phonemes. The patient's inability to distinguish among the distinctive features in a language and the inability to retain a clear phonemic structure of perceived speech constitute the symptoms of "sensory aphasia."

This fundamental set of symptoms caused by such lesions has often been described as the "alienation of word meaning." Because patients with this syndrome are unable to perceive distinct sounds, and are thus unable to retain a clear phonemic structure, they begin to confuse words with a similar sound structure. When they are given the word "golos" (voice), they cannot decide whether what they hear is "golos," "kolos" (ear of corn), "kholost" (unmarried), or "kholst" (canvas). Numerous alternatives surface with equal probability, creating difficulties for patients of this type.

It is important to note that these patients understand and continually pursue the task of comprehension. They actively search for the sense of the utterance and sometimes even try to guess it. Of course, this disturbance of phonemic hearing inevitably leads to great difficulty in identifying the lexical units of speech.

Typically, while patients suffering from sensory aphasia lose the ability to distinguish the meaning of individual lexical units of language because of the disruption of phonemic hearing, they retain the ability to process the subtle intonational-melodic structure of speech. Although these patients are sometimes unable to grasp the topic at certain points in a conversation, they nevertheless can easily distinguish interrogative and declarative sentences and intonation contours which indicate doubt or certainty. This dissociation between the disintegration of decoding lexical components of speech and the relatively good retention of the prosodic components characterizes the comprehension process of these patients suffering from lesion of the left temporal region. It enables them to understand the general situational meaning of the speech addressed to them.

Lesions in the left temporal region sometimes result in a different kind of dysfunctioning in speech comprehension. In cases of "acoustico-mnestic aphasia," the identification of phonemes and the perception of the phonological structure of the word remain relatively unaffected, but traces of words lose their clear sense and easily disappear as a result of the inhibiting influence of subsequent words.

We do not as yet know the physiological mechanisms responsible for these disturbances, but the difficulties of these patients are quite obvious. Especially detailed descriptions are available of the difficulties in decoding speech communications that occur when the syndrome involves the inhibition of auditory-speech traces due to outside influences as well as subsequent speech input. Such patients are quite capable of retaining and understanding individual words or short sentences. However, when given a series of words or a series of sentences, their performance indicates that later words and sentences inhibit the traces of earlier ones. As a rule, such patients are able to retain either the beginning or the end of a verbal series, i.e., they show a strong primacy or recency effect. As a result, perceived speech loses its completeness. Decoding of speech is complicated by difficulties of a mnemonic nature.

When patients of this type hear a complex segment of speech (e.g., a short story), they can reproduce either its beginning or its end and will say that they have forgotten the rest. Even when the story is repeated several times, the reduced number of traces that are retained disrupts the decoding process.

These mnemonic difficulties may be ameliorated or may disappear if one separates items in the communication by long pauses and presents series of words or individual sentences after long intervals. This gives the patient an opportunity to repeat the isolated segments. When this is done, the patient, who is usually unable to understand a long communication, can sometimes understand it.

Of special interest is a highly paradoxical phenomenon that characterizes both groups of patients mentioned so far. Patients who manifest an acute disturbance in decoding the meanings of the lexical items, as well as patients who are able to remember only individual bits of speech, are to some extent able to understand the general sense of a message. However, paradoxical it may sound, these patients understand quite well that in the story "The Hen and the Golden Eggs" the main theme is human failure and disappointment, and that in the fable "The Jackdaw and Pigeons" the theme concerns unacceptable behavior and the resulting suffering from punishment. That is, although they are not able to state clearly with whom precisely all this had occurred, they understand the overall theme. This paradoxical ability to understand the general sense of the communication even though there are disturbances in the decoding and retention of individual phonological and lexical elements may be explained by the fact that in both groups of patients the prosodic structure of speech is preserved. On the other hand, it is possible that the explanation lies in the fact that these patients continue to make active attempts to decode the communication and that these attempts, which are based on the retention of the intonational-melodic structure of the message and on residual sense bits, make possible the decoding of the inner sense of the communication.

THE DISRUPTION OF COMPREHENSION AT THE LEVEL OF LOGICAL-GRAMMATICAL RELATIONSHIPS

The phonological structure and lexical meaning of a language are only some of the aspects required for comprehension. Another aspect, just as essential for comprehending the meaning of a message, is the meaning of logical-grammatical constructions. As we said earlier, logical-grammatical constructions fall into two major groups.

The first of these involves what Svedelius (1897) called the "communication of events." This usually involves a predicatively connected system of words which simply describes actions, properties, or events. Examples of this kind of construction are "The house burns." and "The dog barks."; or more complex sentences, such as "The boy hit the dog." and "The girl drinks tea."

The second type of grammatical constructions is what Svedelius termed the "communication of relationships." Constructions of this type use either inflectional means of expressing relationships—such as the attributive genitive, as in "brat ottsa" (brother of father) and "otets brata" (father of brother)—or constructions which use syntactic words (e.g., prepositions and conjunctions). Examples of these latter constructions are, once again, "kvadrat pod krugom" (a square under a circle) and "vesna pered letom" (spring before summer). Finally, the communication of relations may involve word order—as in "plat'e zadelo veslo" (the dress brushed against the oar) as opposed to "veslo zadelo plat'e" (the oar brushed against the dress)—or comparative constructions—such as "Vanya is stronger than Petya." and "Petya is stronger than Vanya."

The comprehension processes involved in the communication of events are quite dissimilar from those involved in the communication of relationships. The first type of communication involves elements of syntagmatically constructed speech whose comprehension is quite straightforward, whereas the second type is more complex psychologically.

As we have already said, the mechanisms involved in the communication of relationships require the listener to establish a relationship that is conveyed by the construction even though it may differ from the direct meaning of individual words. This is clear in the examples cited above. In those cases, mechanisms such as word order or a change in inflection alter the meaning of the entire construction. Furthermore, the comprehension involved in the communication of relationships often requires the listener to transform a consecutive series of words into one simultaneous whole. The listener must create a simultaneous perception of the single logical structure which the words convey. Different regions of the cerebral cortex are needed to carry out this operation.

The chief function of the temporal regions of the brain is to analyze sound. Thus they are not of central importance in this case. Rather, the operations involved in comprehending logical-grammatical relationships must be carried out by the cerebral mechanisms which make possible spatial or quasi-spatial synthesis. These mechanisms are associated with the tertiary parieto-temporal-occipital regions of the left hemisphere.

Clinicians are well aware that lesions of these cortical regions, which are very underdeveloped in animals and highly developed only in humans, result in acute problems in spatial orientation. Patients who suffer from lesions in these zones continue to see objects quite well and to distinguish between things that are similar in shape. However, they show defects in orientation with respect to their environment. They are unable to distinguish left from right. They lose the ability to understand the significance of the positions of the hands of a clock or to identify the locations of the countries of the world on a map. They also manifest the syndrome known as "constructive apraxia." This is characterized by an inability to reproduce a complex system of spatial relationships, especially if they must synthesize these relationships mentally. Such patients are unable to carry out numerical operations. They become confused when trying to comprehend the substance of a problem requiring mental retention of the digit structure of a number. They cannot distinguish the relationship among the elements and cannot mentally carry out operations going beyond multiples of tens.

Related defects are reflected in the comprehension of grammatical constructions that communicate relationships. The analysis of these patients' difficulties is exceptionally interesting and yields unexpected results. The patients readily understand meanings of individual words and can comprehend sentences that communicate simple events. Thus, they can easily comprehend sentences like the following: "The house burns.", "The dog barks.", or "The boy hit the dog." They can also understand more complex sentences involving a larger number of words, e.g., "Mother and father went away to the theater, and the children and old nurse were left behind at home."

However, these patients encounter great difficulty when faced with grammatical constructions that express the communication of relationships. Patients with cortical lesions in the parieto-occipital regions of the left hemisphere can understand words like "brat" (brother) and "otets" (father), but they are unable to comprehend the construction "brat ottsa" (brother of father) and are even less capable of distinguishing between the constructions "brat ottsa" (brother of father) and "otets brata" (father of brother). They may constantly repeat that the subject matter is a brother and a father, but they are quite unable to understand the relationship between these two components of the grammatical construction.

It often seems to them that the constructions "brat ottsa" and "otets brata" both express the same thing and differ only in their word order. Such patients are not able to penetrate the logical-grammatical scheme of this construction.

A similar picture emerges when these patients are confronted with prepositions that communicate relationships. For example, they cannot comprehend the difference between "kvadrat pod krugom" (a square under a circle) and "krug pod kvadratom" (a circle under a square). When asked to draw a picture of what is described by such constructions, these patients simply draw the two figures vertically in the order that they appear in speech. When asked to draw a circle under a square, they first draw a circle and then a square under it. When patients attempt to understand the difference in the meaning of the two grammatical constructions, they tend to isolate each word and say, "Circle. Well here is the circle . . . under, and this . . . under . . . under . . . square . . . the square is below . . . ." These patients do not combine the successive lexical meanings into a single logical-grammatical structure. As a result, they cannot comprehend the real meaning of these constructions.

Further difficulties arise when such patients are given more complex problems in the communication of relationships. Thus, the sentence "On the branch of the tree is a bird's nest." cannot be understood by them even though it is so simple that it is routinely found in first and second grade Russian textbooks. They might say, "branch . . . tree . . . nest . . . bird." They understand the meaning of each isolated word, but they are unable to combine the meanings into a structure of logical-grammatical relationships.

It follows that more complex constructions, such as those involving complex subordination or noncontiguous components, cannot be decoded by patients of this type. They are quite incapable of understanding seemingly simple constructions, e.g., "V shkolu, gde uchilas' Dunya, s fabriki prishla rabotnitsa, chtoby sdelat' doklad" (literally: To the school, where Dunya was studying, from the factory came a woman worker, in order to give a lecture.). They would be likely to say helplessly, "The school . . . and Dunya was studying . . . and the factory . . . and the woman workers . . . and the report,—but what is it about? I can't understand . . . ." Disorders which occur in cortical lesions of the parieto-occipital regions of the left hemisphere and result in semantic aphasia have been outlined elsewhere in great detail (e.g., Luria, 1971).

The observations cited above reveal an unexpected, but extremely important fact for linguistics. They indicate that the grammatical constructions used in a language fall into two fundamental groups. This distinction is based on differences in the psychological mechanisms and cortical regions involved. The first group is involved in the simple communication of events and relies on predicative links among individual elements. It is an aspect of syntagmatically constructed speech. Grammatical devices in that group do not involve the cerebral mechanisms required for simultaneous synthesis. The second group of grammatical structures is concerned with the communication of relationships. From a psychological perspective, it is quite different. The comprehension of these structures involves the parieto-occipital zones of the left hemisphere. These are essential for the verbal-logical forms of spatial analysis and synthesis. Also they are heavily involved in the comprehension of consecutively presented information and its integration into simultaneous schemes.

It is obvious that an analysis of speech comprehension in patients with cortical lesions in the gnostic regions can have important implications. Such an analysis makes it possible to identify two types of grammatical structures. These seemingly similar structures actually differ both psychologically and in their cerebral organization.

The disorders we have described in connection with the temporal zones differ strongly from those which occur in patients with lesions of the parieto-occipital regions of the brain. However, there is one characteristic common to both types of disorders. In both cases, patients retain the motivation required for an active analysis of incoming text. They try to isolate and compare significant components. Notwithstanding the fact that their lesions disrupt various links in the speech process (the phonemic and lexical structure of the word in the first case, and logical-grammatical constructions in the second), these patients continue to make active attempts to comprehend. They continue to comprehend the intonational-melodic structure of an utterance. They use this information as a clue in trying to analyze individual fragments. Using this method, they are sometimes able to guess the general sense of speech addressed to them.

Among comprehension disorders, we must give a special place to syndromes which result from lesions in the postcentral regions of the speech area in the left hemisphere. These give rise to so-called "afferent motor aphasia." As we have already seen, such patients experience great difficulty in differentiating similar articulemes. They tend to confuse sounds that are similar in their articulation, such as "l" and "d," "l" and "t," or "m" and "b." They also make corresponding mistakes in writing words with these articulemes. Such patients may write "mama" as "baba," "khalat" as "khadat," etc.

It might appear that these patients' difficulties are strictly tied to articulation and do not involve speech comprehension. However, given the important role of production in establishing the meaning of a word, it is not surprising that they have certain difficulties in decoding. These difficulties arise primarily in the comprehension of the lexical composition of speech.

We have described several comprehension disorders in patients suffering from cortical lesions in a gnostic region. We have found that in all of these cases the loss of comprehension has one point in common: The patients manifest numerous difficulties in decoding the hierarchically constructed, *paradigmatic* system of language codes. In some cases, these difficulties are limited to the phonemic and lexical aspects of language, and in others they extend to the logical-grammatical structures. However, the syntagmatic structure of speech, with its intonational-melodic (prosodic) structure, remains basically unaffected. Also, these cases are characterized by the fact that patients approach the problem of decoding in an active way. That is why they can resort to active conjecture when they encounter difficulties in the direct reconstruction of the structure of an utterance. In addition, we have noted that paradoxical fact that a disruption of language codes does not deprive a person completely of the faculty of comprehending the sense of the message. Rather, the disruptions may force a patient to depend on the prosodic structure of the text or on the message fragments which he/she does understand. Even when some comprehension is possible, however, the fact remains that the chief defect of patients suffering from lesions in gnostic regions is the disturbance of paradigmatic language codes.

THE COMPREHENSION OF THE SYNTAGMATIC STRUCTURE OF CONNECTED SPEECH

The difficulties in the processing of the complex system of language codes which result from lesions in the gnostic regions have helped us identify what may be the most important aspects of speech comprehension. These do not, however, exhaust the list of comprehension difficulties. In addition to paradigmatic structure, there is also syntagmatic structure in speech. A disturbance of this aspect of the organization of speech is as interesting as a disturbance in the phonological, lexical, or logical-grammatical codes.

We have already said that the syntagmatic structure of speech production is realized by the frontal regions of the cerebral cortex. Our question here is whether speech disorders associated with frontal lobe lesions are limited to speech production or affect comprehension as well. Until very recently, there was no clear answer to this question. Investigators thought that injury to the frontal regions of the brain, such as the inferior zones of the premotor zone (Broca's region), and the temporal region disturbs the process of speech production but leaves comprehension undisturbed. The validity of this assumption is open to question. It is clear that in any comprehension process the active speech of the listener plays a significant role. Therefore, if the production of syntagmatically organized speech is disturbed, there is every reason to believe that comprehension will also be affected.

The apparent retention of comprehension by patients of this type is explained by the fact that investigators searched for the loss of comprehension by using the same techniques utilized to find a loss among patients with lesions of the posterior, gnostic regions of the brain. In other words, they searched for a loss in the comprehension of lexical and logical-grammatical aspect of speech. In fact, patients in this category may retain the comprehension of paradigmatic structures without any significant change. However, as soon as one turns to comprehension that relies on the syntagmatic organization of speech, observations lead to a quite different conclusion.

Recent studies have produced quite interesting results in this connection. Various types of patients were presented with a variety of grammatical structures—some were correct and some were incorrect. The erros included in these structures were of two types: The mistakes were in the paradigmatic structure of the speech construction or the mistakes were purely syntagmatic. The former included items like "solntse osveshchaetsya zemlei." (The sun is lighted by the earth.), instead of "Zemlya osveshchaetsya Solntsem." (The earth is lighted by the sun.); "Mukha bol'she slona." (A fly is larger than an elephant.), instead of "Slon bol'she mukhi." (An elephant is larger than a fly.); "Stol stoit na lampe." (The table is on the lamp.), instead of "Lampa stoit na stole." (The lamp is on the table.); etc. The study showed that such mistakes could be identified by the patients of this group only after a particularly careful analysis. In this respect, patients suffering from lesions in the frontal regions of the speech area differed sharply from those who suffered from injury to the parieto-occipital regions. The latter judged both constructions presented to them to be correct.

Significantly different results were obtained in cases when the errors were purely syntagmatic. To investigate this aspect of comprehension, patients were given sentences containing mistakes in syntactic agreement among words. For example, they were given the sentence "Parokhod idet po vodoi." (A steamship goes on water.) in which "vodoi" (water) is in the instrumental case even though it can only be in the dative case with the preposition "po" [i.e., it should be "po vode"—J. V. W.]. Our observations showed that these patients experienced considerable difficulty in identifying the mistake in sentences of that kind. When asked to give their opinion about an incorrectly constructed sentence, they said it was correct or "almost correct." Furthermore, when they were asked to correct the sentences, they changed the wrong items. For example, instead of changing "idet po vodoi" to "idet po vode," they were likely to suggest "Parokhod plyvet po vodoi" (A steamship sails on water). That is, they did not correct the syntagmatic error having to do with the case required by the preposition. Thus we see that loss of speech comprehension in these patients is manifested in the inability to reconstruct syntagmatic organization while retaining the ability to understand complex logical-grammatical constructions.

The second characteristic of patients in this group is the disruption of their ability to comprehend the intonational-melodic (prosodic) structure of speech. Remember that this aspect of comprehension is preserved in patients with lesions of gnostic regions of the brain.

THE COMPREHENSION OF THE SENSE (SUBTEXT) OF SPEECH

It now remains for us to discuss briefly a final problem—the problem of the cerebral organization of that aspect of comprehension that is responsible for the transition from the outward meaning of words and grammatical structures to their inner sense of subtext. Unfortunately, there is very little to say about it, because it has remained almost entirely uninvestigated.

In a previous chapter we showed how important this problem is for psychology. We discussed the fact that comprehension of sense differs sharply from the comprehension of the external content of speech and that the study of the depth of reading into the text and the transition to the subtext is one of the basic problems of psychology. An important question in this connection concerns the cerebral mechanisms involved in the process of passing from comprehension of the external meaning of speech to its latent, inner sense.

Psychopathologists are well aware that this transition is severely disrupted in various types of brain lesions. One of the most useful techniques is experimental psychopathology is concerned with how a patient understands the figurative sense of a proverb. In other words, it is concerned with the depth of understanding of a text, or the process of passing from outer meaning to inner sense.

However, these phenomena (which have been widely described in psychopathology) have not been studied in detail in neuropsychological research on patients with focal brain lesions. There is every reason to believe that the transition from the external meaning to inner sense is either impossible or extremely difficult for patients with lesions of the frontal regions of the brain. Lexical and logical-grammatical language codes remain intact in them, but the process of passing from meaning to inner sense and, more particularly, to the motivational aspect of an utterance is severely disrupted.

To date, we do not have sufficient data at our disposal to reveal how comprehension of the sense of communication is affected in patients with lesions in the frontal regions of the brain. However, our earlier observations about the patients' inability to produce organized speech lead us to believe that the process of actively analyzing the general meaning, and then the inner sense, of speech is severely disturbed.

Observations indicate that patients with massive lesions of the frontal regions can easily grasp the meaning of simple constructions used in the communication of events as well as more complex constructions which convey the communication of relationships. For example, these patients experience little difficulty in understanding the sentence "At the edge of the forest the hunter killed a wolf." or constructions such as "spring before summer" or "An elephant is bigger than a fly." However, the patients' comprehension of more complex constructions and their attempts to derive the sense of a communication from its outer meaning are quite another matter.

We know that the process of understanding the meaning of a complex communication requires active analysis, the collation of its parts, returning to earlier text, etc. This active process is especially easy to observe in the process of reading, where the reader's eye movements reveal his/her constant return to parts of the text that had been read earlier and the collation of these parts with subsequent sections.

It is precisely these active processes in comprehension that disappear or are acutely disturbed in patients with lesions of the frontal regions of the brain. They may continue to understand simple fragments of communication, but this comprehension begins to deteriorate when the derivation of the sense requires preliminary active processing of text. It is therefore to be expected that difficulties begin to emerge in the comprehension of passages in which meaning can be understood only by bringing together noncontiguous parts. In this connection, consider the following segment of text: "Birds are very useful; they destroy insects. They protect our gardens." "Birds" and "they" are separated by several words, while the words "insects" and "they" are close to each other. Normal subjects will connect "they" with "birds" and will inhibit the connection between "insects" and "they." But a patient with a serious frontal lobe syndrome, as a rule, cannot do this. He/she is likely to connect the words "insects" and "they" which occupy contiguous positions in the text. He/she would be likely to draw the conclusion that "they" refers to insects and that insects protect our gardens.

Patients with frontal lobe lesions also encounter difficulties in understanding semantic inversions. Thus, a correct understanding of the sentence "I am not used to not observing rules." requires the listener to replace the double negative with a single affirmative construction ("am not used to not observing" = "am used to observing"). Constructions involving double negatives are usually understood incorrectly by patients with injury to the frontal regions of the brain because this intermediate operation of replacing the double negative with an affirmative construction is not carried out. The patient processes the sentence impulsively as a sentence about an aggressive, stubborn person.

Similar difficulties can also be noted in the comprehension of complex logical-grammatical structures, e.g., "brother of father" and "father of brother," or "a circle under a cross" and "a cross under a circle." The only difference here is that unlike patients with lesions of the parieto-occipital regions, patients with frontal lobe lesions make these errors as a result of passivity and their inability to abstract from the directly perceived text.

Even greater difficulties are encountered by patients with frontal lobe lesions in connection with the active processing required to make the transition from text to subtext or from external meaning to inner sense. While easily understanding the external meaning of metaphors, they often experience difficulties in the comprehension of their inner sense. They manifest a tendency toward direct comprehension of the metaphor. For example, they might interpret "an iron hand" in terms of a situation in which a hand holds pincers. That is, they are unable to comprehend the deeper interpretation of this metaphor, which is not connected with a concrete situation. While they may understand the external meaning of the proverb "Not all that glitters is gold.", they have difficulty in finding the deeper sense. If asked (as was done in a study by Zeigarnik, 1973) to select a sentence which expresses a similar meaning, they are likely to choose a sentence that contains the same words (e.g., "Gold shines more than tin.") rather than a sentence which has a similar sense (e.g., "Someone possessing an academic degree is not necessarily outstanding in his/her abilities.").

It is natural that frontal lobe patients who manifest a disturbance in the fundamental mechanism for decoding the general meaning of a communication will experience considerable difficulties in decoding its sense. While they may readily grasp the external meaning, patients of this type frequently do not go beyond the level of an external evaluation of the events described in the text. They are quite unable to go on to the sense expressed in a text. For example, we used a text about young quail in our clinical studies. In the text, a mother quail gave strict instructions to her fledglings not to leave the nest and not to make noise. However, the fledglings did not obey her. They climbed out of the nest and began to cheep, and a dog ate them. The inner sense of this story (one ought to be careful, one must obey one's elders) remains beyond the comprehension of frontal lobe patients. They interpret the story in terms of the information that dogs hunt quails, i.e., they understand only the external events occurring in the story.

It is therefore quite natural that patients with serious frontal lobe damage often understand only the concrete aspects of a text and make no attempt to synthesize its various components or to move from the external text to its deeper subtext. Because of this, comprehension disorders of patients with lesions of the frontal lobes are above all concerned with the depth of reading of a text, i.e., with decoding its inner emotional sense. This is perhaps the most important fact for understanding the role of the frontal lobes in decoding text. We have discussed this phenomenon in greater detail elsewhere (Luria, 1974b, 1975a).

All of these observations indicate that the loss of speech comprehension in patients with frontal lobe lesions differs in a fundamental way from comprehension difficulties found in patients with lesions in the speech areas of the cerebral cortex.

CONCLUSIONS

The changes that occur in speech activity (both production and comprehension) as a result of focal brain lesions have been outlined in a general way. The delineation above indicates that such lesions do not result in a general, diffuse lowering of speech activity. Rather, they may affect any one of the several elements involved in this activity. The data provided by neuropsychologists can be used to provide a better understanding of the structure of speech activity.

We have shown how human speech activity traverses a complex course, starting with the motivation or the need to say something to someone. Subsequent steps include a stage concerned with the general sense or the primary semantic graph which is to be embodied in speech, inner speech with its predicative structure which makes possible the transition to the formulation of an expanded speech utterance, and finally, the expanded speech utterance with all its complexities based on the phonological, lexical, and semantic codes of a language.

Observations have disclosed that speech disorders resulting from focal lesions of the brain are extremely diverse in nature. When the lesion is located in the frontal regions of the brain or in the frontal regions of the speech area, speech production disturbances appear. This may affect the process of transforming an initial intention into an expanded speech utterance, in which case either the motive or the formation of the general intention is affected. It may also affect the transformation of this general intention or the initial semantic graph into a speech utterance by disrupting inner speech. Finally, it may effect the syntagmatic structure of the expanded speech utterance.

On the other hand, a lesion of the posterior gnostic regions of the cerebral cortex does not affect the motive, the initial semantic graph, or the predicative structure of connected, syntagmatically organized speech. In these instances, it is the phonological, lexical, semantic, or logical-grammatical codes of the language that suffer.

Similar facts emerge in our examination of comprehension disorders resulting from brain lesions. As we have seen, the speech activity involved is the reverse of that involved in production. It begins with the perception of an expanded speech utterance. In these cases, focal lesions may lead either to a loss of the phonological structure of speech or to a disorder of its lexical composition. Also, such lesions may disturb the complex logical-grammatical structures involved in converting consecutively presented information into simultaneous patterns.

In disorders of speech production as well as speech decoding, the anterior regions of the brain participate in processes that involve the motive, the intention, inner speech, and connected, predicative syntagmatically constructed speech. Damage to these regions may leave the phonological, lexical, semantic, and logical-grammatical structure of a language relatively unaffected. Conversely, lesions in the gnostic areas of the cerebral cortex do not cause noticeable disorders in connection with the motive and initial semantic graph, and in certain cases, syntagmatically constructed predicative structure. These lesions have their primary effect on the phonological, lexical, or semantic and logical-grammatical codes.

All this supports the notion that individual systems of the left cerebral cortex, in particular the speech areas, participate in different ways in the complex process of speech activity. The different types of lesions allow us to isolate and study various parts of the normally integrated and indivisible processes involved in the psychophysiological structure of speech utterance.

There is no need to emphasize the importance of this analysis of the cerebral organization of speech for psychology and linguistics. It is precisely this that has led to the appearance of a new science—*neurolinguistics*. We can expect a great deal from the development of this subject.

Data about the cerebral organization of speech activity are still scanty. Despite the fact that the study of speech disorders resulting from focal lesions of the brain came into existence more than 100 years ago and has made a significant contribution to neurology, a psycholinguistic analysis of these disorders is yet to be carried out. We can confidently say that today we are at the very first stage of this very complex course.

There is no doubt, however, that this course of study will help us develop an understanding of the complex process of speech which distinguishes humans from animals and which is the key to an analysis of the organization of the most complex forms of human conscious activity.

References

Ach, N. *Uber die Begriffsbildung.* Bamberg: Bucher, 1921.

Akhutina, T. V. *Neirolingvisticheskii analiz dinamicheskoi afazii* [A neurolinguistic analysis of dynamic aphasia]. Moscow: Izdatel'stvo Moskovskogo Universiteta, 1975.

Apresyan, Yu. D. *Leksicheskaya semantika* [Lexical semantics]. Moscow: Izdatel'stvo Nauka, 1974.

Artem'eva, T. I. *Issledovanie vozmozhnosti upravleniya semanticheskimi svyazyami c pomoshch'yu rechevoi instrukstii* [An investigation of the possibility of regulating semantic connections with the help of verbal instruction]. Unpublished diploma work, Moscow State University, 1963.

Austin, J. L. *How to do things with words.* New York: Oxford University Press, 1962.

Austin, J. L. *Sense and sensibilia.* London: Oxford University Press, 1969.

Beiswenger, H. Luria's model of verbal control of behavior. *Merrill-Palmer quarterly*, 1968, 14.

Bellert, I. Über eine Bedeutung für die Koherenz von Texten. In F. Kiefer (Ed.), *Semantik und generative grammatik.* Frankfurt: Athenäum, 1972.

Bernshtein, N. A. *O postroenii dvizhenii* [The construction of movements]. Moscow: Medgiz, 1947.

Bernshtein, N. A. *The coordination and regulation of movements.* Oxford: Pergamon, 1967.

Bever, T. G. The cognitive basis for linguistic structures. In J. R. Hayes (Ed.), *Cognition and the development of language.* New York: Wiley, 1970.

Bever, T. G. The interaction of perception and linguistic structures. In T. Sebok (Ed.), *Current trends in linguistics* (Vol. 12). The Hague: Mouton, 1974.

Bever, T. G., Fodor, J. A., and Weksel, W. The acquisition of syntax: A critique of contextual generalization. *Psychological review,* 1965, 72.

Bierwisch, M. On certain problems of semantic representation. *Foundations of language,* 1969, 5.

Bloomfield, L. A set of postulates for the science of language. *Language,* 1926, 2.

Bloomfield, L. *Language.* New York: Holt, Rinehart and Winston, 1933.

Boskis, R. M. *Glukhie i slaboslyshashchie deti* [Deaf and partially deaf children]. Moscow: Izdatel'stvo Pedagogicheskikh Nauk, 1963.

Braine, M. D. S. The acquisition of language in infant and child. In C. Reed (Ed.), *The learning of language.* New York: Appleton-Century-Crofts, 1971.

Broca, P. Remarques sur le siege de la faculte du langage article. *Bull. Soc. Anthrop.,* 1861, 6.

Bronckart, J. P. Le role regulateur du langage chez L'enfant: Critique experimentelle des travaux de A. R. Luria. *Neuropsychologia,* 1970, 8.

Brown, R. *A first language: The early stages.* Cambridge, Mass.: Harvard University Press, 1973.

Brown, R. and McNeill, D. The "tip of the tongue" phenomenon. *Journal of Verbal Learning and Verbal Behavior,* 1966, 5.

Bruner, J. S. *Beyond the information given.* New York: Norton, 1973.

Bruner, J. S. The ontogenesis of speech acts. *Journal of Child Language,* 1975, 2.

Bruner, J. S., Goodnow, J. J., and Austin, G. A. *A study of thinking.* New York: Wiley, 1957.

Bühler, C. and Hetzer, H. Das erste Verstandniss für Ausdruck in erstem Lebensjahr. *Zschr. f. Psychol.,* 1928, 107.

Bühler, K. *Sprachtheorie.* Jena: Fischer, 1934.

Carroll, J. B. *The study of language.* Cambridge, Mass.: Harvard University Press, 1955.

Carroll, J. B. *Language and thought.* New York: 1964.

Cassirer, E. *The philosophy of symbolic forms.* New Haven: Yale University Press, 1953.

Chafe, W. L. Language and consciousness. *Language,* 1974, 50.

Chafe, W. L. Givenness, contrastiveness, definiteness, subjects, topics, and point of view. In C. N. Li (Ed.), *Subject and topic.* New York: Academic Press, 1976.

Chomsky, N. *Syntactic structures.* The Hague: Mouton, 1957.

Chomsky, N. *Aspects of the theory of syntax.* Cambridge, Mass.: MIT Press, 1965.

Chukovskii, K. *Ot dvukh do pyati* [From two to five]. Moscow: Izdatel'stvo Sovetskaya Rossiya, 1958. (English translation: *From two to five*. Berkeley: University of California Press, 1963.)

Clark, H. H. The influence of language on solving three-term series problems. *Journal of Experimental Psychology*, 1969, 82.

Clark, H. H. Comprehending comparatives. In G. B. Flores d'Arcais and W. J. M. Levelt (Eds.), *Advances in psycholinguistics*. Amsterdam: North Holland, 1970.

Clark, H. H. Semantics and comprehension. In T. A. Sebeok (Ed.), *Current trends in linguistics, Vol. 12: Linguistics and adjacent arts and sciences*. The Hague: Mouton, 1974.

Cole, M. and Scribner, S. *Culture and thought: A psychological introduction*. New York: Wiley, 1974.

Deese, J. On the structure of associative meaning. *Psychological Review*. 1962, 69 (161).

Dilthey, W. *Die Typen der Weltanschauung*. Berlin, 1901.

Eccles, J. *Facing reality*. New York: Springer-Verlag, 1970.

Fillmore, C. The case for case. In E. Bach and R. T. Harms (Eds.), *Universals in linguistic theory*. New York: Holt, Rhinehart and Winston, 1968.

Fillmore, C. Types of lexical information. In D. D. Steinberg and L. A. Jokobovits (Eds.), *Semantics: An interdisciplinary reader in philosophy, linguistics and psychology*. Cambridge: Cambridge University Press, 1971.

Fillmore, C. J. Verben des Resteils. In F. Kiefer (Ed.), *Semantik und generative grammatik*. Frankurt: Athenäum, 1972.

Fodor, J. A. and Bever, T. G. The psychological reality of linguistic segments. *Journal of Verbal Learning and Verbal Behavior*, 1965, 4.

Fodor, J. A., Bever, T. G., and Garrett, M. The development of psychological models for speech recognition. Report on Contract No. AF19 (628)-5705, Department of Psychology, MIT, 1968a.

Fodor, J. A., Bever, T. G., and Garrett, M. The development of psychological models of speech perception. Unpublished manuscript, MIT, 1968b.

Fodor, J. A. and Garrett, M. Some syntactic determinants of sequential complexity. *Perception and Psychophysics*, 1967, 2.

Fradkina, F. I. The emergence of speech in the child. *Uchenye zapiski LGPI im. A. I. Gertsena*, Vol. XII, Leningrad, 1955.

Frisch, K. *Uber die "Sprache" der Bienen*. Jena: Fischer, 1923.

Frisch, K. *The dance language and orientation of bees*. Cambridge, Mass.: Harvard University Press, 1967.

Gal'perin, P. Ya. The development of research on the formation of intellectual actions. In *Psikhologicheskaya nauka v SSSR* (tom 1) [Psychological science in the USSR, Vol. 1, 62]. Moscow: Izdatel'stvo Akademii Pedagogicheskikh Nauk RSFSR, 1959.

Gal'perin, P. Ya. *Vvedenie v psikhologiyu* [Introduction to psychology]. Moscow: Izdatel'stvo Moskovskogo Universiteta, 1976.

Gardner, B. T. and Gardner, R. A. Two-way communication with an infant chimpanzee. In A. M. Schrier and F. Stolinitz (Eds.), *Behavior of nonhuman primates* (Vol. 4). New York: Academic Press, 1971.

Gardner, R. A. and Gardner, B. T. Teaching sign language to a chimpanzee. *Science*, 1969, 165.

Gelb, A. Medizinische psychologie. *Acta Psychologica*, 1937.

Goldman-Eisler, F. Hestitation, information and levels of production. In A. V. S. De Reuck (Ed.), *Disorders of language*. London: Churchill, 1964.

Goldman-Eisler, F. *Psycholinguistics: Experiments in spontaneous speech*. New York: Academic Press, 1968.

Goldstein, K. *Der Aufbau des Organismus*. The Hague: Nijhoff, 1934.

Goldstein, K. *Language and language disorders*. New York: Grune and Stratton, 1948.

Greenberg, J. H. (Ed.), *Universals of language*. Cambridge, Mass.: MIT Press, 1963.

Grice, H. P. Meaning. *Philosophical Review*, 1957, 66.

Grice, H. P. Utterer's meaning, sentence-meaning and word-meaning. *Foundations of Language*, 1968, 4.

Halliday, M. A. K. Language structure and language function. In J. Lyons (Ed.), *New horizons in linguistics*. Harmondsworth: Penguin, 1970.

Halliday, M. A. K. *Explorations in the functions of language*. London: Arnold, 1973.

Halliday, M. A. K. *Learning how to mean: Explorations in the development of language*. London: Arnold, 1975.

Head, H. *Aphasia and kindred disorders of speech* (2 vols.). London: Cambridge University Press, 1926.

Hjelmslev, L. La categorie des cas. *Aarhus*, 1936.

Hjelmslev, L. La stratification du langage. *Word*, 1954, 10.

Howes, D. On the interpretation of word frequency as a variable affecting speech recognition. *Journal of Experimental Psychology*, 1954, 48.

Howes, D. On the relation between the probability of a word as an association and in general linguistic usage. *Journal of Abnormal and Social Psychology*, 1957, 54.

Howes, D. and Osgood, C. E. On the combination of associative probabilities in linguistic context. *American Journal of Psychology*, 1954, 67.

Hull, C. L. Knowledge and purpose as habit mechanisms. *Psychological Review*, 1930, 37.

Humboldt, W. von. Uber das vergleichende Sprachstudium in Beziehung auf die verschiedene Epochen der Sprachentwicklung. *Gesam. Schriften*, 4, 1905.

Humboldt, W. von. Uber die Verschiedenheiten des menschlicher Sprachbaues und ihren Einfluss auf die geistige Entwicklung des Menschengeschlechts. *Gesam. Schriften*, 7, 1907.

Ivanov, V. V. Notes on the typological and comparative-historical investigation of Roman and Indo-European morphology. *Trudy po znakovym sistemam*, IV [Works on sign systems (Vol. IV)]. Tartru: Tartru State University, 1969.

Jakobson, R. O. *Studies in child language and aphasia*. The Hague: Mouton, 1971.

Jarvis, P. E. Verbal control of sensorimotor aspects of performance: A test of Luria's hypothesis. *Human Development*, 1968, 11.

Johonson, E. G. Verbal control of motor behavior in the preschool child: An empirical investigation of Luria's theory. Unpublished doctoral dissertation, University of Sidney, 1976.

Jung, C. G. *Diagnostische Assoziationsstudien* (Vol. 1). Leipzig: Barth, 1906.

Jung, C. G. *Diagnostische Assoziationsstudien* (Vol. 2). Leipzig: Barth, 1910.

Karpova, S. A. *Osoznanie slovesnogo sostava rechi doshkol'nikami* [The conscious understanding of the verbal composition of speech by preschoolers]. Moscow: Izdatel'stvo Moskovskogo Universiteta, 1967.

Katsnel'son, S. D. *Tipolgiya yazyka i rechevoe myshlenie* [The typology of language and verbal thinking]. Leningrad, 1972.

Katz, J. J. *The philosophy of language*. New York: Harper & Row, 1966.

Katz, J. J. *Semantic theory*. New York: Harper & Row, 1972.

Kent, H. G. and Rosanoff, A. J. A study of association insanity. *American Journal of Insanity*, 1910, 67.

Khomskaya, E. D. *Vyrabotka sensornogo uslovnogo refleksa na frazu* [The formation of a sensory conditioned reflex to a sentence]. Unpublished diploma work, Moscow State University, 1952.

Khomskaya, E. D. The investigation of the influence of speech responses on movement responses in children with cerebroasthenia. In *Problemy vysshei nervnoi deyatel'nosti normal'nogo i anormal'nogo rebenka* [Problems in the higher nervous activity of the normal and abnormal child]. Moscow: Izdatel'stvo Moskovskogo Universiteta, 1958.

Khomskaya, E. D. *Mozg i aktivatsiya* [Brain and activation]. Moscow: Izdatel'stvo Moskovskogo Universiteta, 1972.

Kiefer, F. (Ed.), *Studies in syntax and semantics*. Dordrecht: Reidel, 1969.

Kiefer, F. Uber Prasuppositionen. In F. Kiefer (Ed.), *Semantik und generative grammatik*. Frankfurt: Athenäum, 1972.

Kleist, K. *Gehirnpathologie*. Leipzig: Barth, 1934.

Klimenko, A. P. *Voprosy psikholingvisticheskogo izucheniya semantiki* [Problems in the psycholinguistic study of semantics]. Minsk, 1970.

Knebel', M. O. *Slovo v tvorchestve aktera* [The word in the actor's creative work]. Moscow: Izdatel'stvo Russkogo Teatral'nogo Obshchestva, 1970.

Knebel', M. O. and Luria, A. R. Means and ways to code sense. *Voprosy Psikhologii*, 1971, 4.

Kol'tsova, M. M. *O formirovanii vysshei nervnoi deyatel'nosti rebenka* [On the formation of higher nervous activity in the child]. Leningrad, 1958.

Korovin, K. G. *Postroenie predlozhenii v pis'mennoi rechi rugoukhikh detei* [The construction of sentences in the written speech of hard of hearing children]. Moscow: Izdatel'stvo Akademii Pedagogicheskikh Nauk, 1950.

Lakoff, G. *Irregularity in syntax.* New York: Holt, Rhinehart and Winston, 1970.

Lakoff, G. On generative semantics. In D. D. Steinberg and L. A. Jakobovits (Eds.), *Semantics: An interdisciplinary reader in philosophy, linguistics and psychology.* Cambridge: Cambridge University Press, 1971.

Lakoff, G. Linguistics and natural logic. In D. Davidson and G. Harmon (Eds.), *Semantics of natural language.* Dordrecht, Netherlands: Reidel, 1972.

Lashley, K. S. The problem of serial organization in behavior. In L. A. Jeffress (Ed.), *Cerebral mechanisms in behavior.* New York: Wiley, 1951.

Lebedinskii, V. V. Performance of symmetrical and asymmetrical programs by patients with frontal lobe lesions. In A. R. Luria and E. D. Khomskaya (Eds.), *Lobnye doli i regulyatsiya psikhicheskikh protsessov* [The frontal lobes and the regulation of mental processes]. Moscow: Izdatel'stvo Moskovskogo Universiteta, 1966.

Lenneberg, E. G. Cognition in ethnolinguistics. *Language*, 1953, 29.

Lenneberg, E. H. and Roberts, J. M. The language of experience: A study in methodology. *International Journal of American Linguistics*, 1956, 13.

Leont'ev, A. A. *Yazyk, rech' i rechevaya deyatel'nost'* [Language, speech, and speech activity]. Moscow: Izdatel'stvo Nauka, 1969.

Leont'ev, A. A. *Printsipy teorii rechevoi devatel'nosti* [Principles of the theory of speech activity]. Moscow: Izdatel'stvo Nauka, 1974.

Leont'ev, A. N. *Problemy razvitiya psikhiki* [Problems in the development of mind]. Moscow: Izdatel'stvo Akademii Pedagogicheskikh Nauk RSFSR, 1959.

Leont'ev, A. N. *Deyatel'nost', Soznanie, Lichnost'* [Activity, consciousness, and personality]. Moscow: Izdatel'stvo Politicheskoi Literatury, 1975.

Leopold, W. F. *Speech development of a bilingual child* (4 vols.). Evanston, Ill.: Northwestern University Press, 1939-1949.

Lichtheim, L. Ueber Aphasie. *Dtsch. Arch. klin. Med.*, 1883, 36.

Luria, A. R. (Ed.), *Rech' i intellekt v razvitii rebenka* [Speech and intellect in the development of the child]. Kazan: A. V. Lunacharskii poligrafshkola, 1927.

Luria, A. R. *Rech' i intellekt derevenskogo, gorodskogo i besprizornogo rebenka* [The speech and intellect of the rural, urban and homeless child]. Moscow-Leningrad: Izdatel'stvo Gosudarstvo, 1930.

Luria, A. R. *The nature of human conflicts.* New York: Liveright. 1932. (Reprint— New York: Grove Press, 1960.)

Luria, A. R. On the pathology of grammatical operations. *Izvestiya Akademii Pedagogicheskikh Nauk RSFSR*, 1946, 3.

Luria, A. R. *Travmaticheskaya afaziya* [Traumatic aphasia]. Moscow: Izdatel'stvo Akademii Meditsinskikh Nauk SSSR, 1947. (English translation: *Traumatic aphasia.* The Hague: Mouton, 1970.)

Luria, A. R. The directive role of speech in development and dissolution. *Word*, 1959, 15.

Luria, A. R. *The role of speech in regulation of normal and abnormal behavior*. Oxford: Pergamon Press, 1961.

Luria, A. R. *Vysshie korkovye funktsii cheloveka* [Higher cortical functions in humans]. Moscow: Izdatel'stvo Moskovskogo Universiteta, 1962. (English translation: *Higher cortical functions in man*. New York: Basic Books, 1966.)

Luria, A. R. *Mozg cheloveka i psikhicheskie protsessy* [The human brain and mental processes]. Moscow: Pedagogika, 1970. (English translation: *Human brain and psychological processes*. New York: Harper & Row, 1966.)

Luria, A. R. *Poteryannyi i vozvrashchennyi mir* [The lost and regained world]. Moscow: Izdatel'stvo Moskovskogo Universiteta, 1971. (English translation: *The man with the shattered world*. New York: Basic Books, 1972.)

Luria, A. R. *Istoricheskoe razvitie poznavatel'nykh protsessov* [The historical development of cognitive processes]. Moscow: Izdatel'stvo Moskovskogo Universiteta, 1974a. (English translation: *Cognitive development*. Cambridge, Mass.: Harvard University Press, 1976.)

Luria, A. R. *Neiropsikhologiya pamyati* [The neuropsychology of memory]. Moscow: Izdatel'stvo Pedagogika, 1974b. (English translation: *The neuropsychology of memory*. Silver Spring, Md.: V. H. Winston & Sons, 1976.)

Luria, A. R. *The working brain*. Harmondsworth: Penguin, 1974c.

Luria, A. R. *Osnovnye problemy neirolingvistiki* [Basic problems of neurolinguistics]. Moscow: Izdatel'stvo Moskovskogo Universiteta, 1975a. (English translation: *Basic problems of neurolinguistics*. The Hague: Mouton, 1976.)

Luria, A. R. Scientific perspectives and philosophical dead ends in modern linguistics. *Cognition*, 1975b, 5.

Luria, A. R. Basic problems of language in light of psychology and neurolinguistics. In E. Lenneberg and E. Lenneberg (Eds.), *Foundations of language development*. New York: Academic Press, 1975c.

Luria, A. R. and Khomskaya, E. D. (Eds.), *Lobnye doli i regulyatsiya psikhicheskikh protsessov* [The frontal lobes and the regulation of mental processes]. Moscow: Izdatel'stvo Moskovskogo Universiteta, 1966.

Luria, A. R. and Polyakova, A. G. Observations on the development of voluntary action in early childhood. *Doklady Akademii Pedagogicheskikh Nauk SSSR*, 1959, 3 and 4.

Luria, A. R. and Subbotskii, E. V. A contribution to the early ontogenesis of the regulative function of speech. In P. Dixon (Ed.), *Language development*, 1975.

Luria, A. R. and Vinogradova, O. S. An objective investigation of the dynamics of semantic systems. *British Journal of Psychology*, 1959, 50.

Luria, A. R. and Vinogradova, O. S. An objective investigation of the dynamics of semantic systems. In *Semanticheskaya struktura slova* [The semantic structure of the word]. Moscow: Nauka, 1971.

Luria, A. R. and Yudovich, F. Ya. *Rech' i razvitie psikhicheskikh protsessov u rebenka* [Speech and the development of mental processes in the child]. Moscow: Izdatel'stvo Akademii Pedagogicheskikh Nauk, 1956. (English translation: *Speech and the development of psychological processes in the child.* London: Staples Press, 1963.)

McCarthy, D. Language development in children. In P. Mussen (Ed.), *Carmichael's manual of child psychology.* New York: Wiley, 1954.

McCawley, J. D. The role of semantics in grammar. In E. Bach and R. Harms (Eds.), *Universals in linguistic theory.* New York: Holt, Rinehart and Winston, 1968.

McCawley, J. D. Bedeutung und die Beschreibung der Sprachen. In F. Kiefer (Ed.), *Semantik und generative grammatik.* Frankfurt: Athenäum, 1972.

McNeill, D. *The acquisition of language.* New York: Harper & Row, 1970.

Mel'chuk, I. A. Towards a functioning model of language. In M. Bierwisch and K. E. Heidolph (Eds.), *Progress in linguistics.* The Hague: Mouton, 1970.

Mel'chuk, I. A. *Ocherk teorii yazykovykh modelei "Smysl-Tekst"* [Outline of a theory of "Sense-Text" linguistic models]. Moscow: Izdatel'stvo Nauka, 1974.

Miller, G. A. Some psychological studies of grammar. *American Psychologist,* 1962, 17.

Miller, G. A. Some preliminaries to psycholinguistics. *American Psychologist,* 1965, 20.

Miller, G. A. *The psychology of communication: Seven essays.* New York: Basic Books, 1967.

Miller, G. A., Galanter, E., and Pribram, K. *Plans and the organization of behavior.* New York: Holt, Rinehart and Winston, 1960.

Miller, G. A. and Isard, S. Some perceptual consequences of linguistic rules. *Journal of Verbal Learning and Verbal Behavior.* 1963, 2.

Monakow, C. von. *Die Lokalisation im Grosshirn und der Abbau dar Funktionen durch corticale Herde.* Wiesbaden: Bergmann, 1914.

Morozova, N. G. On the comprehension of text. *Izvestiya Akademii Pedagogicheskikh Nauk SSSR,* 1947, 7.

Morton, J. A model for continuous language behavior. *Language and Speech,* 1964, 7.

Morton, J. *Biological and social factors in psycholinguistics.* London: Logos, 1971.

Noble, C. E. An analysis of meaning. *Psychological Review,* 1952, 59.

Osgood, C. E. Semantic differential technique in the comparative study of cultures. *American Anthropoligist,* 1964, 66.

Osgood, C. E., Suci, G. J., and Tannenbaum, P. H. *The measurement of meaning.* Urbana: University of Illinois Press, 1957.

Pestova, G. D. *Ob'ektivnoe issledovanie sistem smyslovykh svyazei* [An objective investigation of systems of semantic connections]. Unpublished diploma work, Moscow State University, 1958.

Piaget, J. *The language and thought of the child*. Cleveland: Meridian, 1955.

Piaget, J. and Inhelder, B. *The psychology of the child*. London: Routledge and Kegan Paul, 1969.

Polyakov, Yu. F. *Patologiya poznavatel'noi deyatel'nosti pri shizofrenii* [The pathology of cognitive activity in schizophrenia]. Moscow: Izdatel'stvo Meditsina, 1974.

Porzig, W. Wesenhafte Bedeutungs beziehungen. Beitrage zu der Geschichte der Deutschen Sprache und Literatur. 1934, Bd. 58.

Potebnaya, A. A. *Iz zapisok po russkoi grammtike* [From notes on Russian grammar]. Khar'kov, 1888.

Premack, D. Language in chimpanzees? *Science*, 1971a, 172.

Premack, D. On the assessment of language competence in the chimpanzee. In A. M. Schrier and F. Stollnitz (Eds.), *Behavior of nonhuman primates* (Vol. 4). New York: Academic Press, 1971b.

Pribram, K. H. and Luria, A. R. *Psychophysiology of the frontal lobes*. New York: Academic Press, 1973.

Razran, G. Stimulus generalization of the conditioned response. *Psychology*, 1949, 46.

Revault d'Allonnes, G. L'attention. In G. Dumas (Ed.), *Traite de psikhologie*. Paris, 1923.

Riess, B. F. Semantic conditioning involving the galvanic skin reflex. *Journal of Experimental Psychology*, 1940, 26.

Rommetveit, R. *Words, meanings and messages*. New York: Academic Press, 1968.

Rommetveit, R. *On message structure: A framework for the study of language and communication*. London: Wiley, 1974.

Rozengart-Pupko, G. L. *Rech'i razvitie vospriyatiya v rannem vozraste* [Speech and the development of perception in childhood]. Moscow: Izdatel'stvo USSR Academy of Medical Sciences, 1948.

Sapir, E. Conceptual categories in primitive languages. *Science*, 1927, 74.

Sapir, E. Grading: A study in semantics. *Philosophy of Science*, 1944, 11.

Saussure, F. de. *Cours de linguistique generale*. Paris: Payot, 1922.

Shcherba, L. V. *Izbrannye raboty po russkomu yazyku* [Selected works on the Russian language]. Moscow, 1957.

Sherrington, C. S. *The brain and its mechanisms*. Cambridge: Cambridge University Press, 1934.

Sherrington, C. S. *Man on his nature*. London: Cambridge University Press, 1942.

Shubert, J. The verbal regulation of behavior. *Journal of Genetic Psychology*, 1969, 114.

Shvachkin, N. Kh. The experimental investigation of early generalizations in the child. *Izvestiya Akademii Pedagogicheskikh Nauk SSSR*, Moscow, 1954, 54.

Shvarts, L. A. The word as a conditioned stimulus. *Byulletin eksperimental'noi biologii i meditsini* [Bulletin of experimental biology and medicine]. Moscow, 1948, 25 (4).

Shvarts, L. A. The problem of the word as a conditioned stimulus. *Byulletin eksperimental'noi biologii i meditsini* [Bulletin of experimental biology and medicine]. Moscow, 1954, 38 (12).

Skinner, B. F. *Verbal behavior.* New York: Appleton-Century-Crofts, 1957.

Slobin, D. I. Universals of grammatical development in children. In G. B. Flores d'Arcais and W. J. M. Levelt (Eds.), *Advances in psycholinguistics.* Amsterdam: North Holland, 1970.

Sokolov, A. A. *Vnutrennyaya rech' i myshlenie* [Inner speech and thinking]. Izdatel'stvo Proveshchenie, 1968. (English translation: *Inner speech and thought.* New York: Plenum, 1972.)

Sokolov, E. N. *Vospriyatie i uslovnyi refleks* [Perception and the conditioned reflex]. Moscow: Izdatel'stvo Moskovskogo Universiteta, 1958.

Sokolov, E. N. (Ed.), *Orientirovannyi refleks i voprosy vysshei nervnoi devatel'-nosti v normi i patologii* [The orienting reflex and problems of higher nervous activity in the norm and in pathology]. Moscow: Izdatel'stvo Pedagogicheskikh Nauk, 1959.

Spanger, E. *Die Frage nach der Einheit der Psychologie.* Abhandl. Preuss. Acad. Wiss., 1926.

Spanger, E. *Der Sinn und Voraussetzungslosigkeit der Geisteswissenschaften.* Abhandl. Preuss. Acad. Wiss., 1929.

Stanislavskii, K. S. *Rabota aktera nad soboi* [The actor's work on himself]. Moscow: Izdatel'stvo Iskusstvo, 1951.

Stanislavskii, K. S. *Rabota aktera nad rol'yu* [The actor's work on a role]. Moscow-Leningrad: Izdatel'stvo Iskusstvo, 1956.

Stern, C. and Stern, W. *Die Kindersprache: Eine psychologische und sprachtheoretische Untersuchung* (4th rev. ed.). Leipzig: Barth, 1928.

Stumpf, C. *Die Sprachlaute.* Berlin, 1926.

Svedelius, C. *L'analyse du langage.* Ph.D. dissertation, Uppsala University, 1897.

Tappolet, E. Die Sprache des Kindes. *Deutshe Rundschau,* 1907.

Taylor, T. Y. *A primer of psychobiology: Brain and behavior.* New York: W. H. Freeman, 1974.

Trier, J. Das sprachliches Feld. *Neue Jahrbucher f. Wissenschaft,* 1934, Bd. 10.

Trubetskoi, N. *Grundzuge der Phonologie.* Prague: Cercle Linguistique de Prague, 1939.

Vinogradov, V. V. Basic types of lexical word meanings. *Voprosy yazykoznaniya,* 1953, No 5.

Vinogradova, O. S. Some features of the orienting response to stimuli of the second signal system in normal and mentally retarded school children. *Voprosy Pikhologii,* 1956, 6.

Vinogradova, O. S. and Eisler, N. V. The manifestation of the system of verbal relationships during the registration of vascular reactions. *Voprosy Psikhologii,* 1959, 2.

Vygotsky, L. S. *Myshlenie i rech'* [Thinking and speech]. Moscow: Sotsekriz, 1934. (English translation: *Thought and language.* Cambridge, Mass.: MIT Press, 1962.)

Vygotsky, L. S. *Izbrannye psikhologicheskie issledovaniya* [Selected psychological research]. Moscow: Izdatel'stvo Akademii Pedagogicheskikh Nauk RSFSR, 1956.

Vygotsky, L. S. *Razvitie vysshikh psikhicheskikh funktsii* [The development of higher mental functions]. Moscow: Izdatel'stvo Akademii Pedagogicheskikh Nauk RSFSR, 1960.

Vygotsky, L. S. *Mind in society.* Edited by M. Cole, V. John-Steiner, S. Scribner, and E. Souberman. Cambridge, Mass.: Harvard University Press, 1978.

Weighl, E. Zur Psychologie sogenannten Abstraktionsprozesse. *Ztschr. f. Psychol.*, 1927, 103.

Weinreich, U. Travels through semantic space. *Word*, 1958, 14.

Wernicke, C. *Der aphasische Symtomencomplex.* Breslau: Cohn und Weigart, 1874.

Wertsch, J. V. Simply speaking. *Papers from the Tenth Regional Meeting of the Chicago Linguistic Society.* Chicago: Chicago Linguistic Society, 1974.

Wertsch, J. V. The influence of perceived speaker intention on the recognition memory of connected discourse. *Journal of Psycholinguistic Research*, 1975, 4.

Whorf, B. L. *Language, thought and reality: Selected writings of Benjamin Lee Whorf.* Edited by J. B. Carroll. Cambridge, Mass.: MIT Press, 1956.

Wittgenstein, L. *Philosophical investigations.* Oxford: Blackwell, 1972.

Wozniak, R. Verbal regulation of motor behavior, Soviet research and non-Soviet replications: A review and application. *Human Development*, 1972, 15, 13-57.

Zeigarnik, B. V. *Patologiya myshleniya* [The pathology of thinking]. Moscow: Izdatel'stvo Moskovskogo Universiteta, 1962.

Zeigarnik, B. V. *Vvedenie v patologiyu* [An introduction to pathology]. Moscow: Izdatel'stvo Moskovskogo Universiteta, 1969.

Zeigarnik, B. V. *Osnovy patopsikhologii* [Foundations of psychopathology]. Moscow: Izdatel'stvo Moskovskogo Universiteta, 1973.

Zholkovskii, A. K. On the rules of semantic analysis. In *Mashinnyi perevod i prikladnaya lingvistika* (No. 8). [Machine translation and applied linguistics (No. 8)]. Moscow, 1964.

Zholkovskii, A. K. A lexicographical description of Somali substantives. In *Narody Azii i Afriki* [Peoples of Asia and Africa], No. 1, 1967.

Zholkovskii, A. K. and Mel'chuk, I. A. The construction of a working model of language ("text-sense"). In *Mashinnyi perevod i prikladnaya lingvistika* (No. 11) [Machine translation and applied linguistics (No. 11)]. Moscow, 1969.

Author Index

Subject Index

263